Map of the WESSEX of the Novels and Poems

Scale of Miles
5   10   15

Septentrio

C000270459

Lumsdon   Christminster

R. Thames

NORTH

The Brown House   Alfredston
Cresscombe
Marygreen

River Thames

WESSEX

Gaymead
Kennetbridge

Castle Royal
Aldbrickham

MID
Marlbury Downs

WESSEX
The Great Plain

Inkpen Beacon

Stoke Barehills   Quartershot

Weydon Priors

Icenway House

Stonehenge

UPPER

Head

Meddenton
Wingreen
ston
lott
The Chase
The Slopes
Chaseborough
Trantridge Cross
urcastle
Knollingwood Hall
Lornton Inn
Warborne
SSEX
Welland
Kingsbere
Heath
Shottsford Forum
Chene Manor
Havenpool
Mynton
Sandbourne
Anglebury
Corvesgate   Knollsea
Cove
tle
ip

Wintoncester

Fernel Hall
WESSEX
Deansleigh Park

Melchester

Southampton

Portsmouth

The Great Bramshurst Forest

Solentsea

The Island

The Channel

Emery Walker sc

THOMAS HARDY

THOMAS HARDY
The World of His Novels

J. B. Bullen

F

FRANCES LINCOLN LIMITED
PUBLISHERS

To Roma, whose idea it was, and who supported the writing with love and enthusiasm.

Frances Lincoln Limited
www.franceslincoln.com

Thomas Hardy: The World of His Novels
Copyright © Frances Lincoln Limited 2013
Text copyright © J. B. Bullen 2013
Photographs copyright © as listed on page 256

First Frances Lincoln edition 2013

A catalogue record for this book is available from the British Library.

978-0-7112-3275-4

Printed and bound in China

1 2 3 4 5 6 7 8 9

Endpapers: *Map of the Wessex of the Novels and Poems* by Emery Walker. The map was added to Macmillan's 1912 Wessex Edition of Hardy's novels and poems.
Title page: Thomas Hardy in the garden at Max Gate, photographed by Hermann Lea.

Contents

References

Throughout the book, the numbers in brackets after quotations refer to page numbers in the novel under discussion. The quotations are all taken from the editions of Thomas Hardy in the Oxford World's Classics under the general editorship of Simon Gatrell and published by Oxford University Press. They are as follows:

Far from the Madding Crowd, ed. Suzanne B. Falck-Yi (2008)
The Return of the Native, ed. Simon Gatrell (2008)
The Mayor of Casterbridge, ed. Dale Kramer (2008)
The Woodlanders, ed. Dale Kramer (2009)
Tess of the d'Urbervilles, ed. Juliet Grindle and Simon Gatrell (2008)
Jude the Obscure, ed. Patricia Ingham (2008)

The poems are taken from *Thomas Hardy: The Complete Poems*, ed. James Gibson (London: Macmillan, 1976).

Introduction

THOMAS HARDY'S NOVELS contain some of the most colourful and engaging characters in literature, from the towering figure of Michael Henchard to the voluptuous Tess Durbeyfield, from the femme fatale Eustacia Vye to the melancholy Jude Fawley. But even more memorable is Hardy's depiction of the landscape, the hills, forests and fields of the West Country recorded with extraordinarily loving and detailed conviction. Why then do some readers find his work impossibly gloomy? The villages and towns bustle with local activity. The cottages are homely and picturesque and the grand houses are drawn with the finesse of a draughtsman's eye. But above all Hardy's stories take us out into the landscape. The sun comes up through the mist on Egdon Heath, or sets in the mysterious depths of the Hintock woods; the wind tears across the open fields of Flintcomb Ash or the north Berkshire Downs. The heat rises in the fertile valley of the Froom and the bitter cold descends on the same river as it passes the outer walls of Casterbridge. The tragedies of Hardy's novels are indeed dark, but that darkness is a foil to the brightness and optimism of life. As Hardy recognized, pleasure, joy and satisfaction are emotions understood only in terms of their opposites, and much of the energy of his writing comes from the stress between these contrasts. He is a writer who celebrates the pleasures of life and of love but he also mourns their passing. To see only the gloom in Hardy is to miss the sense of pleasure and to overlook the enormous positive vitality of his work.

This book takes us back to the world in which Hardy lived and wrote. His early readers thought that it was exclusively rustic and at first he was classed as a provincial writer. It soon became clear, however, that his characters were facing issues that were not confined to the realm of hedges and farmyards. Problems raised by female emancipation in a male world were not exclusively rural; nor were the inroads made by industrial processes into time-honoured methods of production. The double standards of sexual morality were as much an urban as a rural conundrum and so were religious doubt and family strife.

Though Hardy's world and the world of his contemporaries seems very different from ours, when we examine it more closely we can see that the problems faced by the Victorians bear a strange resemblance to our own. For example, nineteenth-century science questioned man's relationship with nature while in the twenty-first century global warming prompts questions about our responsibility for the health of the natural world. In the nineteenth century, industrial processes fundamentally altered the shape of Victorian society no less than the revolution in physics and technology has changed ours. Then there were questions about gender and sexuality. Though Victorian codes of sexual behaviour were strangely unlike our own, it takes very little imagination to see that the underlying issues between men and women remain the same.

But Hardy's novels are not simply about 'issues'. He once pointed out that a novel is an 'impression' not an 'argument', by which he meant his principal focus was not the abstract realm of ideas and concepts. The intellectual challenges of his day were important to him, but his main interest lay in people and their relationship to each other and with their environment. Though he was not a realist writer, the 'impression' in his novels arose from his ability to create believable characters in believable settings. The Wessex world of his creation is a visionary place charged with stories, legends and myths, enhanced with light, colour, sounds, texture and smells and populated by psychologically credible characters. At one point he categorized his most popular works as 'Novels of Character and Environment' in which the argument or the abstract issues emerged from the amalgam of these two elements. Throughout Hardy's writing, character, environment and argument are inextricably connected. The environment is not just a backdrop for the characters. Instead, the villages, buildings, woods and fields play an active part in the plot. Sometimes they set the mood for the drama that unfolds within or around them, sometimes they reflect the temperament, personality or disposition of one figure or another, but there is always a link between the dispositions of Hardy's characters, the scenes in which he places those characters and the underlying issues with which the novels deal.

This interdependence of character and environment has its roots in Hardy's upbringing and childhood and long preceded his concern with contemporary issues. He passed his early years as a rather sickly boy in the hamlet of Higher Bockhampton just outside Dorchester in Dorset. It was a remote place in a somewhat backward county and many of his early experiences came from the games he played by himself on Puddletown Heath, the tract of wild country that lay just behind his parents' cottage. One of his early watercolour paintings called *The Playground of T. H's Childhood* illustrates the spot. Here, the natural world of hills and valleys, insects, birds and butterflies, snakes and wild ponies or 'heath croppers' that lived on the bracken all helped to shape his mind and imagination. The cottage represented another world, the world of human interaction where both his mother and his grandmother told him stories and legends about the local

---

Puddletown Heath, a tract of wild country that lay just behind Hardy's parents' cottage is illustrated in one of Hardy's early sketches called *The Playground of T. H's Childhood*. Watercolour on paper, 10.7 x 13.6 cm.

(The playground of T.H's childhood.)

countryside and his father sang and played the violin. For the first eight years of his life the cottage and the heath constituted his whole world, ultimately becoming the imaginative nucleus of his writing. Together, they acted as a kind of centre of energy pushing out fictional lines of force first into Dorset and then into the surrounding counties of Wiltshire, Hampshire and Cornwall.

It is surprising that a writer who later took on some of the central issues of nineteenth-century intellectual and ethical life should have had a rather meagre formal education. His father, also Thomas, was a builder who came from a long line of builders, and his mother, Jemima, had once been a lady's maid. His mother, who was well read, had ambitions for her son, but she was in no way learned. Hardy joined the parish school in Bockhampton only when he was eight years old, and then two years later diligently walked three miles each way to the British School in Dorchester. In his childhood and early adolescence he developed affections for a number of local girls of his own age, but his most powerful sentimental experience involved his attraction to the voluptuous Julia Augusta Martin. She was already in her thirties, and together with her husband owned the rather grand Kingston Maurward House nearby.

Perhaps even more significantly, he made close friends with the charming Horace Moule, son of the vicar of nearby Fordington. Charismatically intellectual, yet dipsomaniac and probably homosexual, Moule, who was eight years older than Hardy, introduced him to many of the scientific and theological controversies that were challenging Christian faith in this period. Though he was academically unsuccessful, Moule attended both Oxford and Cambridge and produced in Hardy a persistent longing for the university education he never received. Hardy's technical skills in drawing and mathematics together with contacts he had through his father's trade suggested that his best choice of career would be in building or architecture. So in 1856, at the age of sixteen, Hardy abandoned the idea of any formal academic training and was articled to the Dorchester architect John Hicks where, in a liberal and friendly atmosphere, he received a thorough grounding in the trade.

It was his move to London in 1862, however, that was one of the greatest milestones in his life. He joined the architectural office of the prosperous Arthur Blomfield. This was staffed by lively young men with whom Hardy experienced at first hand modern life, modern literature, modern art, modern music and modern architecture. In the same year the capital was buzzing with the huge International Exhibition in South Kensington. In the space now occupied by the Natural History Museum thirty-six countries were represented in the areas of art, industry and technology with Britain leading the way. Hardy was a regular visitor and since he went with many of his family members he may also have taken Eliza Nicholls, a pious twenty-four-year-old lady's maid with whom he had some kind of tender understanding. Hardy was probably very sexually naïve when he went to London, but he learned a great deal through the gossip in Blomfield's office and from the sight of the cohorts of London prostitutes who were making hay in the sunshine of the exhibition. The poetry that Hardy was writing at this time suggests a restless uncertainty about women, and it was not long before the shadowy Eliza, on leaving London, faded from his life.

As Hardy's work at Blomfield's office progressed he had plenty of time to explore the many interests and experiences that London offered. Art was one of them. Drawing he did professionally, but from his boyhood he had had a passion for painting. When he left school, Horace Moule's older brother Henry gave Hardy his first lessons in watercolour. From then on he often took the opportunity of sitting down and attempting to paint the scene before him and though he had no major talent in this direction the artist's way of seeing features prominently in his novels where scenes, both landscapes and interiors, are carefully composed, grouped and lit. What Hardy lacked in Dorset, however, was any major collection of painting, so London was like an Aladdin's cave for him. He regularly visited the National Gallery, where he was particularly impressed by the way in which certain painters managed to create visionary experiences from simple or commonplace scenes. Foremost among them was Joseph Mallord William Turner for whose work Hardy retained a lifelong admiration. He also began a habit maintained throughout his life of visiting the summer exhibitions of the Royal Academy, as well as the special exhibitions put on by smaller galleries in the city. So enamoured was Hardy by the pleasures of painting that he briefly, but seriously, considered changing his career to become an art critic, but architecture was going well. In his first years with Blomfield he won a couple of essay and design prizes, and his very first published piece of writing, 'How I Built Myself a House', was a comic satire on the contemporary fashion for suburban building.

From Black Heath Corner, Hardy's first attempt at sketching from nature, c.1858. Watercolour on paper, 20 x 33 cm.

None of the Hardy family had much interest in art, but music had always played a prominent part in the household. His father was a church musician and the young Thomas had been encouraged, sometimes with his father and sometimes alone, to play his violin for local parties and harvest suppers. Many of the novels involve music making of this kind, from the sheep-shearing supper in *Far from the Madding Crowd* to the mumming at the Christmas party in *The Return of the Native*. But London offered more sophisticated musical pleasures. When Hardy arrived in the capital he soon began to attend concerts and develop new tastes. One of them was a particular liking for opera and he would regularly attend performances of works by Rossini, Verdi, Donizetti, Bellini and others. When, later in the century, Wagner was performed in London Hardy rose to the challenge of this new music. It is likely that he attended the concerts given each year by the German conductor Hans Richter, who specialized in staging sections of Wagner's operas. The impact of the combination of music, spectacle and drama may well have played a part in shaping some of the scenes in *Tess of the d'Urbervilles*.

In the early sixties Hardy came more and more in contact with the great controversies of the day. He said that he was one of the first admirers of that Victorian intellectual bombshell, Charles Darwin's *The Origin of Species*.[1] Strictly speaking this was a book about biology, but when it was published in 1859 and taken up by 'Darwin's Bulldog', the biologist and natural historian Thomas Henry Huxley, its impact on ideas about human evolution became very clear. Huxley's own interpretation of Darwin's work, *Evidence as to Man's Place in Nature*, appeared in 1863 during Hardy's second year in London. The pious and the devout were shocked by the theory that men were descended not from angels but from apes and that nature was not the benevolent creation of a loving God but an arena for a bitter and perpetual struggle for survival. Hardy's contemporaries reacted in different ways to these ideas. Some violently rejected them, others gladly accepted them. Hardy, who had been brought up in a community that respected and admired the precepts of the Church of England, reluctantly came to recognize the likely truth of evolutionary theory and was stoically resigned to the new picture it drew of man's relationship with nature. The first of his novels to deal with this spirit of 'modernism' was *The Return of the Native* in which Eustacia Vye defiantly attempts but fails to resist the onset of the new world. By the time Hardy came to write *The Woodlanders* and poems like 'To Outer Nature' or 'In a Wood' he seems to have accepted the fact that man is necessarily an isolated lonely figure in a world that is largely indifferent to him and in which only the fittest survive.

This scientific rationalism, however, was compensated for Hardy by a new note of defiant, assertive humanism. Second only to the impact on him of *The Origin of Species* was another book also published in 1859. This was the philosopher John Stuart Mill's famous work *On Liberty*, that Hardy claimed to know 'almost by heart'.[2] *On Liberty* was a profoundly anti-authoritarian text urging men and women to live not according to the rules and conventions of the day but according to the dictates of their own hearts and impulses. It challenged the roots of Victorian social convention and questioned its moral rigidity so for Hardy, who came from a rather strict Victorian family living in a conservative backwater, it must have seemed like a breath of life. Sue Bridehead in *Jude the Obscure* is Mill's outstanding representative, but the behaviour and attitudes of other characters like Angel Clare in *Tess of the d'Urbervilles* were influenced not only by Mill's rationalism but by his revolutionary stress on the equality of the sexes.

Angel Clare, of course, fails to live up to Mill's ideas about human liberty because his values, like the harp that he plays, are second hand. In any case he is a figure who materialized from a rather different set of interests that Hardy was beginning to develop in the 1860s. From his childhood he had been fascinated by superstitions and local legends, his mother and grandmother providing him with an oral anthology of Dorset folklore. In the 1860s and 1870s these and other myths began to be taken seriously by scholars working in the new science of anthropology. The art critic and social analyst John Ruskin had long taken a semi-scientific interest in the role of myth-making in human history, but E. B. Tylor's book *Primitive Culture* of 1871 offered a much more systematized study of this field. It was probably Hardy's friend, the evolutionist, folklorist and anthropologist Edward Clodd who introduced him to the work of another pioneer in this area, the Oxford mythographer Max Müller, just as he later directed Hardy to the research of James Frazer and his groundbreaking study of myth, *The Golden Bough* (1890). So myth, legend and folklore, which for Hardy had been little more than a curiosity in his early work, had become for him by the time he wrote *Tess of the d'Urbervilles* the source of a particular kind of hidden wisdom. According to the new mythographers ancient Greek legends, stories from remote tribes and myths originating in the Druidic north revealed patterns and symbols through which it was possible to understand more clearly man's early relations with the earth and the natural world.

In 1867, having had a wide range of architectural experience in London helping with the design of churches, schools, railways and houses, Hardy abandoned the heady and polluted air of the capital and returned to the freshness and simplicity of the countryside. Why he went back to Bockhampton, back to live with his parents, and back to work on church restoration for John Hicks in Dorchester is uncertain. He may have gone because of his affection for his Puddletown cousin Tryphena Sparks to whom he was undoubtedly attached, but he said that studying had weakened him and his state of health had declined. He may, as he claimed later, have become subject to fits of depression and needed the strength of his family around him. Certainly by then he had begun to write his first novel, and together with his architectural duties, authorship may have put too great a strain on his mental resources. But the stress was in vain for his manuscript of *The Poor Man and the Lady* was turned down by a couple of publishers.

Architecture still featured prominently in his life and Hardy continued to earn his living as an architectural draughtsman. When in 1869 John Hicks died, Hardy joined the Weymouth practice of G. R. Crickmay for whom he was commissioned to do more church restoration projects. But Hardy determined to carry on writing, cannibalized his first novel, destroyed the manuscript and wrote a second. Just as this new 'sensation' novel, *Desperate Remedies*, with its extravagant and melodramatic plot was on its way to the publisher, Hardy set off on a fateful journey. Crickmay had been asked to restore the parish church of St Juliot far away on the northern coast of Cornwall and he asked Hardy to go and inspect it. In March 1870 he set off on the tortuous route from Bockhampton. He arrived late in the evening and was greeted by the rector's sister-in-law, Emma Lavinia Gifford, Hardy's future wife, in an encounter that, some forty years later, would be remembered in some of the greatest poems in the English language. But for now, Hardy waited anxiously for news from London about his new book. The first publisher, Macmillan, rejected it, but another firm, Tinsley, agreed to take it. When it came out the reviews were very mixed, and in spite of the fact that Hardy was deeply wounded by some of them he launched on a third book, *Under the Greenwood Tree*. This appeared in 1872. It was a Dorset novel and the confidence gained from writing about a world with which he was familiar led to the creation of a unique authorial voice. Hardy now drew his material from his family history and he wrote about the people and the places he knew when he was growing up. Above all, this is the first book that deals with the disappearance of old customs and habits from a living and vibrant village community. Here for the first time Hardy adopted what might be called the poetics of loss, expressing states of mind that were closely bound up with his own temperament and disposition.

Under the Greenwood Tree was published anonymously and it was not until many years later that Hardy was willing to admit that the village of Mellstock was his local village, Stinsford. This was because only gradually did Hardy's readers realize that it was possible to locate the action of almost all his books, and when his career was well developed they began to take real pleasure in visiting the scenes and seeing those locations with their own eyes. This was encouraged by Hardy's invention of the idea of 'Wessex'. Originally, it was an Anglo-Saxon kingdom that lasted only until the eleventh century, but Hardy revived the term.

A blue plaque on 10 South Street, Dorchester: testimony to the power of Hardy's characterization.

At first it corresponded roughly with the county of Dorset, but for Hardy it was as much a cultural concept as a geographical location referring not just to the place but to all the activities that went on in the area. The idea probably came to him as the result of living in London. Moving away from home gave him a new perspective on his birthplace. Not only did he see its physical features in a fresh light, but its customs, values, language and rural crafts would have been thrown into relief by the fast, colourful urban existence of the capital. So when he first used the term 'Wessex' in his next novel, *Far from the Madding Crowd* (1874), it is no coincidence that it appears in a context where Hardy contrasts the pace of life in London with that of life in the small village of Weatherbury. In London, he says, thirty years in the past are 'old' times; in these 'Wessex nooks', as he calls them, one hundred years might just be called 'old'.

As he went on publishing novels, Hardy continued to use the term Wessex, expanding it in *Tess of the d'Urbervilles* and *Jude the Obscure* to include the counties that border on Dorset, that is Hampshire, Wiltshire and even Berkshire. It was not until 1895, however, that he fully recognized that he had created something quite unique. In a preface to *Far from the Madding Crowd* prepared for the first collected edition of his novels, he explained that Wessex was a 'partly real, partly dream-country', but recognized that it was a country that people actually wanted to visit. He said that since he had received so many inquiries from readers interested in 'landscape, pre-historic antiquities, and especially old English architecture' he felt it necessary to state that they were all, as he put it, 'done from the real'.[3] So the term Wessex is an amalgam of the literal, the material and the imaginative. In fact, Hardy rarely wrote without specific places in mind. He may have shifted them, resurrected them from the past, or changed their scale or their surroundings, but the 'real' element is always present and Hardy's use of specific locations has always held a powerful fascination for readers.

One such 'real' spot provides a splendid example of this. If you stand in front of Barclays Bank at 10 South Street, Dorchester, you will see a curious sight. It is a blue plaque that reads: 'This house is reputed to have been lived in by the Mayor of Casterbridge in Thomas Hardy's story of that name written in 1885.' The idea of putting up blue plaques originated in the mid-1860s. Byron was the first to be honoured in this way, and in 1867 one was placed on his birthplace in Cavendish Square in London. Soon they were rapidly extended to the rest of the country so that now hundreds decorate the buildings of the nation, but looking through the list, none, as far as I am aware, commemorates a fictional character. So what exactly is this one commemorating? A clue lies in the word 'reputed'. The word, implying 'possible', 'probable', 'almost certainly', forms a link between the 'real' world of the solid eighteenth-century brick house and the 'dream' world of Casterbridge and one of its imaginary citizens, Michael Henchard. In other words, the belief that Henchard once lived in this house is a tribute to the power of Hardy's imagination, a power so strong, as the plaque testifies, it induces a willing suspension of disbelief in us all.

The chapters that follow examine this process of transformation. There are a number of excellent, carefully researched guidebooks that take the visitor from place to place in pursuit of identifiable fictional locations. This book visits many of those places and adds some that have never before been recognized. But the point of the approach here is not simply to identify these. What I wish to do is to observe the way in which Hardy uses places as essential elements in the unfolding narratives of six of his best-known novels and how he uses other places in the context of the poems. We will see how Hardy observed and recorded, often with scrupulous fondness, the details of the villages, forests and landscapes of Dorset and beyond and made them into the dream-country of Wessex. How, in other words, he created a world out of natural and built environments, populated it with characters and imbued it with his own intellectual and emotional preoccupations.

Chapter One

Far from the Madding Crowd: Articulate Architecture

ON FRIDAY 23 MAY 1863 a fire broke out in the dairy house of Lower Waterston or Waterson farm, some five miles outside Dorchester in Dorset. It tore through two barns, a granary and into the adjoining ancient manor house. The labourers were working in a remote part of the farm. Seeing the flames rise from the barns, they ran to help and were joined by villagers from nearby Puddletown and Troy Town. One of those, a Mr Danman, worked alongside the farmer, Richard Genge, and for ten hours they tried to put out the fire and drag what remained of the farmer's belongings into the courtyard. But much of the interior of the building was badly damaged, leaving the outer walls intact.

Ten years later Hardy sat down to write a story centred on this same house. Here, too, a fire breaks out in a straw rick nearby, and the farm hands are plunged into a state of confusion as they try to prevent it spreading. In the nick of time a shepherd arrives, takes command, organizes the labourers, climbs the rick and brings the fire under control with his sheep-crook. The shepherd is Gabriel Oak, and the incident occurs at Weatherbury Farm towards the beginning of *Far from the Madding Crowd*. The fire brings Oak into contact once again with the beautiful but impulsive Bathsheba Everdene. Only two months previously she had saved him from suffocation in his shepherd's hut, but she had also rejected his offer of marriage. Since then their social and economic positions had changed dramatically. His flock had been driven over a cliff and he had lost his livelihood. She on the other hand had inherited the prosperous tenancy of Weatherbury Upper Farm. The meeting is embarrassing for both of them, but having proved his mettle in controlling the fire Oak asks for work and she agrees to employ him.

On the day of the fire at Waterston Manor Hardy was in London studying in the architectural office of Arthur Blomfield. He must have known about it, however, because he regularly visited his parents in nearby Higher Bockhampton and had relatives in Puddletown. He would also have been told about it by his friend John Hicks (the Dorchester architect), with whom he worked his first years of apprenticeship. Though the building was not insured, the Earl of Ilchester, who owned it, decided to rebuild the interior, so that by 1867, when Hardy left London to live again with his parents, it had been restored and the farmer, his wife and family had all moved back in.

Hardy began writing *Far from the Madding Crowd* in 1873 in the cramped conditions of his parents' small cottage. In 1874 it was serialized in *The Cornhill Magazine* with illustrations by the artist Helen Paterson. As a trained architectural draughtsman, Hardy took considerable interest in her work. He himself drew local details to use in his stories and before beginning this novel had already sketched examples of agricultural dress, a sheep dip and an 'old-fashioned malthouse'. When he learned that the *Cornhill* was to illustrate the text he thought these drawings might be useful to the artist, and one in particular seems to have caught Paterson's attention. At the opening of chapter thirty-four there is a small woodcut of Waterston, almost certainly based on a sketch by Hardy. Waterston was the object of considerable

Waterston Manor.
Above: A drawing by Helen Paterson for the serial version of *Far from the Madding Crowd*, probably from a drawing supplied by Hardy.
Below: As it is today.

local admiration and Hardy was not alone in drawing this building. As we have seen, in his youth he had been strongly encouraged to paint outdoors by Henry Joseph Moule, the eldest son of the local vicar of Fordington, and just as the novel was appearing in 1874 Moule himself went along to Waterston to do some watercolours of his own.[1]

Today, 'the bower of Oak's new-found mistress, Bathsheba Everdene' is privately owned, but you can see why Hardy found it so attractive. It was, he said, 'a hoary building, of the early stage of Classic Renaissance' and he points out the unexpected, energetic mixture of styles: 'Fluted pilasters . . . chimneys . . . panelled or columnar, some coped gables with finials.' (73) Nikolaus Pevsner, the eminent architectural historian, endorsed Hardy's enthusiasm in his famous *Buildings of England* series, saying that 'among the seventeenth century manor houses of Dorset none is more charming.' It is the words 'surprise' and 'fun' that come to Pevsner's mind to account for Waterston's extraordinarily exuberant mixture of architectural modes and styles.[2]

In his account of the building, Hardy suggests that it has two dominant characteristics. The south front, he says, represents uninhibited pleasure and amusement, while the back, with its farmyard and barns, is its workaday side. When it became a farmhouse, he tells us, 'the vital principle of the house had turned round inside its body'. Even the interior seems to have a life of its own. The main staircase 'was of hard oak, the balusters, heavy as bed-posts . . . and the stairs themselves continually twisting round like a person trying to look over his shoulder'. Noise is everywhere. 'Every window,' says Hardy, 'replied by a clang to the opening and shutting of every door, a tremble followed every bustling movement, and a creak accompanied a walker about the house, like a spirit, wherever he went.' (74) In Hardy's account of the farmhouse it is endowed with such vitality that it is sometimes hard to distinguish between the fabric and its inhabitants.

Looking round Waterston Manor today we can see that it is much tidier and more carefully maintained than it would have been in the nineteenth century. In the 1860s Hardy recorded that 'soft brown mosses, like faded velveteen, formed cushions upon the stone tiling, and tufts of the houseleek or sengreen sprouted from the eaves of the low surrounding buildings'. (73) Now all this has gone, and gone too are the signs of agricultural activity. When Hardy was writing the novel, Richard Genge farmed 506 acres around. He employed nineteen men and women, more or less the same number that Bathsheba inherited, and some of this farming activity can be seen in Joseph Moule's watercolours. When in the mid-1960s John Schlesinger came to make a film version of the book, Waterston was far too carefully manicured to represent a nineteenth-century farmhouse; Schlesinger's choice of the more dilapidated Bloxworth House in southern Dorset is probably a fairly accurate representation of the state of Waterston a hundred years before.

But we have to remind ourselves that Waterston Manor and Weatherbury Farm are not one and the same place, and though the world of fiction closely approaches the world of fact the two are actually very different. Hardy was clear that the village of Weatherbury was modelled on Puddletown, but he also acknowledged that he had taken liberties with its topography. 'The heroine's fine old Jacobean house', he wrote in a preface to a later edition, 'would be found in the story to have taken a witch's-ride of a mile or more from its actual position' but, he adds, 'its features are described as they still show themselves to the sun and moonlight'. (4) Hardy always transforms places, landscapes and buildings to meet the needs of his story. This early novel is often read as a pastoral story with an almost exclusively agrarian setting. As a result the built environment is usually overlooked in favour of the natural one, though in fact buildings and man-made constructions play a significant and important role throughout.

Hardy, though he had left Blomfield's employ, was now, as we have seen, working for G. R. Crickmay in Weymouth. So when, having spent each day measuring, drawing and checking buildings, in the evening he sat down to write *Far from the Madding Crowd*, it is not surprising that he was enormously sensitive to building design and construction in his novel. Interestingly, however, his approach was not what one might have expected from a practising architect. His account, for example, of Weatherbury farmhouse is very different from Pevsner's professionally accurate account of Waterston Manor. Pevsner aims at objectivity, balance and factual accuracy, but though Hardy records many architectural details he chooses them not for their comprehensiveness but for their expressive potential. Pevsner writes engagingly, with amusing anecdotes and strong opinions, but his buildings remain essentially inanimate organizations of stone, brick and wood. Hardy's are very different. Many of his buildings, both in this novel and later ones, are like living entities. They seem to move, they make sounds, and they even have human characteristics. On the outside, the 'body' of Weatherbury farmhouse is 'hoary' and 'sleepy'. Inside it is filled with a 'vital principal' including stairs that resemble 'a person trying to look over his shoulder'. (73)

Why does Hardy do this? And how does it relate to the story of Gabriel Oak, Bathsheba Everdene and Frank Troy? The opening phrase describing the farmhouse as 'the bower of Oak's new-found mistress' gives us a clue. The farmhouse is not just the house she has inherited, or one that she has bought or rented; it is her 'bower', her special, appropriate feminine residence. In other words there is a connection between Bathsheba and the design of the house. Like her, it is unorthodox, wayward and fun. Like her it is beautiful but unusual, and like her it has two contrasting aspects. On the one hand Bathsheba is entirely aware, to the point of vanity, of her own good looks, but on the other she is active, practical and able single-handedly to run a farm. Similarly the house, with its gracious south front and utilitarian back courtyard, has contrasting sides. One is elegant; the other, workaday. So Weatherbury farmhouse perfectly suits a girl who combines a taste for literature and music with a determination to organize a team of farm workers.

Weatherbury farmhouse stands at the heart of *Far from the Madding Crowd*. From this centre radiates a network of other buildings, houses, barns, huts and tents, each one of them endowed with special characteristics that link them to a particular character or to the rural community at large. This architectural network extends across Wessex to include a wide range of building types from the grandest to the most humble, from the ancient to the modern, from the beautiful to the ugly and from the decorative to the utilitarian. The most homely construction, and the one which lies at the greatest social distance from Weatherbury farmhouse, also happens to be the first to appear in the novel, on a cold December day. It stands in a field some twenty miles west of Puddletown on Norcombe Hill in fiction or Toller Down on the map. It has, says Hardy, the puzzling form of a 'dark object under the plantation hedge' looking like 'a small Noah's Ark on a small Ararat'. (15–16)

This is Gabriel Oak's shepherd's hut, a construction standing 'on little wheels, which raised its floor about a foot from the ground'. In the nineteenth

A shepherd's hut, like 'a small Noah's ark', similar to that used by Gabriel Oak.

century flocks of sheep on chalk uplands were used to fertilize the thin agricultural soil and in the winter months, particularly during the lambing season, the shepherd would spend the night with the flock in this specially constructed hut. In recent years shepherd's huts have become hugely popular with people who want an extra room in their garden, and by coincidence, no more than half a mile down Waterston Lane, there is a business for building and restoring them. In 2000 Richard and Jane Plankbridge discovered an original hut on the banks of the river Piddle and set about rebuilding it. They now complete or renovate one hut each month. Looking at the unfinished interior of one of these it is not difficult to make the connection with *Far from the Madding Crowd*.

'The inside of the hut, as it now presented itself,' says Hardy, 'was cosy and alluring, and the scarlet handful of fire in addition to the candle, reflecting its own genial colour upon whatever it could reach, flung associations of enjoyment even over utensils and tools.' These are the tools of Oak's trade and an extension of his personality. 'In the corner,' says Hardy, 'stood the sheep-crook, and along a shelf at one side were ranged bottles and canisters of the simple preparations pertaining to ovine surgery and physic.' 'On a triangular shelf across the corner,' he adds, 'stood bread, bacon, cheese, and a cup for ale or cider' (17), all suggestive of the shepherd's self-sufficiency. Practical, efficient, ordered, caring: the objects exemplify both Oak's personal qualities and his professional activity. When he plays his flute in this hut he resembles a shepherd from the idyllic groves of classical Arcady, and when he brings newborn lambs too weak to survive the cold to warm at the stove, he becomes the good shepherd of the Bible. So much of Gabriel Oak's role is encapsulated in this sheltering, warm interior and it foreshadows the emotional warmth that he later extends to the human flock at Weatherbury, and especially to Bathsheba Everdene.

When Oak loses his sheep he loses his livelihood and he also loses his hut. It is not long after his arrival in Weatherbury, however, that he finds another location that embodies many of the same qualities that Hardy had identified with Oak's hut. In the wake of the fire at the farm, Bathsheba suggests that all the workers come to the farmhouse for a drink. They accept the idea gratefully, but ask that a barrel of ale should be sent instead to the malthouse. As a newcomer Gabriel Oak, too, is directed to the malthouse because it is the centre of communal life. Hardy writes,

Warren's Malthouse was enclosed by an old wall inwrapped with ivy, and though not much of the exterior was visible at this hour, the character and purposes of the building were clearly enough shown by its outline upon the sky. From the walls an overhanging thatched roof sloped up to a point in the centre, upon which rose a small wooden lantern, fitted with louvre-boards on all the four sides, and from these openings a mist was dimly perceived to be escaping into the night air. There was no window in front; but a square hole in the door was glazed with a single pane, through which red, comfortable rays now stretched out upon the ivied wall in front. (56)

Oak's shepherd's hut expresses many of his personal strengths; the malthouse embodies the positive values of the community. It is now February. The weather is still bitter and the unpretentious comfort of the maltster's offers sociable protection against the elements. Hardy's first readers would have readily understood its purpose and its status in the village. Malthouses were once abundant in Britain but since the process of malting has been industrialized they have been either demolished or turned into private houses and their operations are now mysterious to most of us. The Puddletown malthouse, Hardy tells us in a preface to the novel, was pulled down at about the time that he was writing it. Now there are only four in Britain that still use the methods employed by Maltster Warren and the nearest one to Puddletown is Warminster Maltings.

In the malting process, the stored barley from the local farms is steeped in water for several days before being drained in a 'couch' area to continue the process of germination. It is then spread out on two long 'growing' floors under a low ceiling where it is turned several times a day. To maintain a constant temperature the windows are either small or non-existent. After a period of nearly two weeks the malting barley is moved to a drying floor above a kiln and kept at a higher temperature for several days to stop germination and concentrate the sugar. The maltster, who usually lived on the premises, fed the kiln from below with wood or coal, and the heat escaped into the air through the characteristically shaped chimney that Hardy mentions. The maltster would supply malt to local inns, or to large houses like Bathsheba's where they made their own beer. Warminster Maltings was never a one-man operation, but nearby in Chinn's yard, Warminster, there is a former maltings that corresponds in scale to its counterpart in Weatherbury. It too has tiny windows in a line on the right-hand wall marking the level of the two growing floors, and at the far end is the triangular roof of the kiln flu above the drying area. In *Far from the Madding Crowd* Hardy focuses on the glowing warmth of the kiln and the maltster's living quarters. It is an interior of traditional rustic simplicity suggesting time-honoured rituals.

> The room inside was lighted only by the ruddy glow from the kiln mouth, which shone over the floor with the streaming horizontality of the setting sun, and threw upwards the shadows of all facial irregularities in those assembled around. The stone-flag floor was worn into a path from the doorway to the kiln, and into undulations everywhere. A curved settle of unplaned oak stretched along one side, and in a remote corner was a small bed and bedstead, the owner and frequent occupier of which was the maltster. (56)

Meanwhile that occupier, Maltster Warren (for whom Hardy's illustrator, Helen Paterson, provided a portrait vignette), seems to be part of the plant world rather than the human one: 'This aged man was now sitting opposite the fire, his frosty white hair and beard overgrowing his gnarled figure like the grey moss and lichen upon a leafless apple-tree.' (56)

The maltster's is a centre of collective conviviality and mutual support in Weatherbury. It is a place for the exchange of stories, the repetition of village and personal histories and the passing on of local gossip, all encouraged by the warmth from the kiln and free-flowing drink produced by the maltster. On the next occasion we see Oak there he is bursting through the door out of the bleak February weather. In his arms he is carrying newborn lambs abandoned in the snow drifts on Bathsheba's farm and has brought them, as he did to his shepherd's hut, to warm and recover before the fire.

In their different ways, the farmhouse, the shepherd's hut and the malthouse each play a part in the social and agricultural economy of Weatherbury. The vitality of the farmhouse is an emblem of the energy of agrarian labour, the shepherd's hut is linked to rural pastoralism, and the maltster's to the sympathetic and supportive community. These buildings provide what Hardy called in the

A small maltings in the centre of Warminster, now converted to shops.

preface 'continuity in local history'. He believed in 'the preservation of legend, folklore, close inter-social relations, and eccentric individualities', and in recording these ways of life, *Far from the Madding Crowd* helped in that very process of preservation. Hardy attached high value to these locations because their very fabric contained something of the spirit of their former inhabitants and the 'attachment to the soil of one particular spot by generation after generation'. (4–5) Hardy has sometimes been accused of creating a romantic pastoral in his image of Wessex and of ignoring the harsh conditions of the late nineteenth-century Dorset labourer, or the clashes between yeomen and peasantry exemplified by the Tolpuddle Martyrs. But this is to miss the point. *Far from the Madding Crowd* is not an escapist narrative. In endorsing the value of the rural way of life it does not create an ideal alternative. As the story passes through the various seasons it celebrates the round of agricultural labour, the pulse of life and the importance of living in tune with the soil, but within this the inhabitants of Weatherbury are still

The Barracks, Devizes

Le Marchant Barracks just outside Devizes, the likely place to which Frank Troy was posted when he left Dorchester. They have now been converted into flats.

subject to the pain of sexual betrayal, manic obsession and bitter rejection. The maltster's may be a centre of rural harmony but it is around the fire there that the workers first hear of the principal 'lost sheep' of the story. This is Fanny Robin, Bathsheba's youngest servant girl, and it is at the malthouse that her sudden disappearance from Weatherbury farm is first announced.

Fanny Robin is an orphan brought up at the expense of the neighbouring farmer, Boldwood, but working on the Everdene farm. She had been secretly courted by Frank Troy, a sergeant in a cavalry regiment, the Eleventh Prince Albert's Own Hussars, temporarily stationed in Casterbridge barracks. Her disappearance is linked to Troy. The couple had discussed marriage, and it emerges much later that she is pregnant. Without warning, however, Troy's regiment is moved to a 'remote Garrison town'. Though Hardy does not name the town, we can be fairly confident that it is based on Devizes, in Wiltshire, some sixty-four miles from Dorchester. Fanny follows on foot and when she arrives she finds Troy incarcerated in the local barracks where she tries to contact him. The location is a desolate one. 'For dreariness', we are told, 'nothing could surpass a prospect in the outskirts of a certain town and military station, many miles north of Weatherbury . . . on this . . . snowy evening.' The imposing and mono-lithic structure of Le Marchant Barracks just outside Devizes was probably the model for this. It was situated on the London Road on the outskirts of the town, at a spot that must have been much more isolated than it is now. Built in the mid-nineteenth century, in 1959 it became a regimental museum. After a period of disuse it was converted into flats, and then other houses were built in the grounds. From the rear of the building it is possible to see the Kennet and Avon canal close by and in the distance lie the fields and the open hills of Wiltshire. On this February evening, the snow and the darkness simplify the contours of both landscape and building into monotonous regularity. 'The scene was a public path,' says the narrator, 'bordered on the left hand by a river, behind which rose a high wall. On the right was a tract of land, partly meadow and partly moor.' (85)

In the novel Hardy has moved the canal right up to the wall of the barracks and turned it into a river. On the left hand 'were flatness in respect of the river, verticality in respect of the wall behind it, and darkness as to both'. It is as if this were a diagram constructed on an architect's drawing board. Plan and elevation, horizontal and vertical. But the impersonal architectural record is immediately suffused with unhappy emotions. 'If anything could be darker than the sky,' says Hardy, 'it was the wall, and if anything could be gloomier than the wall it was the river beneath.' The repetition of the phrase 'if anything could be' creates a numbing effect, unrelieved by the account of the undecorated surface of the building, cold, unfeeling and hostile: 'The indistinct summit of the facade was notched and pronged by chimneys here and there, and upon its face were faintly signified the oblong shapes of windows, though only in the upper part. Below, down to the water's edge, the flat was unbroken by hole or projection.' (86) The blankness and the absence of ornament deprive the building of life and prepare the way for the entry of the desolate young woman. In order to attract Troy's attention Fanny throws balls of snow at his window. It slowly opens and the blank impersonality of the scene increases: "'Is it Sergeant Troy?" said the blurred spot in the snow, tremulously.' 'This person', we are told, 'was so much like a mere shade upon the earth, and the other speaker so much a part of the building, that one would have said the wall was holding a conversation with the snow. "Yes," came suspiciously from the shadow.' (87) The humans in this scene have become blanks, inanimate objects, just wall and snow, and their loss of identity reflects the sense of rejection and isolation felt by Fanny Robin.

Sad figure though she may be, Fanny Robin returns to the story like a thunderbolt. When she has been abandoned by Troy, she meets him with his new wife, Bathsheba, late one evening on the road from Casterbridge. Not recognizing the couple in the growing dusk, Fanny asks the way to the local workhouse. Troy, who knows the voice, climbs down from the carriage and, risking Bathsheba's suspicions, promises to find money for Fanny and meet her with it in the morning. Fanny's journey to Casterbridge, weary, ill and pregnant, is intensely pathetic and when her only help is a local dog she becomes a figure of even deeper pathos. Part of the Dorchester Union Workhouse still stands, and it was this that Hardy had in mind for the object of her journey.

The workhouse was built in 1836 not long after the notorious Poor Law Amendment Act of 1834, and was designed to bring in the poor under one roof. The charitable aims of the Act were soon lost and the workhouse, for old and young alike, became synonymous with vicious treatment, poor diet, segregation and control. Conditions were kept deliberately harsh to encourage self-sufficiency and to discourage entry. They were, therefore, the resort of the desperate and Fanny Robin, heavily pregnant and without a penny in the world, is indeed desperate. Hardy's account of the workhouse is correspondingly bleak. 'On this much-desired spot outside the town,' he says ironically, 'rose a picturesque building.' He then compares its architecture to the cover for a corpse: 'Originally, this building had been a mere case to hold people. The shell had been so thin, so devoid of excrescence, and so closely drawn over the accommodation granted, that the grim character of what was beneath showed through it, as the shape of a body is visible under a winding-sheet.' (262–3)

The Union Workhouse was built in Damers Road in a characteristically cruciform design, and when most of it was demolished in the twentieth century the remainder was incorporated into the local hospital. From what we see today it is not difficult to recognize Hardy's description. 'This stone edifice', he says, 'consisted of a central mass and two wings, whereon stood as sentinels a few slim chimneys, now gurgling sorrowfully to the slow wind. In the wall was a gate, and by the gate a bell-pull formed of a hanging wire.' The gate in the wall is still there, and though the bell-pull has gone we can follow Fanny's path, through the door, up the steps and to the main entrance inside the wall. Fanny 'raised herself as high as possible upon her knees, and could just reach the handle. She moved it and fell forwards in a bowed attitude, her face upon her bosom . . . A little door by the large one was opened, and a man appeared inside. He discerned the panting heap of clothes, went back for a light, and came again.' Then two women 'lifted the prostrate figure and assisted her in through the doorway'. (263)

The Union Workhouse in Damers Road, Dorchester, built by George Wilkinson in 1836. This later became Damers Hospital.

The barracks and the workhouse mark the trajectory of Fanny Robin's plunge into desolation. The events in front of the blank façade of the barracks represent the beginnings of a downward trend that ends at the door of the even blanker façade of the workhouse. As her story unfolds she is changed from a young and good-looking girl to an impersonal, anonymous shape. The brutal and harsh architecture of the first and the mean and starved design of the second frame her degradation. The appearance of both barracks and workhouse not only expresses the suffering of Fanny Robin herself, but reflects the heartlessness and carelessness of Frank Troy. More than this, however, Hardy suggests a contrast between the socially supportive malthouse and the socially divisive workhouse, and in a rather Dickensian way, he treats the design of the workhouse as an emblem of a cold and unfeeling element within Victorian society. When Dorchester workhouse was opened in 1834 it had a splendid view over the fields south of the town. In the novel, Hardy mentions that 'it was discovered that the view from the front . . . was one of the most magnificent in the county. A neighbouring earl once said that he would give up a year's rental to have at his own door the view enjoyed by the inmates from theirs – and very probably the inmates would have given up the view for his year's rental.' (263) The principal authority on British workhouses, the historian Peter Higginbottom, suggests that the anecdote is probably based upon fact, and refers to the most important landowner in the Dorchester area, Henry Fox-Strangways, 3rd Earl of Ilchester. Ironically, Fox-Strangways, as we have seen, owned the farm at Waterston, or the fictional Weatherbury Farm tenanted by Bathsheba Everdene.

Fanny's flight from Weatherbury takes place in February; her death in the workhouse in October. Exactly halfway between these dates Hardy devotes three chapters to the events of one day, the first of June. These chapters are what might be called the architectonic centre of the story, because each one involves a building. The first is set in the great barn, the second in the farmhouse and the third in a fir plantation immediately behind the house. These three scenes form a kind of triptych that moves through the day, passing from morning to night and from light to dark. The first of the three, 'The Great Barn and the Sheep Shearers', is one of Hardy's most dramatic architectural pieces. In it, ancient and modern, architecture and rural life come together. It is, says Hardy, a 'picture of to-day in its frame of four hundred years ago'. The whole chapter resembles a large painted canvas showing a bustling brilliantly lit rural scene set in a magnificent architectural frame. The sheep shearing takes place in the June sunlight when the barn is temporarily converted for sheep shearing.

But this is no ordinary barn, and Hardy goes out of his way to stress its dignity and antiquity by pointing out its similarities to the local church. The barn 'not only emulated the form of the neighbouring church of the parish, but vied with it in antiquity. Whether [it] had ever formed one of a group of conventual buildings nobody seemed to be aware; no trace of such surroundings remained.' (143) The barn that used to stand at Waterston no longer exists. We know that there was one before 1863 because the newspapers reported that it had been burnt down. Yet it could never have resembled the barn of the novel because a stone building would have left significant traces. Instead we have to travel out of Puddletown to the village of Cerne Abbas, ten miles to the north. Here the tithe barn standing close to the centre of the village was Hardy's model.

We can be sure of this because in 1915 he went with his architect friend Sir Sidney Cockerell to show him what he had had in mind.[3] This beautiful and imposing building is not easy to find. It lies well back from the road at the end of a narrow lane. Leaving the road the lane turns, rises and suddenly opens out into a grassy area and there stands the barn, massive, solid and imposing. Built in the mid-fourteenth century, it was linked to the Benedictine abbey dissolved under Henry VIII of which (as Hardy suggests) no trace remains. It was built by ecclesiastical masons with substantial walls of knap flint and deep-set ashlar buttresses. Originally, it was a much longer building than it is now but stones from the northern end were used in the construction of some of the cottages in the village. The pointed windows on the southern side were inserted in the eighteenth century when that part of the building was first made habitable. Though the roof has been renewed, the huge interior of the old barn looks much as it did in the nineteenth century, where the two porches resembling the transepts of a church with their large doors, north and south, would have had the threshing floor between them. These doors were opened not only to allow entry for the carriages loaded with grain, but to create a draught across the threshing floor when the wheat was separated from the chaff. As the present owners tell me, even now when the doors are open, the wind sweeps in and a strong breeze is channelled across the floor. Hardy's interest, however, focuses on the porches, the roof and

Cerne Abbas tithe barn, Barton Farm, dates from the late fourteenth century. Left: The interior, with the 'dusky, filmed, chestnut roof, braced and tied in by huge collars'.
Below: The exterior, showing the 'range of striding butresses'.

the walls. The porches are simple and monumental. Their primitive appearance suggests a kind of unpretentious integrity. They are 'lofty enough to admit a wagon laden to its highest with corn in the sheaf, [and] spanned by heavy-pointed arches of stone, broadly and boldly cut, whose very simplicity was the origin of a grandeur not apparent in erections where more ornament has been attempted'. (143) He then moves to the roof. The main roof at Cerne Abbas collapsed in the 1880s and was not recreated in its original form, but under the porch we can see something of the early complexity of the woodwork.

As Hardy describes them, the beams seem to be charged with huge force and energy all kept tightly under control by counter-forces. 'The dusky, filmed, chestnut roof, braced and tied in by huge collars, curves, and diagonals, was far nobler in design, because more wealthy in material, than nine-tenths of those in our modern churches.' Outside, the walls seem to be marching past in steady, heavy movement. 'Along each side wall', says Hardy, 'was a range of striding buttresses, throwing deep shadows on the spaces between them, which were perforated by lancet openings.'

In Hardy's mind, though the barn resembles both the church and the castle, it is superior to them in one important respect: that it continues to fulfill the function for which it was built. For Hardy the church suggests 'worn out religious creeds' and the castle is a monument to the violence and strife of a past age. In contrast, the barn, dedicated to the basic necessities of existence, represents something as permanent as life itself. In the structure of the barn, he says, 'medievalism and modernism had a common stand-point'. The barn is a symbol of the timelessness of agrarian life, and like the barn, Weatherbury village itself 'was immutable'. In Weatherbury 'three or four score years were included in the mere present, and nothing less than a century set a mark'. (144) The barn, therefore, embodies continuity and stability. It provides a record of collective memory and helps guarantee the identity of the community. 'The barn', Hardy tells us, 'was natural to the shearers, and the shearers were in harmony with the barn.'

Having established the metaphorical 'frame' for the sheep shearing, Hardy turns to the picture within that frame. What Hardy describes is an ancient ritual but one that has ecclesiastical overtones. It is a kind of secular church service. For the purpose of the day the two ends of the building, 'answering ecclesiastically to nave and chancel . . . were fenced off with hurdles' to enclose the sheep.

If the barn resembles the church, then the sheep represent the congregation, with Gabriel Oak as simultaneously the good shepherd and officiating priest. In this 'picture of to-day in its frame of four hundred years ago' (144) Oak and his muse, Bathsheba, are positioned in the foreground with the farm-workers and sheep in the background, creating a pictorial group representative of harmony and balance between labour and affection.

In the tithe barn at Cerne Abbas the dark and cavernous interior is lit only by the narrow openings in the sidewalls. Near the great doors, however, the sun pours in, creating a dramatic contrast between dark and light. In the novel, Hardy uses that contrast to transform the sheep shearing into a ritual of sacred dignity. 'Here the shearers knelt,' he tells us, 'the sun slanting in upon their bleached shirts, tanned arms, and the polished shears they flourished, causing these to bristle with a thousand rays strong enough to blind a weak-eyed man.' (144)

In the sheep-shearing scene the architectural frame of the barn is given as much prominence as the communal ritual that takes place within it. In the second scene of this triptych, the sheep-shearing supper at the farmhouse, the architectural element is less dominant. Nevertheless the structure of the house plays a subtle role in the social balance of the farming community. The bright day has faded into evening, and for the 'supper a long table was placed on the grass-plot beside the house, the end of the table being thrust over the sill of the wide parlour window and a foot or two into the room'. Bathsheba 'sat inside the window, facing down the table. She was thus at the head without mingling with the men.' (151) When Gabriel Oak takes his place at the far end of the table the balance is complete. In this odd arrangement, Bathsheba maintains her superior position by remaining inside the house, yet simultaneously dining with the workers. Outside, the workers eat in their own way with Gabriel at the helm.

Like the scene in the barn this communal activity is also carefully lit. Activity has drifted into passivity in an image of classical tranquillity. The sun, says Hardy, 'went down in an ochreous mist' and the workers, as 'they sat, and talked on . . . grew as merry as the gods in Homer's heaven. Bathsheba still remained enthroned inside the window . . . [and] sometimes looked up to view the fading scene outside.' (156) It is a moment held in suspension, out of time and as Bathsheba sings to the accompaniment of Gabriel's flute, past, present and future conjoin: 'The shearers reclined against each other as at suppers in the early ages of the world.' The pastoral idyll is disturbed, however (as it always is in this novel), by a different note. Boldwood appears unannounced and the mood darkens when, uninvited, the farmer takes it upon himself to leave the table and enter the house to join Bathsheba on the other side of the window. Hardy's illustrator, Helen Paterson, chose to illustrate this moment in the serialization of the novel, and one can see clearly the way in which the window of the farmhouse acts as a fulcrum between the classes.

In the woodcut Bathsheba is singing 'The Banks of Allan Water' whose verse runs: 'For his bride a soldier sought her,/And a winning tongue had he/ on the banks of Allan Water/None was gay as she!' The song, which originates

Helen Paterson's illustration of the sheep-shearing supper in *Cornhill Magazine* from 1874.

in ancient Scottish oral traditions, tells the story of a Miller's daughter who is betrayed by her soldier lover and who dies of grief. 'Subsequent events', we are told, cause this verse 'to be remembered for many months . . . by . . . those who were gathered there'. (157) Indeed they are, but for Bathsheba the sudden appearance of the soldier in the next scene comes as an unexpected shock.

The third scene of the triptych, 'The Same Night: the Fir Plantation', balances the first one in the barn because it, too, is located just outside Weatherbury farmhouse. Whereas the earlier one took place in bright sunshine, however, this is cast in profound darkness. At first it might not appear to involve a building at all, but as Hardy makes clear its location is 'a vast, low, naturally formed hall, the plumy ceiling of which was supported by slender pillars of living wood, the floor being covered with a soft dun carpet of dead spikelets and mildewed cones'. (161) The fir plantation did not grow spontaneously but was essentially man-made and planted to 'shelter the premises from the north wind'. In other words it is what might be called 'natural architecture' and Hardy makes splendidly imaginative use of it in this extraordinary incident.

Throughout *Far from the Madding Crowd* Hardy plays on the contrasting relationship between dark and light. Of its fifty-seven chapters, at least thirty-one are set in conditions where vision is partly or totally obscured. Others take place in bright sunlight. The sun in the sheep-shearing scene, for example, is 'strong enough to blind a weak-eyed man', but it is followed by a night as dark as 'the Ninth Plague of Egypt' in the fir plantation. On this same night before going to bed, Bathsheba makes her inspection of the farm. She takes with her a so-called 'dark lantern'. The lantern illustrated here is characteristic of this type, which gets its name from a shutter on the lens that can be opened and closed at will rather like a modern torch.

A nineteenth-century 'dark lantern' from the Pitt Rivers Museum, Oxford.

As Bathsheba makes her way back to her house through the plantation, she hears footsteps. She waits silently for the person to pass, but the path is narrow, something tugs at her skirt and she is pulled up against the stranger. Her lace hem has become caught in his spur. He asks her if she has a lantern. She admits that she has, and,

> a hand seized [it], the door was opened, the rays burst out from their prison, and Bathsheba beheld her position with astonishment. The man to whom she was hooked was brilliant in brass and scarlet. He was a soldier. His sudden appearance was to darkness what the sound of a trumpet is to silence. Gloom, the *genius loci* at all times hitherto, was now totally overthrown, less by the lantern-light than by what the lantern lighted. (162)

The event is of course a highly theatrical one, with the plantation providing the theatre and the lantern the stage lighting. Like a theatrical event, this too is a kind of deception. Bathsheba is deceived by the brilliance of Troy's appearance, 'Dazzled by brass and scarlet', (203) as later Boldwood perceptively observes. It is no coincidence either that the two meet at 'the darkest point of [Bathsheba's] route' (161). This is a brilliant stroke on Hardy's part in this rich psychological drama expressed through the material details of the setting. The darkness in the fir plantation is both physical and mental. It is pitch black amongst the trees, and Bathsheba's self-awareness is equally obscure. In his novels Hardy often draws on the connection between night and mental blindness. Here, however, with a subtle twist, Hardy stresses Bathsheba's personal shortcomings by placing the plantation 'just outside her own door'. (161) Very clearly she has little understanding of either herself or her own motives. Her mind is like the 'dark lantern' she carries, the gloom a symbol of her psychological limitations, and her physical entanglement with Troy's spur anticipates her disastrous sexual involvement with him. Again, the detail is so rich. The male phallic spur gets entangled with the trimming, or 'gimp', of her dress by chance. The encounter has no emotional content. It is simply an arbitrary coupling. But Troy's aggressive, mechanical, militaristic sexual persona is expressed through that potentially wounding spur, a spur that contrasts strongly with the shears that Gabriel Oak had deftly and authoritatively wielded at the sheep shearing earlier in the day. As Troy tries half-heartedly to unravel himself the two people, male and female, lit by the lantern, form a tableau with prophetic significance. The light 'radiated upwards into their faces, and sent over half the plantation gigantic shadows of both man and woman, each dusky shape becoming distorted and mangled upon the tree-trunks till it wasted to nothing'. (162) At this moment the architecture of Hardy's 'naturally formed hall' provides a screen on which images of the future are projected. The theatre has become a phantasmagoria, and the picture thrown upon its walls shows the couple, transformed into anonymous grotesques, with their relationship fading away into obscurity.

The entanglement that began in the fir plantation in June is consummated in July by the precipitous secret wedding in Bath. The couple return to Weatherbury with Troy now master of the farm. On his first morning there he greets Oak and a farm worker, Jan Coggan, from an upper window of his new residence, Weatherbury farmhouse. Realizing that Bathsheba is now Troy's wife Oak is speechless with rage and despair. Troy tries a casual conversation about the changes he wants to introduce to Weatherbury. 'A rambling, gloomy house this,' he says. Oak disagrees: 'But it is a nice old house.'

'Yes – I suppose so,' says Troy, 'but I feel like new wine in an old bottle here. My notion is that sash-windows should be put throughout, and these old wainscoted walls brightened up a bit; or the oak cleared quite away, and the walls papered.' Again Oak disagrees: 'It would be a pity, I think.' 'Well, no,' Troy comes back, giving his reasons.

A philosopher once said in my hearing that the old builders, who worked when art was a living thing, had no respect for the work of builders who went before them, but pulled down and altered as they thought fit, and why shouldn't we? 'Creation and preservation don't do well together,' says he, 'and a million of antiquarians can't invent a style.' My mind exactly. I am for making this place more modern, that we may be cheerful whilst we can. (233–4)

The relationship between creation and preservation has always been a vexed architectural issue. It was widely discussed in the nineteenth century and it troubled Hardy. When he was writing *Far from the Madding Crowd* he was a still a practising architect extensively involved in church 'restoration', a word that he came to believe was synonymous with vandalism. Later he became a member of the Society for the Protection of Ancient Buildings, founded by William Morris and Philip Webb in 1877, whose aim was to protect buildings from modernizing or invasive restoration. Hardy was entirely in sympathy with their view that additions to ancient buildings formed a part of their collective cultural heritage. Speaking in later years he lent his support to careful conservation, and resisted any changes that happened to be 'convenient and fashionable for the occupiers of the moment'. 'The policy of "masterly inaction"', he said, 'was never practised to higher gain than by [those] who simply left their historic buildings alone.'[4] Troy's attitude to the past is a callous one. He is introduced into the novel as 'a man to whom memories were an encumbrance, and anticipations a superfluity' (166) and what is clear from his views on modernization is that he has no sense of the part played by the farmhouse in the life of the community, and no respect for the memories that are held within its ancient fabric. His plans for Weatherbury farmhouse, however, are rapidly thwarted and never come to fruition.

By October, Fanny Robin has reappeared in the story. She has died in the workhouse, and has been brought back to Weatherbury where Bathsheba opens her coffin, discovering not only her body but that of her infant child. Troy flees the house and arranges for a headstone to be carved by a stonemason in Casterbridge. After the funeral he goes to Weatherbury churchyard and in an act of what the narrator calls 'absurd' posthumous repentance on the heels of 'previous indifference', he plants bulbs and flowers on Fanny's grave. Hardy was particularly attached to Puddletown church, the model for Weatherbury church. When the first collected edition of his works appeared in 1895 he commissioned a picture by H. Macbeth Raeburn as the frontispiece of the novel with the church standing prominently in the foreground. The caption reads: 'The Weatherbury of the story drawn on the spot.' The Weatherbury church now takes its revenge on Troy in a famous night scene in which, as the soldier sleeps in the porch, a storm rises and a gargoyle spouts water over the grave, destroying his efforts of the previous day. The appearance of this architectural detail is important. On the one hand it encapsulates the magnificent vitality of gothic workmanship.

Above: *Weatherbury* by Henry Macbeth Raeburn, frontispiece for the
1895 Osgood McIlvaine edition of *Far from the Madding Crowd*. Opposite:
Fifteenth-century gargoyle in the church of Sydling St Nicholas.

It was 'of the most original design that a human brain could conceive'. Yet it is
also repellent, demonic, partly man, partly monster. 'It was too human', says the
narrator,

> to be called like a dragon, too impish to be like a man, too animal to be
> like a fiend, and not enough like a bird to be called a griffin. This horrible
> stone entity was fashioned as if covered with a wrinkled hide; it had short,
> erect ears, eyes starting from their sockets, and its fingers and hands were
> seizing the corners of its mouth, which they thus seemed to pull open to
> give free passage to the water it vomited. (306)

As the powerful, but threatening life force concentrated into this sculptured monument brings retribution upon Troy, a strange reversal takes place. He himself is turned into a gargoyle. When he discovers what has happened in the night, his 'brow became heavily contracted. He set his teeth closely, and his compressed lips moved as those of one in great pain.' 'Troy's face', Hardy writes, 'was very expressive, and any observer who had seen him now would hardly have believed him to be a man who had laughed, and sung, and poured love-trifles into a woman's ear.' (308)

History and his past actions have caught up with him. In the past, memory had been an 'encumbrance' to him and he had been as disdainful of people as he had been of ancient buildings. The gargoyle forces him to face something of the anguish that he has inflicted upon others. In other words, the work of the medieval mason brings the past into the present, and the gargoyle establishes links between them that Troy would have preferred to have ignored.

Leaving the graveyard at Weatherbury church Troy walks to the coast, his mind filled with guilt and despondency. He decides to go swimming, abandons his clothes on the shore and is carried out to sea by a current. He fails to return and is presumed drowned. In fact he has been rescued and is persuaded to spend six months at sea with his rescuers. When he comes back to Britain, he is repelled by the idea of returning to Weatherbury and instead joins a travelling circus. In the September of that same year one of his performances takes place at a large sheep fair at Greenhill not far from his original point of departure, Weatherbury. Bathsheba, Boldwood and many of the farm workers attend. A circular tent of 'exceptional newness' has been erected for a performance of 'Turpin's Ride to York' in which Troy, once a skilled cavalryman, plays the leading role.

Peeping through a slit in the canvas before he is due to go on stage Troy is startled to see his wife in the audience. Desperate to conceal himself, he adds make-up, disguises himself more heavily and persuades the manager to speak his lines on the pretence that he has a bad cold. He goes through the performance undetected, in a role that comes naturally to him, the early eighteenth-century highwayman Dick Turpin. Like Turpin, Troy has robbed both Boldwood and Bathsheba of money, and it was through his wife's finances that he bought himself out of the army. Throughout the novel he has been involved in dissimulation and trickery, and it is in the refreshment tent after the performance that he plays his final deception. The reception area was highly respectable and divided into first, second and exclusive areas. Bathsheba and Boldwood, suspecting nothing, go into the exclusive area. Everything there is created to give the illusion of luxury and permanence. It has 'chairs and a table, which, on candles being lighted, made quite a cozy and luxurious show' and even the barman looks as if 'he had never lived anywhere but under canvas all his life.' (336) But it is fake, and what appears substantial is in fact temporary; it is form without substance, giving the diners a false sense of privacy. Troy puts this to his advantage by going round to the back of the tent to eavesdrop on Bathsheba and Boldwood as they take tea close to the outer canvas of the tent. Able to hear clearly, in order to see her he 'took a penknife from his pocket and softly made two little cuts crosswise in the cloth'. To his amazement he finds himself 'within twelve inches of the top of Bathsheba's head'. For her part she has no idea that she is being watched. She leans against the canvas so that 'it was pressed to the shape of her shoulder and she was in fact, as good as in Troy's arms'. (336)

With this episode, the novel has, in a sense, come full circle. This temporary structure of 'exceptional newness' is the counterpart of Gabriel Oak's shepherd's hut. One is brash and insubstantial, while the other, equally temporary, suggests nurture and integrity. These two locations form the outer edge of the network of buildings in *Far from the Madding Crowd* and between them lies a range of equally expressive locations. Their importance is highlighted by the fact that not all buildings in the novel are employed by Hardy in this same way. The two churches, All Saints' and All Souls', in the 'garrison town' where Troy waits for Fanny and where Fanny waits for Troy are just venues for a mistake, and their architectural appearance is of no particular significance. Much the same might be said of Casterbridge cornmarket, Boldwood's farmhouse, Oak's cottage in Weatherbury and the tavern called the Buck's Head. The great barn itself, however, provides the most striking example of the difference between expressive and non-expressive architecture. The first time it appears it forms the centrepiece of one of Hardy's most important statements about the connection between the life of a community and its architecture. On the second occasion it is almost invisible. This is on the evening before the summer storm that threatens to wreak havoc with the ricks on Bathsheba's farm. Troy, celebrating his recent marriage, gets all the farm hands drunk. The carousal takes place in the barn, yet as readers we hardly notice that it is the same barn that played such a prominent part in the sheep-shearing episode.

Far from the Madding Crowd promotes the values of personal integrity, social consistency and dignified labour in the rural context. The principal antagonist to those values is Frank Troy, whose bright red jacket is repeatedly contrasted with the ochres and greens of the countryside. His behaviour is directed entirely to the fulfilment of selfish ends and he has no respect for individuals or the wider community. He wilfully causes pain to Boldwood, he indirectly causes anguish to Oak, he exploits Bathsheba's naivety, and he casually destroys Fanny Robin. His famous sword exercise in the 'hollow amid the ferns' is a mesmerizing act of seduction, and as readers we are as dazzled as Bathsheba by this erotic performance. But we should not forget that it is an intensely aggressive act designed to disembowel the enemy. Fanny Robin has already fallen victim to Troy's heartless sexual aggression and in the hollow among the ferns Bathsheba is about to go down a similar path. In Weatherbury Troy uses his sword-like sensibility to cut through the small community, destroying all in its path. He is a man with no roots. His stopovers are always temporary. In the army he moves from barracks to barracks, his stay in Weatherbury is fleeting, and the last we see of him before he is shot in Boldwood's drawing room is in a tent. Standing against this are the values represented by the antiquity of the sheep-shearing barn. This acts as a memorial to the continuity of rural culture where human labour moved to the rhythm of the seasons. The people of Weatherbury are in harmony with the barn, so they are in harmony with themselves.

When Hardy moved back to Dorset after five years in London he seems to have observed the slow pace of rural life in a new light and in *Far from the Madding Crowd* he registers that life. Hardy was no rustic nor even gentleman farmer, but he was familiar with the day-to-day life of the agricultural community and though he was never centrally part of it he recognizes the value of living close to the land and according to patterns dictated by nature. Hardy's practice as an architect left its mark all over the text of the novel, and everywhere he has an eye for building and construction. But he was also sensitive to the symbolic meaning of buildings and what they represent within the community. Unlike Troy he understands the significance of a sympathetic relationship between man and his environment. One of the things that *Far from the Madding Crowd* tells us is that the conjunction between man and architecture is not a simple set of equivalents or parallels. Instead it involves concordances and subtle reciprocities between the animate world and the inanimate one. In Hardy's next novel, *The Return of the Native*, his focus shifts away from the built environment in an agricultural setting to a much wilder natural environment. Its geographical location in Dorset is very close, but its position in the mental map of Wessex is quite remote.

Chapter Two

The Return of the Native: Man's Place in Nature

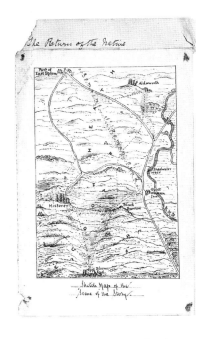

The map provided by Hardy for the first edition of *The Return of the Native* (1878).

EGDON HEATH, THE CHIEF GEOGRAPHICAL feature of *The Return of the Native,* is just a little to the south-west of Puddletown or Weatherbury, but the psychological distance between them is enormous. Gone is the agricultural world of sheep shearing and hay making in the valley of the Piddle. Instead furze cutting, harsh, primitive and humble, is the only trade, and the higher land is windswept, cold and lonely. In the earlier novel Hardy was ready to move locations from their geographical position. Bathsheba's house was shifted close to the village of Weatherbury and the tithe barn at Cerne Abbas was placed within the confines of her farm. The locations in *The Return of the Native* are more precisely placed and Hardy even provided a map for the first edition to pinpoint all the major spots. It is true that he made several significant adjustments to the topography, but comparison with a modern Ordnance Survey map makes it clear that the action of the novel takes place on Puddletown Heath, three miles to the east of Dorchester.

The map as Hardy drew it consists of hilly terrain with a scattering of isolated cottages and a single weir. There is no village, no grand house, no church, no farmhouse and no meeting place such as the maltster's in *Far from the Madding Crowd*. In keeping with a story where so much takes place out of doors and characters interact by moving around the heath, its surface is etched with the criss-crossing of paths and roads. The most important feature of Hardy's map, however, is its orientation. Instead of using the traditional north/south directions, the top is easterly and the bottom is westerly. The reason for this is clear. At the base of the map we find Blooms-End cottage, the home of Mrs Yeobright and her niece Thomasin, and the birthplace of Clym Yeobright. All the other locations radiate from this point. Mistover, the home of Eustacia Vye to the left, the Quiet Woman, Damon Wildeave's home to the right, Alderworth, the married home of Clym and Eustacia directly above, and immediately in the centre there is the Bronze Age tumulus of Blackbarrow (or Rainbarrow as Hardy later called it).[1] Blooms-End, then, is the geographical fulcrum and psychological focal point of the narrative. It is the place to which Clym Yeobright returns, and it is here that the first and fateful meeting between Clym and Eustacia Vye takes place. It is entirely appropriate, therefore, that it should have the most prominent and weightiest position at the bottom of the map.

But Blooms-End is important in other ways. It is located on the spot in Higher Bockhampton where Hardy was born and grew up. Though unlike the Hardys' cottage Mrs Yeobright's cottage is an 'old, irregular, thatched house, facing the heath, and commanding a full view of the valley' (109), for both Hardy and for Clym Yeobright their parental cottage symbolized home and *The Return of the Native* asks far-reaching questions about the idea of 'home', what it really means, where it might be found and whether it can be retraced after a significant absence. For Hardy this was as much a personal as a literary issue. His parents' cottage with its adjacent heath was his birthplace and the place where his imagination had first been nurtured. Growing in experience he came to realize more and more just how much he owed to this obscure country spot and as he matured as a novelist he recognized that the springs of his writing lay here. If Puddletown Heath was home to Hardy, so Egdon Heath is home to the characters of *The Return of the Native*. In other words the spot occupied by Blooms-End and Hardy's cottage represents an intersection of fact and fiction, of life and narrative, and of landscape and imagination.

When he was sixteen Hardy wrote a poem about this cottage with the rather lofty title 'Domicilium', the Latin for home. The verse paints a pastoral and idyllic picture in which the cottage is protected by trees, embowered in the nearby flowering plants, and rooted in the landscape.

> It faces west, and round the back and sides
> High beeches, bending, hang a veil of boughs,
> And sweep against the roof. Wild honeysucks
> Climb on the walls, and seem to sprout a wish
> (If we may fancy wish of trees and plants)
> To overtop the apple-trees hard by.
>
> Red roses, lilacs, variegated box
> Are there in plenty, and such hardy flowers
> As flourish best untrained. Adjoining these
> Are herbs and esculents; and farther still
> A field; then cottages with trees, and last
> The distant hills and sky.

A delicate, undated drawing of the cottage by Hardy, probably from the 1890s, shows that little had changed over the years. The building stands in an intimate relationship with the garden by which it is surrounded on three sides. In the distance, on the fourth side and above the roof we can see the outline of Puddletown Heath. In the poem this is described as ancient and rugged.

> Behind, the scene is wilder. Heath and furze
> Are everything that seems to grow and thrive
> Upon the uneven ground. A stunted thorn
> stands here and there, indeed; and from a pit
> An oak uprises, springing from a seed
> Dropped by some bird a hundred years ago.

Top: Drawing done by Hardy in the 1890s of his parents' cottage at
Higher Bockhampton. Pencil on paper, 14 x 19 cm.
Above: Hardy's bedroom in the cottage at Higher Bockhampton.

Hardy goes on to recall the words of his paternal grandmother telling him how in her youth the spot had been even more isolated and how

> . . . Snakes and efts
> Swarmed in the summer days, and nightly bats
> Would fly about our bedrooms. Heathcroppers
> Lived on the hills, and were our friends;
> So wild it was when first we settled here.[2]

Today the cottage looks much as it did in Hardy's day. It belongs to the National Trust and is the last house in the unmetalled lane that runs through the village. It was built by John Hardy, Hardy's great-grandfather, made of cob (gravel, sand, clay, flint, chalk and straw), protected by cement at the back, brick at the front and covered in wheat straw thatch. It is very small, but when Hardy was born it was even smaller. Downstairs the space was divided to provide a kitchen, parlour and even a small office where his father, and later his brother, managed the affairs of the family's building firm. Though the conditions were cramped and space limited, Hardy's parents entertained in the low-ceilinged parlour, and even had parties with dancing and music. An old-fashioned, cavernous inglenook fireplace provided heat from a large furze or peat fire, and in front of it stood a settle to guard against drafts from a door which, in Hardy's day, opened straight from the front garden. Upstairs there were rooms for the parents and children and adjoining the building was a minute cottage for Hardy's grandmother. When the old lady died in 1857, Hardy's father linked the two places, enlarging the space for the family. The tiny room in which Hardy was born is much as it was when he grew up, as is the bedroom that he later shared with his brother Henry. Here the young Thomas often perched on the deep window seat that looked across the garden, and it was in this room that he read, drew, painted, wrote poetry and even completed two novels, *Under the Greenwood Tree* and *Far from the Madding Crowd*. Both Hardy and his siblings were strongly attached to this spot. His brother and two sisters, Mary and Kate, continued to live there long after he had moved out and it was not until 1912 that, all unmarried and still living together, they tore themselves away and moved to a house just a few miles across the valley of the Frome.

Before his marriage in 1874, Hardy had been able to come and go at will from this cottage, often staying there for long periods. After his marriage he had to be more circumspect. From the outset, Hardy's mother, Jemima, had disliked his fiancé Emma Gifford for her social pretensions, believing that she brought no youth, wealth, or intelligence to her son. For her part Emma was taken aback when she discovered how unsophisticated and 'countrified' were Hardy's parents. The mutual suspicion between the two women meant careful advance preparation for any meeting and the idea of 'home' for Hardy began to lose its exclusive connection with Higher Bockhampton.

After his marriage Hardy made more changes. Physically the location of the cottage standing near heath and hills was unaltered, but Hardy was not the same person who had passed a rather isolated childhood there. It was not just that he had become an adult, architect, author and married man navigating the tricky waters between his strong-minded mother and his wife. He and Emma now needed a new place they could call home. Ever since a Continental honeymoon they had occupied rented accommodation in places where they had no roots. They first settled briefly in Surbiton before going to Westbourne Grove and then on to Swanage. Abandoning Swanage in May 1876, the couple set off on a second Continental journey, this time travelling down the Rhine to Heidelberg and back via Belgium and Holland. Emma was becoming weary of travelling. 'Going back to England,' she wrote in her diary, 'where we have no home & no chosen county.'[3] Finally, in July 1876, after more indecision, they settled in the small town of Sturminster Newton about fifteen miles from Higher Bockhampton, and not long after they moved in Hardy began *The Return of the Native*.

Physical changes had been accompanied by mental ones, and Hardy's attitudes and values had also shifted since he sat and wrote in his cottage bedroom. Under the influence of his friend Horace Moule and his period in sophisticated London society he had come into contact with some of the most radical and advanced theories of the nineteenth century, theories that would change man's outlook on the world.

He had probably been introduced to the Moule family by the eldest brother, Henry, with whom, as we have seen (p.22), he shared an interest in watercolour painting. But it was the fourth brother, Horace, eight years older than Hardy, to whom he was more attracted, and as early as 1857 Horace started lending him books. The father, the formidable Reverend Henry Moule, had been vicar of Fordington since 1828. All his sons had been brought up in a rigorous intellectual climate, but Horace, intelligent, gifted and suave, often clashed with his father about modern ideas in science and theology. In contrast, Hardy, like the other members of his family, had grown up in the simple beliefs of the local Anglican Church, and its rituals and dogmas were deeply interwoven into his personality. When Moule told him about the publications of the rationalist biblical historians David Strauss and Ludwig Feuerbach, writers who reinterpreted Christ and his life in humanist rather than divine terms, Hardy's faith was strongly tested. It was tested further when Moule gave him a famous collection of articles published in 1860 with the innocuous title of *Essays and Reviews*. This launched a further challenge to the authenticity of the text of the Bible and sent shockwaves through the Church so great that the Church contemplated prosecuting its authors for heresy. The turbulence created in the faithful was intensified by the publication in 1859 of Charles Darwin's *The Origin of Species* of which Hardy claimed to be an early admirer. Its message about evolutionary processes, about the impersonal forces of nature and the ruthless survival of the fittest, all radically changed the Victorian attitude to what people believed was man's place in the natural world. In Darwin's work (at least as it was interpreted by the biologist T. H. Huxley), man was beginning to seem more like an ape than an angel. The effect these views had on society was not immediate, but it was profound.

Traditionally, man had occupied the place of honour in the great chain of being as God's most outstanding creation, and the natural world was the home that God had given him to rule over as he wished. But advances in the science of geology, especially in the work of Charles Lyell, suggested something different. Fossil finds indicated that the earth was much older than originally supposed, that man was a recent comer, and that the creation story in Genesis was a fanciful myth. This put in question the whole view of the natural order. Suddenly, instead of being the most prominent figure in the natural landscape, man was a tiny entity dwarfed by the vast eons of time that stretched out behind him. Darwin's research further destabilized the traditional view of divine beneficence. Men had long believed in what Shakespeare had called 'great creating nature'. She was a goddess who sustained and nurtured man, not only supplying his physical needs but also offering him spiritual comfort. The sense of nature's metaphysical and imaginative power was felt most strongly at the beginning of the nineteenth century in the poetry and painting of the Romantics. Hardy had grown up reading Coleridge, Shelley, Keats and other writers of the period, all of whom, in their different ways, were passionate about the living, healing force of the natural world. Wordsworth summed this up when he described nature as a power 'whose dwelling is the light of setting suns,/And the round ocean and the living air,/And the blue sky and the mind of Man'.[4] Darwin's work challenged this positive and sympathetic attitude from the standpoint of botany and biology. In a famous passage that seemed to question so many of the old assumptions he wrote:

> We behold the face of nature bright with gladness, we often see superabundance of food; we do not see or we forget that the birds which are idly singing round us mostly live on insects or seeds, and are thus constantly destroying life; or we forget how largely these songsters, or their eggs, or their nestlings, are destroyed by birds and beasts of prey; we do not always bear in mind, that, though food may be now superabundant, it is not so at all seasons of each recurring year.[5]

Nature, the comforting source of the material and psychological needs of man, had become in Tennyson's famous words 'red in tooth and claw'. This was all new to Hardy. He had grown up in a rural spot intimate with the natural world and had observed at first hand its face, 'bright with gladness'. But as he read the works of Lyell, Darwin and other scientists a shadow fell across that face. So when he came to write about Egdon Heath in the first chapter of *The Return of the Native*, a chapter entitled 'A Face upon which Time makes Little Impression', the physiognomy of nature had darkened. It was now no longer 'bright with gladness' but had become, instead, a 'near relation of night'. (9)

The opening of *The Return of the Native* is a truly remarkable piece of writing. No other novel by Hardy, and possibly no other nineteenth-century novel, devotes four pages to landscape alone. There are no houses, no people (other than a phantom furze cutter) and no animals. Yet the prose, like the musical prelude to some great opera, is deep and resonant.

A Saturday afternoon in November was approaching the time of twilight, and the vast tract of unenclosed wild known as Egdon Heath embrowned itself moment by moment. Overhead the hollow stretch of whitish cloud shutting out the sky was as a tent which had the whole heath for its floor.

The heaven being spread with this pallid screen and the earth with the darkest vegetation, their meeting-line at the horizon was clearly marked. In such contrast the heath wore the appearance of an instalment of night which had taken up its place before its astronomical hour was come: darkness had to a great extent arrived hereon, while day stood distinct in the sky. Looking upwards, a furze-cutter would have been inclined to continue work; looking down, he would have decided to finish his faggot and go home. The distant rims of the world and of the firmament seemed to be a division in time no less than a division in matter. The face of the heath by its mere complexion added half-an-hour to eve; it could in like manner retard the dawn, sadden noon, anticipate the frowning of storms scarcely generated, and intensify the opacity of a moonless midnight to a cause of shaking and dread. (9)

The two most prominent features of Egdon Heath are its darkness and its loneliness. It is a 'relation of night', it 'meets the evening gloom in pure sympathy' and has a 'vast dark surface'. (13) The story opens in twilight, it reaches a climax in the darkness of night a year and day later, and many of the most important events are played out at night. It is also a lonely place. 'Solitude', says Hardy, 'seemed to look out of its countenance and it had a lonely face, suggesting tragical possibilities.' (11) The word 'lonely' punctuates the text again and again, and loneliness seems to be a condition endemic to those who live close to the heath.

Though Hardy's emphasis in the opening paragraphs of the book lies on the physical appearance of the heath, surprisingly this is not expressed in the usual terms of landscape. Instead, Egdon is given a human face. It has (as the heading for the first chapter tells us) 'A Face' with an 'Atlantean brow'. It is 'haggard', 'wild' and 'grim'. Sometimes the old face is 'swarthy', sometimes it is 'full of watchful intentness'.

Winfrith Heath remains today as nearby Puddletown Heath appeared in the 1870s.

In personifying Egdon like this Hardy suggests that it has a special rapport with the human world, or 'a peculiar and kindly congruity' (10) as he calls it. The idea is central to Hardy's writing. Throughout his fiction Hardy creates an interactive relationship between man and the landscape he inhabits. He assumes that the emotional and psychological rapport between man and his environment is not just one way, but that often each can be interpreted in the terms of the other. Egdon is an outstanding case of this, appealing to a special kind of individual who, like the heath, itself is 'majestic without severity, impressive without showiness . . . grand in its simplicity'. (10) But, Hardy asks, what could be the attraction of a place so dark and lonely? And his answer resonates not only through this novel, but also through his later ones. 'Haggard Egdon', he says, 'appealed to a subtler and scarcer instinct, to a more recently learnt emotion, than that which responds to the sort of beauty called charming and fair.' Places that were once labelled as areas of outstanding natural beauty, he explains, have lost their charm for modern man. 'Indeed,' he says,

it is a question if the exclusive reign of this orthodox beauty is not approaching its last quarter. The new vale of Tempe may be a gaunt waste in Thule: human souls may find themselves in closer and closer harmony with external things wearing a sombreness distasteful to our race when it was young. The time seems near, if it has not actually arrived, when the chastened sublimity of a moor, a sea, or a mountain will be all of nature that is absolutely in keeping with the moods of the more thinking among mankind. And ultimately, to the commonest tourist, spots like Iceland may become what the vineyards and myrtle gardens of South Europe are to him now; and Heidelberg and Baden be passed unheeded as he hastens from the Alps to the sand dunes of Scheveningen. (10)

Earlier generations took delight in the landscape of southern Europe and in other parts of the world that are benign, warm and colourful. But this had all changed. Under the influence of modern scientific rationalism and the new biblical criticism the world had become a less benevolent place, and it was the contours of barren, bleak and hostile locations which fitted this modern sensibility.

Hardy found confirmation of these ideas when he saw some landscape paintings at an exhibition at the French Gallery in London in 1875. At first, he said, the pictures seemed dull and rather dreary, but on closer inspection the indifferent treatment of landscape held a strange fascination for him. 'This accords', he wrote, 'with my feeling about, say, Heidelberg and Baden *versus* Scheveningen . . . Paradoxically put, it is to see beauty in ugliness.'[6] Where beauty was once enjoyed in locations such as Baden-Baden, now it might be found on the Dutch coast at Scheveningen, and it so happens that he and Emma had visited both Baden Baden and Scheveningen during their recent Continental tour. Emma confirmed in her diary that Scheveningen held little interest for her, and the guidebook dismissed it as 'a desert of undulating sand-hills' and 'coarse grass'.[7]

In *The Return of the Native* Hardy is at pains to stress that though the dark, brooding quality of Egdon has an affinity with the contemporary intellectual mood, the place itself is actually extremely old. In other words, it is aesthetically modern but geologically ancient. In geological terms, the so-called Reading beds that emerge from the chalk of the surrounding area are hard to cultivate because the soil does not retain nutrition. This is borne out in contemporary works on local agriculture such as William Stevenson's early nineteenth-century account of Dorset farming, where he says that the area around Puddletown Heath 'is a most dreary tract of heath land, and is scarcely capable of any improvement in the hands of the agriculturalist'.[8] Similarly Egdon, says Hardy, was 'the enemy of civilization', untouched by 'pickaxe, plough, or spade'. Yet in spite of this, or perhaps because of it, it stands as it has always stood, lonely and neglected, providing the unchanging bedrock for all the growth and decay that has taken place on it and around it. 'The sea changed, the fields changed, the rivers, the villages, and the people changed, yet Egdon remained.' (12)

At what point in his life Hardy began to feel this about Puddletown Heath is not known, but two watercolours, both painted near his parents' cottage, represent it as bleak and lonely in dull tertiary colours, olive green and grey. The first, *From Black Heath Corner* (p.14), is his earliest attempt at watercolour, and may be the one that he did under the instruction of Henry Moule. It was painted on a spot looking back down a valley near the cottage. The other,

Hardy, *Rainbarrow and the Heath* (1871). Watercolour on paper, 17.3 x 26.7 cm.

Rainbarrow and the Heath, dating from 1871 shows the monotonous undulating hills of furze, gorse and heather, with a single lonely figure of a cowhand reclining, almost camouflaged, in the middle distance.

If we take the sandy bridle path that leads across the open heath from behind the Hardys' cottage and walk up to the spot where the trees begin it is not difficult to sense how Hardy managed the shift between the literal and the metaphorical representation of the heath in this novel. This stretch of land with its bracken and heather has been kept cleared and free from both trees and rhododendrons so that it resembles what would have been familiar to Hardy's eyes in his youth. At the top of the slope the path divides into four separate tracks. A turn to the right takes us up an incline through a densely wooded area that then opens out once again. This gives extensive views across the alluvial valley of the river Frome, quite different in character from the heath, and behind, to the north-west, a ridge that has been cleared of trees marks the location of what Hardy called 'Mistover Knap', the site of Eustacia Vye's cottage. Immediately beside us on the right is a low fence. Over the fence and beyond it, a narrow path leads through the dense and prickly gorse up to a Bronze Age tumulus. This is Rainbarrow or Blackbarrow. At its foot, growing out of the gorse, beaten and broken, there is a blasted fir tree and on its summit stands a low holly tree. On the other side of the tumulus the ground falls steeply away through bracken and trees to the river. The silence is intense, the stillness profound. As the sun goes down in the west, darkness fills the valleys and even today this feels a very lonely place. Returning to the path, and retracing our steps slightly, we come to the site of a Roman road that drops away down the ridge and is lost in the heath. The surface is pale with embedded flints, and in the dwindling light, as Hardy suggests, it bisects the 'vast dark surface like the parting-line on a head of raven hair'. (13) If we now follow the old Roman road down to the valley floor and turn round to look back and upwards to the tumulus we get some sense of what Diggory Venn sees when, in the first chapter of the novel, he transports Thomasin Yeobright to the Quiet Woman after her failed marriage ceremony. 'The scene before the reddleman's eyes was a gradual series of ascents,' Hardy tells us, culminating in a barrow. At the top a 'bossy projection of earth above its natural level occupied the loftiest ground of the loneliest height that the heath contained'. Rainbarrow was 'the pole and axis of this heathery world'. (17)

As the reddleman watches, Hardy creates a vertical timeline from what he sees before him. At the lowest point on the line is the heath. Here ancient, amorphous rock and heather create 'hillocks, pits, [and] ridges'. On that stands the prehistoric Bronze Age barrow, 'like a wart on an Atlantean brow'. But what catches Venn's attention is a figure that appears in silhouette on top of the barrow completing the picture: 'What the barrow was to the hill supporting it, the object was to the barrow. It rose from the semi-globular mound like a spike from a helmet.' Geological time passes into prehistoric time, historic time into contemporary time culminating in a human representative of the modern world: 'There the form stood, motionless as the hill beneath. Above the plain rose the hill, above the hill rose the barrow, and above the barrow rose the figure.' (17) Held for an instant like a tableau, the 'vale, the upland, the barrow, and the figure above' created, says Hardy, a perfect 'unity'. Suddenly and unexpectedly, however, the figure moves; the tableau is disturbed, revealing the figure's sex. It is a woman.

The woman is, of course, Eustacia Vye. Motionless on the timeline she is an abstraction but when she moves she becomes an individual with a life and a history, and it is not long before we discover why she comes alone to this spot. Eustacia Vye was born on the south coast at Budmouth. As a young orphan she had been deposited on the heath and brought up by her grandfather but had never felt at home there. She sees herself as an alien and it is from this alienation her tragedy arises. 'Inwardly and eternally unreconciled' to the heath she longs persistently to be somewhere else, somewhere more fashionable and exotic. Egdon has become a kind of Hades for her. It is 'her cross' and her 'cruel master'. Her tragedy is that she is torn between two worlds, an old one and a new one, and both of them find expression in her physical appearance. On the one hand she is classical. On Olympus she would have 'done very well with a little preparation'. She has 'Pagan eyes' and a mouth sculpted with such fineness that it might have been discovered 'lurking underground in the South as fragments of forgotten marbles'. (66) Her father was from Corfu, so by nature she faces south. By nurture, however, her habitat is the north, for since coming to the heath she has imbibed 'much of what was dark in its tone'. (67) Again, this is expressed in her appearance. In the twilight the heath seems like a 'head of raven hair' that 'added half-an-hour to eve' (9), and Eustacia's hair also 'closed over her forehead like nightfall extinguishing the western glow'; like the furze, to see it 'was to fancy that a whole winter did not contain darkness enough to form its shadow'. (66) Like the heath, too, Eustacia is profoundly lonely. Egdon has a 'lonely face, suggesting tragical possibilities' and as Eustacia stands on Rainbarrow, she is 'a lonely person', the 'queen of the solitude'. (18)

Loneliness affects almost all those living on the heath. On Hardy's map we can see that Egdon is indeed a 'vast tract of unenclosed wild' dotted with isolated and 'lonely' dwellings. It is as if the loneliness of Egdon and its inhabitants symbolizes the modern condition in a world from which God has withdrawn. Though Eustacia and Wildeve enjoyed each other as 'hot lovers' before the story opens their affair was born largely out of lust and boredom and as a means of staving off loneliness. In the opening scenes the couple fill their time with an erotic power game that waxes and wanes onward through the narrative. As the story develops, however, each believes their salvation to lie somewhere beyond the confines of the heath and beyond the confines of the map. Eustacia pines for Budmouth or Paris; Wildeve plans to go to America. But in the modern world of *The Return of the Native* these places have no real existence; they live only in the realm of romantic fantasy. In reality, only the heath exists. This is the world of the new biology from which romance has been banished, and when characters like Diggory Venn or Clym, for example, leave it, they pass into an existential void, temporarily disappearing from the story.

A figure that enters the story from one of these margins of existence is, of course, Clym Yeobright himself. Disillusioned by the materialism of the diamond trade in Paris he is as anxious to return to the heath as Eustacia is to leave it, and their contrasting responses to the wilderness of Egdon is an index of their conflicting mental attitudes. Clym loves it in all its detailed richness, whereas Eustacia hates it in the abstract. Where Eustacia faces outwards, forever pining for what she cannot have, Clym, like Hardy, had been so 'interwoven with the heath in his boyhood that hardly anybody could look upon it without thinking of him'. (166) Like Hardy, too, Yeobright lived close to the heath.

> He was permeated with its scenes, with its substance, and with its odours. He might be said to be its product. His eyes had first opened thereon: with its appearance all the first images of his memory were mingled, his estimate of life had been coloured by it. His toys had been the flint knives and arrow-heads which he found there, wondering why stones should 'grow' to such odd shapes; his flowers, the purple bells and yellow gorse: his animal-kingdom, the snakes and croppers; his society, its human haunters. Take all the varying hates felt by Eustacia Vye towards the heath, and translate them into loves, and you have the heart of Clym. (171)

Clym finds the heath a congenial and friendly place, and like his cousin Thomasin loves its 'grim old face'. (335) His mother, too, looks upon it as on 'the face of a friend' (38), but for both Eustacia and Wildeve it is merely an inanimate prison. These highly polarized responses, encouraged by Hardy's personification of this tract of land, prompted the first readers of the book to suggest that the heath is actually one of story's dramatis personae. In fact it is not. Hardy may have given it human attributes and it may be humanized by the central characters, but as Hardy warns us really 'the storm was its lover, [and] the wind . . . its friend'. It remains indifferent to mankind, acting as a screen on which humans project their hopes, fears, pleasures and anxieties. At one of the most dramatic climaxes in the story when Clym discovers Eustacia's role in the death of his mother, the heath stands unconcerned and unmoved. He is stunned by the news and sees before him 'the imperturbable countenance of the heath, which, having defied the cataclysmal onsets of centuries, reduced to insignificance by its seamed and antique features the wildest turmoil of a single man'. (312)

Climbing back to Rainbarrow and retracing our path past the Roman road on the right we come to another track that descends into the valley below. This is the route that Eustacia regularly uses between her cottage and Rainbarrow, and it is not difficult to see why a young woman of nineteen wearing a fashionable bustle, dainty shoes and a fine blouse would find the damp, mist and rain of this place repellent. As the road descends the steep bank on the left is filled with tangled rhododendrons and the drop on the right is dense with tall firs. When it reaches the valley bottom it ascends again towards the site of Mistover Knap. In Hardy's day this would have all been open to the wind, and the wilderness of the heath could have been seen rolling away for miles towards the south coast. Mistover Knap itself is a high ridge that marks the northern line of the heath, and where the trees have been cleared Rainbarrow can be clearly seen to the south. Eustacia's cottage, however, cannot be precisely located, though Tony Fincham, the most recent authority on Hardy's Wessex, points out a low earthen wall near the path and a wall that encloses a pond.[9] He suggests that this is all that remains of what might have been the garden of a simple cottage.

It was to the full as lonely a place as Rainbarrow, though at rather a lower level; and it was more sheltered from wind and weather on account of the few firs to the north. The bank which enclosed the whole homestead, and well protected it from the lawless state of the world without; it was formed of thick square clods, dug from the ditch on the outside, and built up with a slight batter or incline, which forms no slight defence where hedges will not grow because of the wind and the wilderness, and where wall materials are unattainable. Otherwise the situation was quite open, commanding the whole length of the valley which reached to the river behind Wildeve's house. High above this to the right, and much nearer hitherward than the Quiet Woman inn, the blurred contour of Rainbarrow obstructed the sky. (60)

Unlike either the Quiet Woman or Blooms-End, Eustacia's cottage is embedded in the heart of this primitive world, and radiating from its darkness is the bonfire she organizes for 5 November. She pays the young boy, Charley, to feed the flames with solid logs in contrast to the furze used on the other bonfires in the area so that it would burn longer and more brightly than its competitors. This fire is significant. Throughout the novel the light from fires, candles and embers forms a connected pattern associated with Eustacia. Fire, light and life are closely linked in mythology, and as the bonfire on Rainbarrow blazes into the sky Hardy points out that the practice of fire lighting has very ancient origins. The Bronze Age funeral pyres that consumed the bodies of the dead at Rainbarrow about four thousand years ago were superseded by ritual fires to the pagan gods, Thor and Woden. These were followed in turn by the fires of the Druids, then the Saxons. However, fire making, he says, has a wider significance than a religious one. 'To light a fire . . . is the instinctive and resistant act of man when, at the winter ingress, the curfew is sounded throughout Nature.' It is an act of resistance against the natural cycle of life and death, and 'indicates', he says, 'a spontaneous, Promethean rebelliousness against that fiat that this recurrent season shall bring foul times, cold darkness, misery and death. Black chaos comes, and the fettered gods of the earth say, Let there be light.' (21)

It is as if light and fire were a protest against the encroaching darkness of the modern condition. Prometheus, it will be remembered, stole fire from the gods, gave it to mankind and was punished by being chained eternally to a wild rock. On several occasions Eustacia is described as 'Promethean', and like Prometheus she is chained to the rocky substance of Egdon. Her sign is the unconventional, defiant bonfire at Mistover and her rebelliousness finds expression in her wider disdain for social convention. With no compunction she dresses as a man, a Turkish knight, to take part in the Christmas mumming and she is careless about the explicitness of her sexual relationship with Wildeve. Eustacia's vitality is expressed primarily in that smouldering sexuality. Her spirit, we are told, is 'flame-like' and sparks rise from it into her 'dark pupils'. (66) When the bonfire on Rainbarrow has died down she returns to it and blows on the embers. Though 'the light raised by her breath', says Hardy, is slight, its effect is sexually alluring. 'A momentary irradiation of flesh was all that it had disclosed of her face. That consisted of two matchless lips and a cheek only, her head being still enveloped.' (57) As a woman who believes that 'a blaze of love, and extinction, was better than a lantern glimmer of the same which should last long years' (69) she goes back to her own bonfire at Mistover hoping that Wildeve will be drawn there like a moth to a candle. He duly appears and she uses its illumination to enhance her physical appearance: 'She seized the moment, and throwing back the shawl so that the firelight shone full upon her face and throat, said with a smile, "Have you seen anything better than that in your travels?"' But Eustacia, as Hardy points out, 'was not one to commit herself to such a position without good ground. He said quietly, "No".' (63)

Eustacia's sexuality, her beauty, her fiery 'smouldering rebelliousness' (67), charms many of the males in the novel and though she may be dragged down into pits of gloom by the cold northern place in which she is forced to live, her sexual magnetism propels the story forward. This allure is directed first at Damon Wildeve, then at Clym Yeobright and, on both occasions, the heath is her arena for mating. When she sets her sights on Clym their meetings, like those previously with Wildeve, take place in the bracken, and on a warm afternoon in early summer she arranges a special rendezvous with Clym halfway between Blooms-End and Mistover.

To find this spot we have to leave Mistover and return to the crossing of the paths at the top of the valley to the east of Bloomsend. Here we can see a number of what are called 'swallet holes' in the surface of the land, dips and declivities caused by the erosion of soluble areas of rock by rainwater. These then become filled with vegetation or trees and it is in one such hollow that Clym waits for Eustacia. As he sits there he finds himself enclosed in a nest of vivid green created by the ferns that (like the attraction of this couple) are young and luxuriant but without fruit or flowers. The ferny vegetation round him, though so abundant, was quite uniform; it was a grove of machine-made foliage, a world of green triangles with saw-edges, and not a single flower. The air was warm with a vaporous warmth, and the stillness was unbroken. Lizards, grasshoppers, and ants were the only living things to be beheld. The scene seemed to belong to the ancient world of the carboniferous period, when the forms of plants were few, and of the fern kind; when there was neither bud nor blossom, nothing but a monotonous extent of leafage, amid which no bird sang. (200)

The primitivism of this pre-human world dominated by foliage and insects is a feature of the antiquity of the heath and its primeval complexion, suggestive of the instinctive nature of Clym's desire for Eustacia. His pursuit of the girl, fuelled by sexual desire, has induced in him a kind of unreflective, mental torpor.

Walking hand in hand they reach the southern edge of the heath, the 'nether margin' as Hardy calls it, where the land flattens out into the valley of the Froom. In the intense illumination of the scene created by 'the sun, resting on the horizon line', Clym can see groups of gnats 'rising upwards and dancing about like sparks of fire'. (202) The gnats refer back to the primitive world of insects that Clym saw earlier amongst the ferns. At dusk male gnats form large mating swarms called 'ghosts', lit up here like 'sparks of fire'. Though the fire suggests the innate vitality of life created by sexual energy, it suggests too the brevity of life, the brevity of desire and the brevity of all existence.

Clym proposes to Eustacia. She accepts, but instead of the anticipated sense of elation, Clym is overpowered by an unexpected sentiment that seems to emanate from 'the dead flat of the scenery'. Looking out beyond the margin of the heath and into the valley of the Froom he recognizes 'something in its oppressive horizontality which too much reminded him of the arena of life; it gave him a sense of bare equality with, and no superiority to, a single living thing under the sun'. (204) Those living things include, of course, the insects that live on the heath. Having committed himself to marriage with Eustacia he has woken to the fact that his life is being determined by a biological process as common to insects as man – sexual reproduction.

Insects feature prominently in this novel; in fact Egdon Heath is alive with gnats, flies, bees, butterflies, grasshoppers, glowworms and mayflies or 'ephemerons' and though their lives are short, they a play crucial role in the natural economy of the heath. Insects also figure importantly in Charles Darwin's *The Origin of Species* where Darwin attributed to them great power in shaping ecological change and development. He spoke of how the process of transporting pollen between the flowers of plants and trees placed them at the heart of the struggle for existence, and he admired 'the slave-making instinct of certain ants; and the cell-making power of the hive-bee'. 'These two latter instincts', he said, 'have generally and justly been ranked by naturalists as the most wonderful of all known instincts.'[10] Another admirer of ant behaviour is Mrs Yeobright. She is walking away from Alderworth back to her home in Blooms-End, having failed to bring about a reconciliation between herself and her son and daughter-in-law, when she sees on the ground a colony that 'had established a thoroughfare across the way' and 'where they toiled a never-ending and heavy-laden throng'. (278) She makes the connection between insect life and human life. 'To look down upon them', she thought, 'was like observing a city street from the top of a tower' and she remembered that generations of the same insects had been doing this on the same spot for years. Though Darwin does not develop the comparison, Hardy clearly sees parallels between insect and human. Already, Clym's pursuit of Eustacia has resembled the behaviour of mating gnats, and the entomologist in Mrs Yeobright, on her journey out to Alderworth, sees mayflies lost, like her son, in the grip of sensual pleasure.

> Occasionally, she came to a spot where independent worlds of ephemerons were passing their time in mad carousal, some in the air, some on the hot ground and vegetation, some in the tepid and stringy water of a nearly dried pool. All the shallower ponds had decreased to a vaporous mud amid which the maggoty shapes of innumerable obscene creatures could be indistinctly seen, heaving and wallowing with enjoyment. (266–7)

Though the scale of human and insect life is very different both here and elsewhere in his novels, Hardy employs this difference to illustrate the diminutive, vulnerable status of man in the context of the vastness of nature. When, for example, Clym and Eustacia have moved to Alderworth, Clym's eyesight fails and he becomes a furze cutter. Dressed in appropriate leather clothing, and working in the huge stretch of vegetation, he is just 'a brown spot in the midst of an expanse of olive-green gorse, and nothing more' (244), and later, when Mrs Yeobright goes to look for him, once again he appears 'of russet hue', hardly more 'distinguishable from the scene around him than the green caterpillar from the leaf it feeds on'. (267) Similarly, other figures are reduced to insignificance by the large and indifferent forces of nature. Like an exotic beetle, Thomasin goes alone to her own wedding, 'a little figure . . . diminishing far up the valley – a pale blue spot, in a vast field of neutral brown – solitary, and undefended . . .' (156), and as Eustacia and Wildeve walk down a slope after a clandestine encounter on the heath, 'their black figures sank and disappeared from against the sky. They were as two horns that the sluggish heath had put forth from its crown, like a mollusk, and had now again drawn in.' (85)

Though Hardy's characters are sometimes dwarfed in a blank and indifferent landscape, that same land, for those who have eyes to see, is filled with vitality and life. One of those who sees that life is Diggory Venn and another is Clym Yeobright, who, paradoxically, perceives more clearly when his eyesight has begun to fail. When their honeymoon period is over Clym sets to work to prepare himself for his mission to bring education to the heath dwellers. His reading is relentless and gradually his eyesight begins to weaken. His short-sighted condition, however, is both literal and metaphorical. He is myopic in his estimation of Eustacia and equally near-sighted about his plans for reform as he prepares to improve the mental state of the heath dwellers with no thought for their impoverished material condition. All he can do now are the most menial tasks and he is forced to take up furze cutting. 'This man from Paris', says Hardy, 'was now so disguised by his leather accoutrements, and by the goggles . . . that his closest friend might have passed by without recognizing him.' (244) Casting off his former identity he rediscovers his childhood self through his physical closeness to the fauna of the heath.

His familiars were creeping and winged things, and they seemed to enroll him in their band. Bees hummed around his ears with an intimate air, and tugged at the heath and furze-flowers at his side in such numbers as to weigh them down to the sod. The strange amber-coloured butterflies which Egdon produced, and which were never seen elsewhere, quivered in the breath of his lips, alighted upon his bowed back, and sported with the glittering point of his hook as he flourished it up and down. (244)

In a strange way Clym's blindness has brought him insight and has brought him, too, back into harmony with the heath, giving him an, albeit temporary, sense of peace and tranquillity.

Clym's furze cutting takes place not far from the cottage at Alderworth. This was modelled on Culpeper Cottage, situated on the map some six miles east of Hardy's birthplace, and lying about half a mile south of the small village of Briantspuddle. The public footpath across the heath runs right in front of the building, but to increase its sense of isolation Hardy created one cottage of what are actually two adjacent buildings once attached to the local brickworks.

When Clym first visits this cottage he does so under considerable duress. It happens on the day after his engagement to Eustacia, following his confession of the arrangement to his mother. The news devastates her since she is fully aware of the unsuitability of the match, and mother and son have a row of wounding proportions. Feeling obliged to move out of Blooms-End, he sets off to find somewhere else to live. The weather has changed from the previous day, and as he crosses the heath the heavy rain and tempestuous wind seem to have turned June into November. Clym's mental anguish finds a sympathetic response in a nearby plantation of fir and beech, one that had been enclosed from heathland in the year of his birth. (203) Both Clym and the trees are suffering, and the young man's mental anguish is expressed through the injury inflicted by the wind on the trunks and branches. The trees 'laden heavily with their new and humid leaves, were now suffering more damage than during the highest winds of winter'. 'Each stem was wrenched at the root, where it moved like a bone in its socket, and at every onset of the gale convulsive sounds came from the branches, as if pain were felt.' (205) The connection between the animate and the inanimate is made through corporeal metaphors and in a similar way another clump of trees expresses the anguish of Clym's mother. The nine trees growing on a high knoll just above Culpeper Cottage are called 'The Devil's Bellows'. Here the unhappy Mrs Yeobright pauses while following her son in her one and only visit to Alderworth. She sees a clump of Scotch firs and feeling 'distressingly agitated,

Above left: Culpeper Cottage, near Briantspuddle, the model for Alderworth, the home of Clym and Eustacia. Above right: The 'Devil's Bellows', a clump of nine trees just above Culpepper Cottage.

weary, and unwell' (268), she sits down beneath them. They were 'singularly battered, rude, and wild, and for a few minutes Mrs Yeobright dismissed thoughts of her own storm-broken and exhausted state to contemplate theirs'. Like the fir and beech trees that Clym passed, these, too, have been damaged in tempestuous weather, and again Hardy expresses this damage in terms of bodily pain: 'Some were blasted and split as if by lightning, black stains as from fire marking their sides, while the ground at their feet was strewn with dead fir-needles and heaps of cones blown down in the gales of past years.' But there is an important difference between Hardy's treatment of the two events. The relationship between Clym and the wounded trees in the copse is one of sympathy; the connection between Mrs Yeobright and the trees in the Devil's Bellows is one of identity. Like them she is gathered into the general travail of nature, and like them she has been besieged by forces that Darwin warned were everywhere in nature, destroying as well as creating. Even on that hot day in August the trees register the anguish of existence and though 'no perceptible wind was blowing', says Hardy, they 'kept up a perpetual moan which one could hardly believe to be caused by the air'. (268)

No scene in the novel is more closely connected to Darwin's concept of the struggle for survival than the last moments of Mrs Yeobright as she crosses and re-crosses the heath in the intense and potentially destructive heat. On this day, 'the sun had branded the whole heath with its mark . . . Every valley was filled with air like that of a kiln . . .' The sky has turned from sapphire to 'metallic violet' and the air pulsates silently. (266) The summer season promotes the life cycle of plants and animals inducing simultaneously, fertility and death. As Mrs Yeobright approaches Clym's cottage, in the garden 'there lay the cat asleep on the bare gravel of the path . . . The leaves of the hollyhocks hung like half-closed umbrellas, the sap almost simmered in the stems, and foliage with a smooth surface glared like metallic mirrors.' (269) On seeing her outside the cottage, Eustacia appears to refuse to open the door, and the old lady staggers back on to the heath.

> Mrs Yeobright's exertions, physical and emotional, had well-nigh prostrated her . . . The sun had now got far to the west of south, and stood directly in her face, like some merciless incendiary, brand in hand, waiting to consume her . . . all visible animation disappeared from the landscape, though the intermittent husky notes of the male grasshoppers from every tuft of furze were enough to show that amid the prostration of the larger animal species an unseen insect world was busy in all the fullness of life. (278)

As one of the 'larger animal species' she approaches a death induced partly by man's action and partly by the 'merciless' hand of nature while the mating of the grasshoppers in the furze continues unabated. Though Mrs Yeobright views the heath as a beneficent home, in evolutionary terms she is dispensable, because as Darwin often pointed out, 'heavy destruction inevitably falls either on the young or old'.[11]

The strong sunlight that illuminates this episode contrasts with the many passages of darkness in the book. Both light (or heat) and darkness (or cold) can be identified with the power of the natural world, which, as Darwin stressed, can be vicious and competitive. Mrs Yeobright's death takes place in intense light; another death, Eustacia Vye's, occurs in equally intense darkness.

It is 6 November, a year and a day after the opening scene on Rainbarrow. A storm is brewing. Leaving her cottage at Mistover, Eustacia takes the familiar path to Rainbarrow. This is where she stood at the opening of the novel, her shape complementing heath and barrow in an architectural unity. Now that unity asserts itself again, but in different terms. 'Never', says Hardy, 'was harmony more perfect than between the chaos of her mind and the chaos of the world without' and 'the wings of her soul were broken by the cruel obstructiveness of all about her'. (340–41) It is as though the storm were a measure of Eustacia's desperation to leave Egdon for ever, but to avoid that simple connection it is through Thomasin Yeobright's eyes we experience its full force. Thomasin climbs the path from Blooms-End cottage up to Rainbarrow and follows Eustacia's route down the slope towards the Quiet Woman.

> She was soon ascending Blooms-End valley and traversing the undulations on the side of the hill. The noise of the wind over the heath was shrill, and as if it whistled for joy at finding a night so congenial as this. Sometimes the path led her to hollows between thickets of tall and dripping bracken, dead, though not yet prostrate, which enclosed her like a pool . . . On higher ground, where the wind was brisk and sustained, the rain flew in a level flight without sensible descent, so that it was beyond all power to imagine the remoteness of the point at which it left the bosoms of the clouds. Here self-defence was impossible, and individual drops stuck into her like the arrows into Saint Sebastian. (349)

Since 'the storm was its lover, [and] the wind . . . its friend' (11), this November night belongs to the heath, and as Eustacia descends the slope from Rainbarrow south towards the Quiet Woman she, like the wind, is effectively entering its embrace. Though her appointment is with Wildeve, it is Egdon Heath that is really her lover, her demon lover. She has already contemplated suicide twice in the story, and her downward path towards the watery vortex in Shadwater weir is, in a sense, no more than the heath claiming its own.

Shadwater weir on the Frome.

We can still see the bank behind which Wildeve sheltered while waiting for Eustacia, but in order that he and Clym should hear her falling into the water Hardy has moved the weir closer to the road. Shadwater, or the Nine Hatches, stands as Hardy describes it, 'a large circular pool, fifty feet in diameter, into which the water flowed through . . . huge hatches, raised and lowered by a winch and cogs . . . The sides of the pool were of masonry, to prevent the water from washing away the bank.' On this night, however, as the forces of nature create a violent whirlpool at its centre, it is 'shaken to its foundations by the velocity of its current'. (355) In the first scene of the book Eustacia emerged upwards on to Rainbarrow as the most recent phase of the evolutionary principle. Now she descends downward to extinction in the dark waters of the river. But in her death her connection to the heath is re-established. As her body lies in the Quiet Woman, she is observed by Diggory Venn and the young Charley. 'Her black hair was looser now than either of them had ever seen it before, and surrounded her brow like a forest. The stateliness of look which had been almost too marked for a dweller in a country domicile had at last found an artistically happy background.' (361) In that 'artistically happy background' it might be said that Eustacia has at last come home. Clym had returned home, and had accommodated himself to life on the heath. The other heathlanders also manage to come to some kind of terms with this harsh environment. Only Eustacia and Wildeve are unable to recognize that, whether they like it or not, they are unable to escape or resist the modern condition. Egdon Heath is where they belong and where Eustacia reigns as queen.

With her death the light of the novel goes out and the narrative concludes with a number of ultimately unexciting compromises. Diggory Venn gets his girl and Clym abandons his idealistic plan for educational reform to become a hedge-preacher on 'morally unimpeachable subjects'. The novel ends, however, where it began, on the summit of Rainbarrow.

> The commanding elevation of Rainbarrow had been chosen for two reasons; first, that it occupied a central position among the remote cottages around, secondly, that the preacher thereon could be seen from all adjacent points as soon as he arrived at his post, the view of him being thus a convenient signal to those stragglers who wished to draw near.

The spot that at the beginning of the novel was dark, romantic and windy has become utilitarian and practical. It has been chosen not because it is mysterious, but because it can be seen clearly from afar and instead of the wild, impetuous, poetic Eustacia a more pedestrian figure has taken her place. In spite of her affinity with the heath, Eustacia has become extinct. Her protest against the darkening landscape and its pragmatic Darwinianism has failed and she has been swept away. In her place comes a new figure, with the face of the future. Clym survives because he is able to adjust to the world of scientific rationalism, but his spirit is broken and his existence a colourless one: 'The speaker was bareheaded, and the breeze at each waft gently lifted and lowered his hair . . . He wore a shade over his eyes, and his face was pensive and lined.' (389)

In *The Return of the Native* Hardy seems to have accepted the consequences of the changed attitudes to man, society and nature promulgated by new theology and the new science, but he mourns the passing of the old values. The flawed, Promethean figure of Eustacia Vye was destined to be extinguished, but in that extinction a glory passes away from the earth.

Chapter Three

The Mayor of Casterbridge:
A Place more Dorchester than Dorchester Itself

FROM PUDDLETOWN HEATH of *The Return of the Native* Hardy moved the setting of his new novel, *The Mayor of Casterbridge*, only three or four miles west but as soon as it was published in 1886 Hardy's readers recognized that he had used Dorchester as a model for Casterbridge. This was not contemporary Dorchester, however, but the town as it appeared to Hardy as a young boy in the mid to late 1840s. This was the Dorchester of his parents, at the time when Hardy was about six or seven years old. Such was the impact of the novel that it placed the town on the British literary map, and in 1910 the town council showed its gratitude by offering Hardy the Freedom of the Borough. During the acceptance ceremony he made a speech in which he addressed the relationship between the real Dorchester and the fictional Casterbridge. He was anxious to point out that there was a real difference between the two and that Casterbridge was what he called 'a dream place' not a reality.[1] Yet he saw the absurdity of denying all connection between the two, admitting that maybe Casterbridge was in some ways more Dorchester than Dorchester itself. The idea Hardy was expressing here is that Casterbridge is not a representation of Dorchester. It is not, he argued, a 'photograph'. Instead it is an imaginative presentation of certain aspects of the town as he remembered it in the 'dream' of his childhood. In his novel, Hardy was not aiming at material accuracy or the replication in words of a physical environment. Rather, he was creating an appropriate setting for a series of dramas that take place within an imaginative location. We have already seen how important this was in his writing, and how he used both natural and man-made places to reflect the psychological state, personal standing, attitudes and values of his characters. Buildings in particular, he felt, could express something about the people who inhabit them and could add a new dimension to our understanding of their lives.

In *The Mayor of Casterbridge* Hardy stresses the importance of the built environment almost from the start. As Susan and her daughter Elizabeth-Jane come into the town for the first time it is the physical appearance or the 'topography' (27) that most impresses Elizabeth-Jane. The couple are approaching from the east along the London road when Elizabeth-Jane is startled by the way in which the distant buildings are huddled all together and shut in by a square wall of trees, 'like a plot of garden' she says, as 'compact as a box of dominoes'. From above, Hardy adds, Casterbridge appears as an almost abstract 'mosaic-work of subdued reds, browns, greys, and crystals, held together by a rectangular frame of deep green'. (27)

The compressed, packed-in distribution of buildings in Casterbridge is old-fashioned but benevolent. Originally the design was adopted to defend its inhabitants from invaders, but as times changed its compactness had turned around upon itself and had created a tightly knit social community. At a metaphorical level, the close construction of these buildings within such a carefully circumscribed area suggests the way in which, in Casterbridge, human lives impinged and continue to impinge on each other both physically and psychologically. For better or for worse everyone knows the business of everyone else, and as the narrative develops, character, plot and topography all become enmeshed in a tight web of cause and effect. Just as the streets of the town create a network of interlacing routes, so the persistently crossing paths of the characters produce unexpected consequences involving personal likes, dislikes, confessions, deceits and revelations.

Hardy had often travelled down the road on which Susan Henchard and her daughter found themselves on that late summer evening. As a young man he had walked every day from his parents' cottage at Higher Bockhampton to his school in Dorchester but one journey, many years later in 1883, must have produced in him some of the sentiments felt by Elizabeth-Jane and her mother. Like them, Hardy and his wife were homeless. Ever since their marriage in 1874 they had occupied rented accommodation and the idea of home was important to him. In *The Return of the Native* he dealt with the idea of home and what it meant in the context of man's place in the natural world. In *The Mayor of Casterbridge* he treats the idea of home in the context of the built environment. To do this Hardy transfers his own sense of homelessness to all the major characters, as each one endeavours to remedy the situation by trying to establish a permanent home in the town. Michael Henchard is not a native but attempts to put down roots by adopting an imposing residence in Corn Street; Lucetta Templeman hails from Jersey, where the old house in which she had been born had been demolished for the sake of 'improvements'. She confesses wistfully to Farfrae that she no longer has a 'home to think of' and is looking for what she calls 'an ark' (149), and as for Farfrae himself, he is 'farfrae home', a migrant when the novel opens, travelling between Scotland and America. Hardy's personal antidote to his rootlessness was to build a house in his native town of Dorchester. The location never appealed to his wife, Emma, who hailed from Cornwall, but around 1882, before arriving in the town, he negotiated with the Duchy of Cornwall to buy a plot on its south-eastern side. During the building work he and Emma rented the now demolished Shire-Place Hall, and as soon as the couple took up residence he threw himself into writing *The Mayor of Casterbridge*.

As Dorchester had effectively drawn Hardy back to his childhood roots, so Casterbridge acts like a magnet, attracting to it all the major characters of the novel. It draws Susan and Elizabeth-Jane as it had attracted Michael Henchard sixteen years previously. It entices Farfrae, who although he is desperate to make a fortune elsewhere is persuaded by Henchard to remain. It also exerts a pull on Lucetta Templeman who, though she attempts to move away, is persistently prevented from doing so. Even characters of lesser significance succumb to its influence: Newsome, Jopp, the old firmity women, and many others all find themselves caught up in Casterbridge society.

The attraction of Dorchester is emphasized in the more stylized form of Casterbridge. It was for Hardy an ancient, social palimpsest. Its solid and reassuring appearance and its compact layout, untouched by modernism, offered an image of cultural continuity. Its very fabric involved, as Hardy wrote about his own architectural work, 'the preservation of memories, history, fellowship, fraternities'.[2] So Casterbridge bore the impress of countless previous generations and its unplanned architectural randomness was indicative of a culture that had developed organically rather than rationally. Throughout the town building materials were used accretively and unsystematically, with 'houses of brick-nogging

. . . slate roofs patched with tiles, and tile roofs patched with slate, with occasionally a roof of thatch'. All the buildings 'derived their chief support from those adjoining' (28), creating the sense of a community where citizens, like the buildings they inhabit, sustain their neighbours.

But it was also a highly diverse culture. Above, the stories are haphazard. Below, that diversity is reflected in the shops that line the street, shops displaying a wide range of specialized tools: 'Scythes, reap-hooks, sheep-shears, bill-hooks, spades, mattocks, and hoes at the iron-monger's; bee-hives, butter-firkins, churns, milking stools and pails, hay-rakes, field-flagons, and seed-lips at the cooper's . . .' (28) The extensive list is indicative of the rich nature of Casterbridge's commercial life, dependent on specialist, individual skills not on centrally organized mechanisms. The whole impression of energetic and vibrant antiquity is strengthened when, on the day after their arrival, Elizabeth-Jane goes in search of Henchard's house. As she passes along the street, Hardy breathes such life into the bricks and mortar that the pedestrians, including Elizabeth-Jane, are forced into an interactive dance movement around the base of the buildings.

> Old-fashioned fronts, which had older than old-fashioned backs, rose sheer from the pavement, into which the bow windows protruded like bastions, necessitating a pleasing *chassez-dechassez* movement to the time-pressed pedestrian at every few yards. He was bound also to evolve other Terpsichorean figures in respect of door-steps, scrapers, cellar-hatches, church buttresses, and the overhanging angles of walls which, originally unobtrusive, had become bow-legged and knock-kneed. (57)

The word that sums up this diversity, unexpectedness and variety is 'picturesque' and it is one that occurs frequently in the novel. The agricultural suburb of Durnover, 'a curious congeries of barns and farmsteads', is described as 'picturesque'; Elizabeth-Jane's colourful use of old dialect words is 'picturesque'; and when Farfrae's rational methods of bargaining begin to take over, Hardy tells us that 'the rugged picturesqueness of the old method disappeared with its inconveniences'. (85) Throughout the story, however, the feeling that the old things are attractive, diverse and traditional is persistently balanced by the sense that they are also inefficient, inaccurate and unreliable.

This ambivalence about the conservatism of the town carries over to a similar ambivalence about its relationship with the surrounding countryside. On the one hand the town is the 'pole, focus and nerve-knot of the surrounding country life' (59) as carriers, carters, yeomen, farmers, dairymen and agricultural workers constantly pass through it. Yet on the other hand it is strongly demarcated from the country. Susan and Elizabeth-Jane notice that it is separated by an almost mathematical line and enclosed in a dense stockade of limes and chestnuts. Inside that stockade the town has 'a sense of great snugness and comfort' as the lamplight glimmers through the trees, giving the countryside beyond 'a strangely solitary and vacant aspect'. (28) However, the strong distinction between town and country was not, Hardy insists, a radical opposition. Though he claims that Casterbridge 'was the complement of the rural life around, not its urban opposite' (54), the story is actually centred almost entirely within the boundaries of the town. In contrast to *Far from the Madding Crowd* and *The Return of the Native* where the action takes place in the countryside, the emotional core of this story, its psychological centre, lies firmly within the urban environment and within the dense stockade of trees that surrounds it.

At first sight Casterbridge appears ancient and timeless, yet there is another side to it that is much more precarious. When Hardy was writing *Far from the Madding Crowd*, he was conscious of recording the details of an agrarian culture that was slowly disappearing. Here, too, he was aware that the culture about which he was writing no longer existed untouched by change. 'The reader will scarcely need to be reminded', he says in a preface written in 1919, 'that time and progress have obliterated from the town that suggested these descriptions many or most of the old-fashioned features here enumerated.' (58) But what was true of 1910 was also true of 1883, and as Hardy reached back in his memory to the town of his childhood he was recording something: not just the buildings, but a whole way of life that, to some extent, had passed away.

In 1883, Hardy's desire to memorialize the past was put into a new perspective by a dramatic event that took place during the building of his own house, Max Gate. He was visiting the site on the Wareham Road when men digging the foundations came across three Romano-British skeletons laid out in separate graves. The experience must have been very moving for him since Hardy claimed that he was actually present when the skeletons were 'lifted up from their rest of, I suppose, fifteen hundred years'. Each body, he said, was placed with perfect accuracy into an oval hole, strongly suggestive of 'the chicken in the egg shell' and around the skeletons lay one or two personal belongings.[3] Suddenly the past was projected into the present, and this find provided startling evidence of a civilization that had developed and had passed away on the very spot where he and his wife were to live! Hardy's fascination with archaeology was not a recent one. During the two years he was living in Wimborne before moving to Dorchester he had already joined the Dorset Natural History and Antiquarian Field Club. The group met regularly, but one day in May 1884, when Hardy was still writing *The Mayor of Casterbridge,* he took part in a special day-long event. It involved the exploration of a number of Roman locations in Dorchester. The club journal recorded that it began at the headquarters in the county museum where a 'Mr Cunnington read a paper on "Ancient Dorchester" illustrated by a plan of Roman Durnovaria.' The group then walked to Fordington Church where Hardy's close friend, Henry Moule, now curator of Dorset County Museum, gave a second paper. This was followed by a trip to Maumbury Rings, and an archaeological tour led by Mr A. Pine. The group then had lunch at the King's Arms Hotel, after which, the record tells us, 'Mr Thomas Hardy read a short paper on some interesting Roman remains lately found by himself during the excavation of a building in Fordington Field.'[4] Each of these contributions to the archaeological field trip highlighted the intimate connection between modern Dorchester and Roman Durnovaria and in *The Mayor of Casterbridge* Hardy drew out similar connections between ancient and modern. 'Casterbridge', he wrote, 'announced old Rome in every street, alley, and precinct. It looked Roman, bespoke the art of Rome, concealed dead men of Rome.' Remembering his own experience in the garden of Max Gate, he continued:

It was impossible to dig more than a foot or two deep about the town fields and gardens without coming upon some tall soldier or other of the Empire, who had lain there in his silent unobtrusive rest for a space of fifteen hundred years. He was mostly found lying on his side, in an oval scoop in the chalk, like a chicken in its shell; his knees drawn up to his chest; sometimes with the remains of his spear against his arm, a fibula or brooch of bronze on his breast or forehead, an urn at his knees, a jar at his throat, a bottle at his mouth; and mystified conjecture pouring down upon him from the eyes of Casterbridge street boys and men, who had turned a moment to gaze at the familiar spectacle as they passed by. (67)

The novel is punctuated with reminders of the town's Roman past. The four roads that lead into the town are essentially Roman; in the suburb of Durnover wheat-ricks overhang the old Roman street; Henchard rents a cottage for Susan near the old Roman wall in West Walks, and though Susan and Elizabeth-Jane are unaware of the fact at the time, the stockade of gnarled trees which they first notice framing Casterbridge are 'but the ancient defences of the town, planted as a promenade'. Finally, when Susan Henchard dies her dust is mingled with the 'dust of women who lay ornamented with glass hair-pins and amber necklaces, and men who held in their mouths coins of Hadrian, Posthumus, and the Constantines'.[5] (124–5)

Dorchester in the 1880s, with the Roman city of Durnovaria marked in blue beneath.

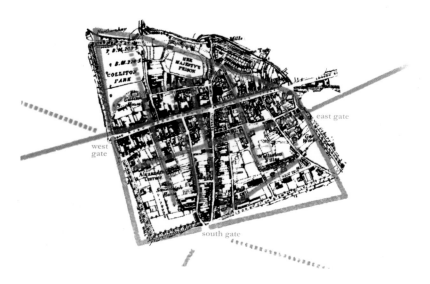

Throughout *The Mayor of Casterbridge* there are reminders not only of the Roman past of the town but also of both its Neolithic origins, and its later medieval phases. In a sense, in his representation of this place 'more Dorchester than Dorchester itself' Hardy was creating a kind of literary archaeology. In the novel the reader is offered just one of the historical layers of the town, but everywhere there is the sense that life has gone on here very much the same way in the past as in the present. The most substantial reminder that Dorchester had been a Roman town lay in its street plan. This grid network continued largely unchanged since the Middle Ages and persisted into the nineteenth century and beyond. As in the Roman period it was in the urban centre that the material and emotional life of the town was concentrated. Further out, on the periphery of Casterbridge are places less integrated into the community and where human relations are poorer or limited. Beyond these again are areas that are desolate, 'beyond the pale', places that are often associated in the novel with violence, and even dissolution.

Hardy is quite specific about the precise centre of Casterbridge and if we stand in modern Dorchester where High Street East meets High Street West we can feel it today. Down South Street we can see a straggling line of market stalls – a butcher's, a florist's, a greengrocer's and some others. On Saturday this increases considerably and is a remnant of something much older. When Hardy moved to Dorchester in 1883 the market was very much more extensive and regularly spilled out on to the High Street. Forty years previously when he was a boy it was even more substantial, effectively blocking the High Street twice each week, once on Wednesdays and again with a larger hiring fair on Saturdays. Fifteen hundred years earlier this was the site of another market, the Roman forum, and Hardy's account of Casterbridge market area is filled with reminiscences of that ancient history.

For the inhabitants of Casterbridge, the market place is 'the node of all orbits'. It is the central meeting place or 'carrefour', where all paths cross. Like the forum that lies beneath it, it is 'the regulation Open Place in spectacular dramas, where the incidents that occur . . . to bear on the lives of the adjoining residents'. (155) It is in the market place that Henchard and Farfrae meet again after their first bitter dispute, it is at this point that Henchard's cart collides disastrously with Farfrae's, it is here that Farfrae first displays his seed drill, and on this spot the disastrous 'skimmity ride' has its tragic conclusion. In a novel that is focused on the shifting balance of human interaction, the market place is the most highly charged location. As everybody passes through, it not only serves as a point of contact between characters, but at another level, it joins our present imaginatively with Hardy's, Hardy's own with that of his childhood, and all of us with the medieval and Roman worlds that lie beneath.

Very close to this spot in Dorchester at the junction of the four ways stand two buildings that play particularly important roles in the narrative. One is the dignified and substantial house at no. 10 South Street, in which Michael Henchard was reputed to have lived. The other is High Place Hall, the residence of Lucetta Templeman, overlooking Corn Street.

The architecture and appearance of Henchard's house, now occupied by Barclays Bank in South Street, are closely interwoven with the mayor's temperament and his position in Casterbridge society. Like most of the buildings in the town it is 'old fashioned' and expresses an honest openness and a transparency between private life and public life. 'The front doors of the . . . houses', writes Hardy, 'were mostly left open at this warm autumn time, no thought of umbrella stealers disturbing the minds of the placid burgesses. Hence, through the long, straight, entrance passages thus unclosed could be seen, as through tunnels the mossy gardens at the back.' (57) When Elizabeth-Jane reaches the mayor's house for the first time she finds it, like the others, with 'the front door . . . open', where she can see 'through the passage to the end of the garden – nearly a quarter of a mile off'. (59) The mossy gardens are integral to the houses. They are filled with flowers. The 'glowing . . . nasturtiums, fuchsias, scarlet geraniums, "bloody warriors," snapdragons, and dahlias' (57), are indicative of the harmony between the rural and the urban environments, but beyond this Elizabeth-Jane can see more. She passes through a door in the garden wall studded with rusty nails where 'generations of fruit trees' have been grown and into Henchard's store yard. This is filled with bursting wheat sacks suggestive of his considerable material success, while at the same time the easy and uninterrupted passage between house, garden and yard offers a strong statement about the integration of life, leisure and labour. In common with the other houses in Casterbridge 'backed by crusted grey stone-work remaining from a yet remoter Casterbridge than the venerable one visible in the street' this one, too, is embedded in history. The combination of old-fashioned fronts with 'older than old-fashioned backs' (57) suggests material and cultural continuity extending back through the Middle Ages, and even further to ancient Rome.

Henchard's House, 10 South Street,
Dorchester, now Barclays Bank.

In the late 1840s, 10 South Street was
lived in by a member of what the local
directory called the 'gentry'. William Tapp
was not the mayor, but he was one of the
two senior aldermen. He lived there with
his wife and practised as a surgeon. This
house, faced with dull red and grey old
brick Hardy tells us, is 'one of the best'. Its solid Georgian style and its symmetrical
and foursquare outer facade reflects the conservative values of the rural town and
in the novel the interior echoes the exterior. Henchard has furnished it with pieces
'associated with the names of Chippendale and Sheraton', objects that express
the aesthetic values of previous generations. But its most prominent piece is a
neo-classical chimneypiece. This is covered with wood carvings comprising gar-
landed lyres, shields, quivers and a draped ox-skull flanked by the heads of Apollo
and Diana, all of which signify, once again, the persistent presence of Rome in
Casterbridge. Like the house itself the fittings impart a sense of rich substantiality,
yet they are at the same time rather ponderous and overbearing. Both the house
and its interior convey a sense of tradition and orthodoxy rather than carefully
considered personal taste.

Henchard's house provides the topographical pivot for the first part of *The
Mayor of Casterbridge*. It is here that he first invites Farfrae, having persuaded him
to stay in Casterbridge, and it is here that Elizabeth-Jane, ignorant of the relationship between them, comes to tell Henchard of the arrival of her mother in the
town. When Henchard begins publicly to court his former wife, he places her and
Elizabeth-Jane in a small cottage on the periphery of the town in West Walks, but

then when they get re-married he installs them in the centre in his Corn Street residence. The marriage, however, is a matter of duty rather than love and Henchard attempts to compensate for his 'lack of deeper emotion' by attending to the appearance of the house. So he has the iron railings 'painted a bright green, and the heavy-barred, small-paned Georgian sash windows enlivened with three coats of white'. (82) But the impact that the two women have on his life is very small, and that, too, is expressed in terms of their presence in the house. It was, Hardy tells us, 'large, the rooms lofty, and the landings wide' but 'the two unassuming women scarcely made a perceptible addition to its contents'. (82) After the death of Susan Henchard, and Henchard's discovery of the fact that Elizabeth-Jane is not his daughter, the psychological focus of the story shifts. Lucetta Templeman comes to take up residence in Casterbridge and Elizabeth-Jane soon joins her in High Place Hall.

Many years previously Lucetta had an affair with Henchard. As a result she became a fallen woman with a damaged reputation. Hearing of the death of his wife, and in an attempt to repair her reputation, she comes to Casterbridge to seek him out. Since she was brought up in the Channel Islands her tastes are somewhat French and a large and recent inheritance allows her to indulge those tastes. In contrast to Henchard's bourgeois dwelling Lucetta has a far more aristocratic place. It is, writes Hardy, an example of 'dignity without

Above: Hermann Lea's photograph of Colliton House (High Place Hall), 1913. Below: The Romano-Celtic mask formerly above the brew-house door of Colliton House is now in Dorset County Museum.

great size', suggesting that 'blood built it, and wealth enjoys it'. (130) The original for High Place Hall, Colliton House, stands a quarter of a mile away on the edge of Colliton Park, Dorchester. For the purpose of the novel Hardy shrank this rather grand building and placed it adjacent to the market place. Made of stone rather than brick, it is a late seventeenth- or early eighteenth-century Palladian building with a facade that is simple, rational and reasonable. In contrast to the appearance of openness and integrity of Henchard's house, however, High Place Hall has a different aspect. At the back there is an alley where all kinds of surreptitious activities went on connected with its dark and brutal past. 'By the alley,' says Hardy, 'it had been possible to come unseen from all sorts of quarters in the town . . . the old play-house, the old bull-stake [and] the old cock-pit.' (131) So it is the word 'intrigue' that Hardy chooses to sum up the most prominent characteristic of this part of Lucetta's new residence. Intrigue demands a disguise, and above a narrow doorway there is a sculpted mask. The original used to be in Glyde Path Road and was incorporated into the arch of the eighteenth-century building. Its short animal ears and gaping mouth identify it as the ancient Romano-Celtic fertility god, Cernunnos. In 1947 the mask was moved into the County Museum, where it can be seen that its grotesque appearance probably owes as much to wind and weather as, according to Hardy's suggestion, the stones of little boys. It is, however, not simply an archaeological memento. It is also an emblem of Lucetta herself, who has come to Casterbridge in disguise. In order to conceal her fallen identity as Lucette Le Sueur she has taken on the name of the respectable Lucetta Templeman with the specific purpose of hiding her 'disreputable' past with Henchard.

On meeting Lucetta, Elizabeth-Jane (oddly for one so observant) notices High Place Hall for the first time, and though 'her admiration for the architecture . . . was entirely on account of the inmate it screened' she is even more struck by Lucetta's taste for interior decoration. The inside of the house had been transformed. This exotic, half-French woman has imported a sofa with cylindrical pillows, an elegant card table, and a piano with brass inlayings. (141) When Henchard sees the same furniture he is even more taken aback. Not only is his own markedly antique, but when he is confronted with such sophistication he feels so exposed that even his 'accents and manner' appear to him crude and boorish. Lucetta prophetically tells him that it would be fifty years before such 'Aesthetic' designs would be available in Casterbridge. One of the heralds of the new vogue was Oscar Wilde, and Lucetta's choice of furniture may well have been retrospectively inspired by his visit to Dorchester in 1883. Wilde, who met Hardy at the time, came to give a lecture on 'The House Beautiful', in which he said that advanced people should avoid 'early English' furniture. It may be 'honestly made and better than modern styles,' he said, but is too heavy and massive for contemporary, advanced taste. 'A lighter and more graceful style of furniture is more suitable for our peaceful times,' Wilde told his audience,[6] and it is very much this style that Lucetta, an aesthete *avant la lettre,* has imported into Casterbridge.

Though Lucetta and Elizabeth-Jane, the latter having no real interest in possessions, may have differed in their taste in furniture, the position of High Place Hall is very much to the liking of them both. It had previously lain empty because potential residents found its public location right above the market place noisy and 'unseemly'. But from this 'gazebo' as Lucetta calls it, the goings-on could be watched at leisure. Sitting in the window the two women have 'a raking view' which affords them a front seat in 'dramas' of the town.

This central crossing point is indeed a theatre. It was once the place where classical drama took place and now the whole dramatis personae of the agricultural and urban world sweep through. During the Roman period, the inhabitants of Durnovaria went to the amphitheatre for violent spectacles, but to the forum for daily drama. From their vantage point in High Place Hall Lucetta and Elizabeth-Jane use the same spot for domestic entertainment as they watch first for Henchard, then for Farfrae. As Lucetta's involvement with each man becomes more complicated, however, she exchanges her role of spectator for that of participant.

From the *carrefour* outside Lucetta's house we can look down the High Street East and identify three further locations, all inns or taverns, that are connected with the wider ethos of the Casterbridge community. First there is the early nineteenth-century front of the King's Arms with its splendid bow windows billowing proudly out into the road. Further down the High Street is the site of the Three Mariners, which together with a third hostelry, Peter's Finger, in the disreputable area called Mixen Lane, serve to represent three definable strata in the town's society. The King's Arms (where Hardy gave his paper on Roman Dorchester) is a place for the gentry. It is here that Henchard stages his mayoral banquet for 'the gentle people and leading volk' (31) on the night of Susan and Elizabeth-Jane's arrival in town.

 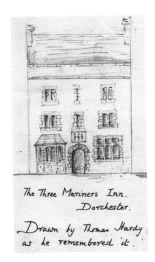

The Three Mariners Inn.
Dorchester.

Drawn by Thomas Hardy
as he remembered it.

Above left: The King's Arms still stands in Dorchester High Street. Above right: Hardy's drawing (c.1885) of the demolished Three Mariners Inn. Pencil on paper, 9 x 7 cm.

Henchard has his proudest moment here, but it is also where he has to face his creditors in the sale of his bankrupt property.

The second inn, the Three Mariners, is a humbler lodging and it is here that Susan Henchard and Elizabeth-Jane take themselves when they first come to Casterbridge. Hardy's affectionate account of its architecture was drawn from memory, as was the pencil sketch that he produced to remind himself of its picturesque details:

> This ancient house of accommodation for man and beast, now, unfortunately, pulled down, was built of mellow sandstone, with mullioned windows of the same material, markedly out of perpendicular from the settlement of foundations. The bay window projecting into the street, whose interior was so popular among the frequenters of the inn, was closed with shutters . . . (40)

In Hardy's account of the inn the picture that emerges is one of ancient, quiet distinction where the alliteration of the soft letter 'm' in the first sentence resonates between words to emphasize the gentle unobtrusive architectural design. The building has now gone, but it was the interior that, for Hardy, was so significant. Here, the occupants were tightly packed into a small space of lively and genial chaos, and like a microcosm of Casterbridge itself, the inn had grown in a haphazard and improvised way. The space demanded by 'intrusive beams and rafters, partitions, passages, staircases, disused ovens, settles, and four-posters', he explains, 'left comparatively small quarters for human beings' (42), and the warren of staircases and passages lead to small rooms subdivided into smaller rooms. Farfrae is given one of these, immediately adjoining that of Elizabeth-Jane and her mother. The result is that when Henchard visits him on the night of their arrival in Casterbridge, each word of their conversation can be heard through the temporary wall. Like life in the town, privacy at the Three Mariners is illusory, and the concealment of acts both present and past, impossible.

Though both the King's Arms and the Three Mariners are close to the physical centre of Casterbridge as well as the psychological centre of the novel, their ethos is very different. Unlike the King's Arms, the Three Mariners is warm, sociable, and reminiscent of the gregarious masculinity of the maltster's in *Far from the Madding Crowd*. The patrons of the Three Mariners are what Hardy calls the 'secondary worthies' of the town. They form the backbone of the community, and have a rich tradition of local gossip, stories and history. Even here, however, there are clear social divisions. The respectable master tradesmen occupy seats in the bow window, whereas an 'inferior set' of men sit on benches against a wall. When Farfrae, an outsider, sings to them, however, he cuts across the class division and moves both groups with his sentimental Scottishness.

The ethos of the life in and around the Three Mariners is summed up by the inn sign that hangs over the Tudor arch outside the building. This is an emblem of both the inn itself and the town as a whole. It represents three sailors in such an old, primitive style that they appear to be 'persons of two dimensions only' standing in 'paralyzed attitudes'. They have been there so long that they have suffered 'warping, splitting, fading, and shrinkage', but their woebegone condition is a mark of respect not neglect. The sign has never been restored for 'the lack of a painter in Casterbridge who would undertake to reproduce the features of men so traditional'. (40) In other words the sign is an icon of continuity and, like the inn itself and the wider world of town beyond it, has its roots in values and attitudes that reach back into the past, but values that are being slowly eroded by the processes of time and change.

The third inn, Peter's Finger, lies on the periphery of Casterbridge in an eastern suburb, at yet further remove from the central point of the market. Socially one stage lower than the Three Mariners it is the resort of the socially disaffected, the disgruntled and the disappointed. Unlike the easy access to both the King's Arms and the Three Mariners, the main entrance to Peter's Finger is apparently unused. The front door is kept shut, and the step perfectly clean. The real entrance is elsewhere, up a nearby alley, a mere slit, where there is a narrow door, 'shiny and paintless from the rub of infinite hands and shoulders' (237), through which people can come and go unseen. Those who patronize Peter's Finger wish to remain anonymous; the company is unsavoury, even criminal, and it is in this location that the skimmity ride is planned with the aim of bringing down Farfrae and Lucetta by exposing Lucetta's affair with Henchard.

Both Lucetta and Henchard are closely associated with their respective residences, one in Corn Street, the other overlooking the market place. Farfrae, in contrast, has only undetermined and un-locatable 'lodgings' in Casterbridge. Even when he comes to marry Lucetta and moves with her into Henchard's former house he acquires none of the qualities of that house nor the attributes of the furniture he has purchased. Consequently, throughout the novel his character remains strangely insubstantial. His energetic, mercurial personality may charm the inhabitants of Casterbridge in ways denied the mayor, but that charm never raises the passions incited by Henchard. It is perhaps characteristic of Farfrae, then, that his standing is vastly increased through his invention of an ingenious temporary structure in West Walks.

In response to an unnamed national event both Farfrae and Henchard decide to stage public celebrations. With no thought for the vagaries of the weather Henchard chooses a site on 'a square earthwork' outside the periphery of the town. Hardy himself identified this as the Bronze Age Poundbury Hill Fort just to the west of the town. The mayor arranges a substantial day of competitive games, prizes and 'a stage for boxing, wrestling, and drawing blood generally' (97), but as the day progresses, so the weather deteriorates and the

Hardy's vignette of West Walks, Dorchester, for 'Her Death and After' in *Wessex Poems* (1898).

event is washed out. Farfrae is cannier. He uses the natural architecture of the Walks, 'vaults of living woodwork' (102) as Hardy calls them, to construct a 'pavilion' using rick cloths. Hardy is architecturally specific about it. 'The densest point of the avenue had been selected,' he says, 'where the boughs made a closely interlaced vault overhead; to these boughs the canvas had been hung, and a barrel roof was the result.' (99) By spreading this patchwork along the Walks, Farfrae creates an open-air ballroom in the form of a gigantic tent made without poles or ropes. The end facing the wind is enclosed, the other is open, and in it he places a string band. The result is 'like the nave of a cathedral with one gable removed', though 'the scene within was', says Hardy, 'anything but devotional'. (99) In contrast to Henchard's games of masculine, physical prowess Farfrae organizes a sophisticated event with romantic overtones. Henchard, 'being by nature something of a woman hater' (74), persistently fails to understand women or respond to their needs, whereas Farfrae appeals to men socially and to woman sexually. Just as he had charmed the men of the Three Mariners with his vocal performance, here in West Walks he charms the women with his performance as a 'wild Highlander'. At the Three Mariners his singing had been a theatrical show; now his dancing is equally dramatic. He throws himself into the reels that, to Henchard's jealous disgust, create obvious excitement in the women. Elizabeth-Jane is one of those who is dazzled and the heightened emotion generated by the event brings him to the brink of a proposal of marriage to her.

The Walks create an enclosure that surrounds Casterbridge on three sides, and along, or just outside them, are a number of locations that play important roles vis-à-vis the more prominent sites at the centre. Two of these are more or less contiguous yet they represent polar opposites in terms of the values of the novel. The first is the agricultural suburb of Durnover (whose name derives from the Roman Durnovaria), modelled in part on the parish of Fordington. 'Here', the narrator tells us,

> . . . wheat-ricks overhung the old Roman street, and thrust their eaves against the church tower; green-thatched barns, with doorways as high as the gates of Solomon's temple, opened directly upon the main thoroughfare. Barns indeed were so numerous as to alternate with every half-dozen houses along the way. Here lived burgesses who daily walked

the fallow; shepherds in an intra-mural squeeze. A street of farmers' homesteads – a street ruled by a mayor and corporation, yet echoing with the thump of the flail, the flutter of the winnowing-fan, and the purr of the milk into the pails – a street which had nothing urban in it whatever – this was the Durnover end of Casterbridge. (87)

Antiquity combines with plenitude in this utopian picture of a golden age. Part classical, part biblical, this account of Durnover brings town and country together in perfect harmony. The language reinforces the sense of equilibrium as carefully modulated, balanced sentences create the feeling of order and calm: 'Here lived burgesses who daily walked the fallow; shepherds in an intra-mural squeeze.'

A number of converted barns still stand at the end of Fordington High Street and in the vicinity of Little Britain, but the sense of deep and dreamy pastoralism has vanished. The connection between abundance and fertility nevertheless makes it the appropriate setting for the carefully staged rendezvous between Elizabeth-Jane and Farfrae. In the hope of creating a love match Susan Henchard writes an anonymous note to both, asking them to go to the granary on Durnover Hill, the hill down which runs Fordington High Street. They meet in one of the barns, and though nothing comes of this encounter in the short term, the seed is sown and much later in the story Farfrae makes Elizabeth-Jane his wife.

The second location is Mixen Lane, 'the mildewed leaf in the sturdy Casterbridge plant'. (236) To reach this area you have to come down from the higher ground of Fordington Hill, cross the river at King's Bridge, and turn left up the narrow Mill Street. Though parts of this area still contain some early buildings, most of it has now been cleared away to build a group of modern flats. But in the nineteenth century the place was the home of notoriety. This, says Hardy, was 'a less picturesque side to the parish'. It was, he says, 'the Adullam of all the surrounding villages', and the residence of the disaffected, the rebellious and the impecunious. Here,

Vice ran freely in and out certain of the doors in the neighbourhood; recklessness dwelt under the roof with the crooked chimney; shame in some bow-windows; theft (in times of privation) in the thatched and mudwalled houses by the sallows. Even slaughter had not been altogether unknown here. In a block of cottages up an alley there might have been erected an altar to disease in years gone by. (236)

In these uneasy and staccato sentences, the details of the buildings of Mixen Lane are used synechdochally (the part for the whole) to suggest the residence of personified, social aberrations, vice, recklessness, theft and murder. Their deity is disease, an allusion to an event that took place in 1854. That year saw a terrible cholera outbreak on this eastern boundary of Dorchester. It was thought (wrongly) to have been caused by miasmal air, and Henry Moule, the vicar of Fordington, heroically devoted himself to its eradication. In *The Mayor of Casterbridge* this slum location is a source of metaphorical, rather than literal

Hermann Lea's 1913 photograph of Mill Street (Mixen Lane), Fordington.

disease. When the disaffected and out-of-work employee Jopp reads Lucetta's letters to the denizens of Peter's Finger, the story of her affair with Henchard comes out. The poisoned narrative then spreads 'like a miasmatic fog through Mixen Lane, and thence up the back streets of Casterbridge' (248), leading eventually to the skimmity ride that precipitates the death of Lucetta.

In *The Mayor of Casterbridge* Mixen Lane is the first of a number of desolate locations, strung out like dark beads on the rivers Frome and Cerne, on the east and north of the town. Each location is characterized by its architectural qualities and each one plays a significant part in the personal tragedy of Michael Henchard. If Mixen Lane embodies collective suffering, then two sites further along the river embody personal suffering. These are the bridges crossed by the eastern road into Casterbridge. They have what Hardy calls 'speaking countenances' where the architectural physiognomy of each one tells a different story. On each bridge

> Every projection . . . was worn down to obtuseness, partly by weather, more by friction from generations of loungers, whose toes and heels had from year to year made restless movements against these parapets, as they had stood there meditating on the aspect of affairs. In the case of the more friable bricks and stones even the flat faces were worn into hollows by the same mixed mechanism. The masonry of the top was clamped with iron at each joint; since it had been no uncommon thing for desperate men to wrench the coping off and throw it down the river, in reckless defiance of the magistrates. (206)

The first bridge, Swan Bridge, built of brick, lay nearest the town (its original collapsed in 1954 but another still crosses the river Cerne at this spot) and it is this one that is chosen by the lowest characters. These are citizens who have no shame and who are happy to out-stare their adversaries. Down-at-heel characters like Jopp, Mother Cuxom and Abel Whittle stand here waiting for their luck to turn. The other bridge, modelled on Grey's Bridge on the Frome, is further from the town, further from the eyes of townspeople and further from the psychological centre of the novel. This is the site chosen by shabby gentility, bankrupts and hypochondriacs who, instead of facing passers-by in the eye like

Grey's Bridge on
the London Road,
Dorchester.

those on the first bridge, stare in blank melancholy over the parapet and down at the flowing water of the river. It is to this spot that Henchard comes when he loses his business to Farfrae followed rapidly by his house, his furniture and his woman, and it is from this spot that Farfrae himself pulls the former mayor back into his employ and back into the centre of the narrative.

A little further upstream is another place that 'embodied the mournful phases of Casterbridge life'. (118) On the death of his wife, Susan, Henchard discovers that Elizabeth-Jane is not his daughter. Instantly, he leaves his house, walks to the first bridge on the High Street, turns left up the 'Schwarzwasser of Casterbridge' and towards an old water mill. Human melancholy is expressed here in terms of the microclimate and the local architecture. 'The whole way along here was sunless,' says the narrator, 'even in summer time; in spring, white frosts lingered here when other places were steaming with warmth; while in winter it was the seed-field of all the aches, rheumatisms, and torturing cramps of the year.' (118) Across the river at the bottom of a hill lay the ruins of a Franciscan priory, whose defunct millrace still made the water roar down the back-hatch 'like the voice of desolation' and behind Henchard, high on a cliff on the other side of the river, rose a building like a pedestal lacking its statue. This was the county gaol, and the missing feature was the corpse of a hanged man. Henchard was impressed with 'the lugubrious harmony of the spot with his domestic situation'

Top: Hangman's Cottage, which Hardy as a boy used to watch 'with fear and fascination'. Above: Ten Hatches weir in the meadows to the east of Dorchester where Henchard was 'intending to make his death-bed'.

and moving on quickly, passed the so-called Hangman's Cottage, which Hardy as a boy used to watch with 'fear and fascination'.[7] Later in the story Henchard returns to the same spot after the furmity woman has publicly exposed his old crime of wife-selling. This time, however, the visit is more permanent since Henchard, unable to endure his shame, abandons his house in Corn Street and goes to live in the cottage of the disaffected Jopp near the Priory Mill. This 'was built of old stones from the long dismantled Priory, scraps of tracery, moulded window-jambs, and arch-labels, being mixed in with the rubble of the walls'. (205) Henchard's life, like his adopted dwelling, is in ruins, the ruins this time of medieval rather than Roman origin, but ruins nonetheless. With the arrival of Elizabeth-Jane's biological father, Henchard's life takes further turn for the worse and, contemplating suicide, he goes into the water meadows outside Casterbridge. He arrives at a sluice called 'Ten Hatches'.

> The river here was deep and strong at all times, and the hatches on this account were raised and lowered by cogs and a winch. A path led from the second bridge over the highway . . . to these Hatches, crossing the stream at their head by a narrow plank-bridge. But after nightfall human beings were seldom found going that way, the path leading only to a deep reach of the stream called Blackwater, and the passage being dangerous. (276)

Taking off his coat and hat he prepares to jump but is prevented by the appearance of a strange image of himself floating 'as if dead' in the water. It is the dummy that had been used in the skimmity ride and at the sight of it he draws back from certain death.

Each of these river locations, the two bridges, the Priory Mill, Jopp's cottage, the prison and Ten Hatches, mark Henchard's progressive alienation from the Casterbridge community, and each is placed on the edge of the town outside the central node of human society. But there is a further group of sites that are extramural, and that stand even further outside the perimeter of the town. Many of them involve secrecy or outright deception, and all of them are either lonely or unpopulated. One of Henchard's strangest journeys is to such a place. He decides to visit a 'weather-prophet'. Driven by his superstitious nature, the corn merchant is passionate about the conditions for the forthcoming harvest but to consult the prophet he feels obliged to go in disguise to a spot utterly remote from human habitation. 'The way to his house', Hardy explains,

> was crooked and miry – even difficult in the present unpropitious season . . . The turnpike-road became a lane, the lane a cart-track, the cart-track a bridle-path, the bridle-path a foot-way, the foot-way overgrown. The solitary walker slipped here and there, and stumbled over the natural springes formed by the brambles, till at length he reached the house, which, with its garden, was surrounded with a high, dense hedge. (173)

The isolation of the prophet's house is a sign, not so much of the alien nature of his activities, but of the alien nature of Henchard's mental state, and his expedition to this out-of-the-way place suggests just how far Henchard has set himself apart from his own community. But this is not the first time that he had sought places for deeds that had to be hidden from the eyes of the citizens of Casterbridge. On two previous occasions the so-called Casterbridge Ring provided an eerie location for his meetings with women.

The model for Casterbridge Ring is the Maumbury Rings, the amphitheatre standing just to the south of Dorchester. When in 1883, Mr A. Pine conducted Hardy and the other members of the Dorset Field Club around this monument they had to walk a little out into the country where Pine would have told them that it had been constructed around AD 70 after the Roman invasion. It is now believed to be much older than this, and probably Neolithic in origin, but whatever their date they held considerable fascination for Hardy. He read about them in his copy of John Hutchins's *History and Antiquities of the County of Dorset,* where he made a tiny, but careful drawing of the ground plan, and annotated the text with his own comparison between its size and the dimensions of the Coliseum in Rome.[8] Today, however, the Ring stands within the Dorchester suburbs in the angle between two branches of the railway line that Brunel constructed in such a way as to avoid cutting through the monument. In the 1840s they were much more isolated than they are now, so they appear as

. . . melancholy, impressive, lonely, yet accessible from every part of the town, the historic circle was the frequent spot for appointments of a furtive kind. Intrigues were arranged there; tentative meetings were there experimented after divisions and feuds. But one kind of appointment – in itself the most common of any – seldom had place in the amphitheatre; that of happy lovers. (67–8)

This is a spot with unsavoury associations. There are the gladiatorial games, the death of wild animals, the public executions, and Hardy mentions in particular the chilling story of the young Mary Channing whose heart burst from her body during her execution by burning. Few locations in the novel have such a long, unbroken historical pedigree, right down to 'pugilistic encounters almost to the death' of the recent past. But the Ring also has a metaphorical role in the book, and as the architectural historian Claudius Beatty pointed out, the words Hardy uses to describe it, 'melancholy', 'impressive' and 'lonely', might equally be applied to Henchard himself. It is significant that he should choose to meet first his former wife, Susan, and later Lucetta Templeman, in a place where wild animals were slaughtered. Henchard himself is described in the book as both 'leonine' and 'tigerish' and when he sees Lucetta pathetically waiting for him at the centre of the Rings he recognizes that she is, as he puts it, 'very small deer to hunt'. (232) The Ring

Hardy's plan of the Maumbury Rings, drawn in the margin of his copy of John Hutchins's *History and Antiquities of the County of Dorset*.

is a reminder not only of the latent violence of the story but that it connects specifically to the darker side of Henchard's nature.

Few characters move very far beyond the confines of Casterbridge, but as Henchard's fortunes flag, his existence in the town becomes more and more unbearable for him. Learning that Elizabeth-Jane's biological father, Richard Newsome, is returning to Casterbridge to claim her as his rightful daughter he finally makes up his mind to leave. Elizabeth-Jane accompanies him as far as the second bridge out of Casterbridge and he sets off towards the east. He is soon torn, however, between 'the centrifugal tendency imparted by weariness of the world' and 'the centripetal influence of his love for his stepdaughter'; the magnetism of the town begins to assert itself once again. So,

> instead of following a straight course yet further away from Casterbridge, Henchard gradually, almost unconsciously, deflected from that right line of his first intention; till, by degrees, his wandering, like that of the Canadian woodsman, became part of a circle of which Casterbridge formed the centre. (296)

What finally draws him back is the news of Elizabeth-Jane's impending marriage but on catching sight of Newsome dancing at the celebration he is distraught. Unseen by the other guests, 'he rose to his feet' and using an appropriate architectural simile Hardy says he 'stood like a dark ruin'. (302)

So often associated with ruins in this novel, Henchard ends his days in one. Leaving Casterbridge for the last time, he travels eastward once again, this time accompanied by the faithful former employee Abel Whittle. The landscape into which he travels is, like Henchard himself, wild and primitive and one where the only signs of former habitation are the numerous tumuli that dot the landscape. Elizabeth-Jane and Farfrae go in pursuit of him and after some twenty miles they catch up. But it is too late: he has died in a derelict, abandoned cottage. Of all humble dwellings, says Hardy, this was

> surely the humblest. The walls, built of kneaded clay originally faced with a trowel, had been worn by years of rain-washings to a lumpy crumbling surface, channelled and sunken from its plane, its gray rents

held together here and there by a leafy strap of ivy which could scarcely find substance enough for the purpose. The rafters were sunken, and the thatch of the roof in ragged holes. Leaves from the fence had been blown into the corners of the doorway, and lay there undisturbed. (307)

The homelessness that afflicted all the characters at the start of the novel has now, in Henchard, taken its ultimate toll. His existential isolation finds an emblem in the deserted and ruined cottage; its dissolution is reminiscent of the fate of those houseless people in Mixen Lane, driven there by the collapse of their roof-trees, and its location, so remote from Casterbridge, is a measure of his exclusion from human society. The very clay of its walls suggests the earth to which the former mayor has returned, and in doing so his dust will be mixing with that of the men and women of Imperial Rome buried in the nearby tumuli, some of whose skeletons Hardy discovered lying beneath the soil of his own garden.

Chapter Four

The Woodlanders:
That Wondrous World of Sap and Leaves

FOR HARDY'S NEXT NOVEL, *The Woodlanders,* we have to travel north out of Dorchester and along the road towards Yeovil. This is the 'forsaken coach-road' mentioned on the first page of the novel, running 'almost in a meridional line from Bristol to the south shore of England'. At the time Hardy was writing coach passengers had forsaken it in favour of the railway, but in the wake of another invention, the motor car, the road gained a new lease of life by becoming the busy A37. After about fifteen miles there is a narrow turning to the left that leads to the compact village of Melbury Osmond. Entering the village, we pass the cottages, the church and churchyard and drive through a small ford. Suddenly, the lane comes to an abrupt halt before sturdy metal gates. We can go no further. Through the gates, however, we can glimpse the Melbury estate, containing the woods and farmland of the former Earls of Ilchester. The contrast between the enclosed domestic world of the village and the rolling open spaces of parkland and forest is striking but in the nineteenth century the separation between villagers and aristocracy was even greater. The riches of the Earls of Ilchester lay on one side of the gate, and the poverty of the villagers could be seen on the other. The owners of the Melbury estate had played a part in the highest ranks of British society since the Middle Ages, but in the nineteenth century the farm labourers, like many of the farm labourers of Dorset, were amongst the poorest in the country, eking out an existence at the very lowest levels of society. Few places, therefore, illustrated so graphically the famous lines from 'All Things Bright and Beautiful', 'The rich man in his castle/The poor man at his gate'.

Right next to the gate of Melbury Park is a cottage once owned by Henry Stephen, the 3rd Earl of Ilchester. In the early years of the nineteenth century this was rented to John and Maria Swetman, Thomas Hardy's maternal great-grandparents. Here, the Swetmans struggled to bring up seven children, one of whom, Betty, caused them great anguish. In 1804 she found herself pregnant by George Hand, a local labourer who was idle and often drunk, and Betty was catapulted into marriage in the nearby village church of St Osmond. Her father hugely disapproved. He cut off his daughter without a penny, and even though the couple went to live just up the lane at Barton Hill Cottages, he offered no financial support. As a result Betty Hand's own children, among them Jemima, Hardy's mother, grew up in grinding poverty. Jemima was born in 1813. Like her mother she was married in St Osmond's church to Thomas Hardy senior and she, too, was pregnant at the time. A copy of their marriage certificate hangs in a frame just inside the church door telling us that the ceremony took place on 22 December 1839. A little over five months later, on 2 June 1840, Thomas Hardy the younger was born sixteen miles away in the parish of Stinsford.

The world of Hardy's childhood and boyhood in and around Stinsford had supplied the imaginative context for a number of his previous novels. For *The Woodlanders* he abandoned the land of his father's family and explored the land of his mother's. When he was a child the Melburys – Melbury Osmond, Melbury Sampford and Melbury Bubb – were, for him, remote places that he knew in none of the intimate detail in which he understood the countryside around Higher Bockhampton. But they had something mysterious about them; they existed in the depths of countryside far away from the bustle of Dorchester. Much of his knowledge of the area, therefore, must have come from the tales told to him by his mother and grandmother together with what he gleaned from his copy of John Hutchins's *History of Dorset*.[1] His mother must have told him how she, like the characters in *The Woodlanders*, grew up surrounded by the extensive forests and cider orchards, all in the shadow of the great house at Melbury Sampford. The country settings for *The Woodlanders* are quite different, therefore, from those of *Far from the Madding Crowd* or *The Return of the Native*. In this new novel it is much harder to specify them accurately or to pin them down precisely. They exist in a slightly indistinct realm of 'sap and leaves' and the curious reader has to work harder to identify the landmarks and locations.

There are two principal reasons for this, one pragmatic and the other imaginative. The pragmatic one is connected with Henry Fox-Strangways, the 5th Earl of

Ilchester. When he died in 1905 Hardy revealed that Fox-Strangways, whose home was Melbury House, had been angry with him for using a scandalous family legend as the basis for Hardy's short story 'The First Countess of Wessex'. How and when Fox-Strangways expressed this anger we do not know, but we can reasonably assume that his feelings about *The Woodlanders* were similar. The possibility of comparisons between his twenty-five-year-old wife, Mary Dawson, and Hardy's character, the twenty-eight-year-old, dissolute, former actress Felice Charmond, must have been profoundly irritating for him and Fox-Strangways was a powerful man. Not only was he one of the richest landowners in the country, but his social and political connections spread across the land. In Dorset alone he owned numerous estates including large tracts of Puddletown Heath near Hardy's parents in Higher Bockhampton.

Soon after the book was first published Hardy confessed to his friend the critic and poet Edmund Gosse that Great Hintock was Melbury Osmond and that Little Hintock a hamlet that lay two miles away.[2] When, in 1895, he came to revise the book for the first collected edition of his novels, Hardy realized that he had been playing with fire and made several radical changes to these locations. First, he moved the action five miles east, away from Melbury House and Bubb Down Hill towards High Stoy Hill. Then he attempted to erase any references that would specifically identify places on the Earl's estate. Finally, to further distract his readers, he claimed to have forgotten exactly where the story was set. In a preface to a later edition of the book he mentioned that he had had so many requests for information about the location that he went off in search of it himself, spending, as he told them, 'several hours on a bicycle with a friend in a serious attempt to discover the real spot'. (4) The image of Hardy cycling around north-west Dorset in search of the location of one of his own novels is certainly an amusing one and it is hardly surprising that the attempt ended in failure!

There was, however, an aesthetic reason for the blurring of the geography of the Hintocks. On several occasions during the writing of the book Hardy recorded that his interest in the physical and material world had diminished and he had become progressively more concerned with the invisible forces that lay beneath the surface of things. Referring specifically to landscape painting he said that he felt that beautiful effects had lost their attraction for him, and he now wanted to see 'the deeper realities underlying the scenic'. Though nature, he said, was played out as a 'beauty' it still held an appeal for him as a 'mystery'. In *The*

Woodlanders he hoped to express these 'abstract imaginings' and take novel writing into a new phase by adopting the 'thoughts of the analytical school'. Characters might then become what he called 'visible essences' or spectres, defined less by their manners and gestures and more by the half-conscious workings of their minds. People, he said, are really 'somnambulists' and 'the material is not the real'. The real, he added, is optically invisible 'because we are in a somnambulistic hallucination that we think the real to be what we see as real'.[3]

The result of Hardy's new focus was that the solid market town of Casterbridge with its river, bridges, walks and buildings gives way to the seasonal flux and change of the woodlands, with their sunshine, shadow, fog, mist, storm and where (as many of the characters discover) directions disappear and it is easy to get lost. The characters themselves are also less precisely defined than previously and the boundaries between them and their environment less clearly marked. George Melbury and Giles Winterborne have none of the forceful impact of Michael Henchard or Gabriel Oak and the seductress Felice Charmond none of the erotic magnetism of Eustacia Vye. In *The Woodlanders* characters are known more by their temperament, class and disposition than by their physical appearance, and the complex, but compelling plot unfolds principally around the psychological forces that link characters to each other and that unite them with their woodland setting. They are indeed like somnambulists.

Though *The Woodlanders* may have little of the topographical precision of *The Mayor of Casterbridge,* we can nevertheless identify many of the scenes, buildings and locations in the story. Having registered that Melbury Osmond, the village of Hardy's mother's family, was the inspiration for Great Hintock, we can now retrace our steps back to the 'forsaken coach-road' between Dorchester and Yeovil. From here we can follow the route taken by Mrs Dollery's van in the opening scenes of the novel as she transports Barber Percombe to find the poor country girl Marty South in Little Hintock. He is making the journey in a rather bizarre attempt to persuade Marty to sell her hair to make a wig for Mrs Charmond, the local landowner. But the girl's village is hard to find. The road Mrs Dollery takes is a small one and today is no more than a bridleway called, from an incident in the seventeenth century, Murderer's Lane. It leads away from the highway, up into Bubb Down woods, woods that Hardy in the early editions of the book called Rubdown, and descends the eastern slope of the hill. From here

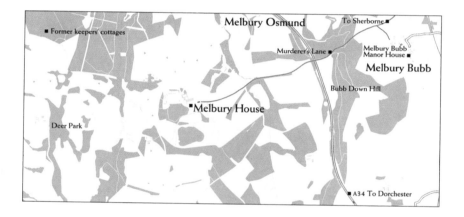

Top: View of Melbury Bubb (Little Hintock) from Bubb Down Hill with 'gardens and orchards sunk in a concave'. The manor house can be seen on the left. Above: Map showing the Melburys and the path of Grace's walk from Melbury Bubb to Hintock House along Murderer's Lane crossing the 'forsaken coach-road' running between Dorchester and Bristol.

Little Hintock, Hardy writes, 'could be discerned in the dusk about half a mile to one side, gardens and orchards sunk in a concave, and as it were nipped out of the woodland'. (7) On the Ordnance Survey map we can identify this as Melbury Bubb and today it is even smaller and more isolated than it was in the nineteenth century. Percombe gets off where the road branches. He leaves the van to go on to Sherton-Abbas (Sherborne), and as he walks down into the hamlet he can detect the smell of cider making, a local activity confirmed by nineteenth-century maps that show this area rich in apple orchards. Before reaching Marty's cottage, however, the lane took him alongside and past the most substantial building in the hamlet. It was, says Hardy, 'a dwelling-house of respectable, roomy, almost dignified aspect.' This is the seventeenth-century home of George Melbury, the timber merchant, his second wife Lucy and his daughter Grace who, when the novel opens, is away at school. Though the west-facing garden-front, Hardy says, 'remained much as it had always been . . . on the east facing side',

the principal house-door opened on the square yard or quadrangle towards the road, formerly a regular carriage entrance, though the middle of the area was now made use of for stacking timber, fagots, hurdles, and other products of the wood. It was divided from the lane by a lichen-coated wall, in which hung a pair of gates, flanked by piers out of the perpendicular, with a round white ball on the top of each. (22)

In Melbury Bubb, the manor house stands on this spot as it did in the 1880s. The western garden front with its porch and entrance looks back up towards Bubb Down Hill, and on the other side, the eastern side, what Hardy describes as a working yard is now mainly turfed over and planted with apple trees and a vegetable garden. But the lichen-coated wall remains. It still divides the house from the lane, though a small, low door has replaced a much larger opening through which carriages and wagons came and went. In the novel, the Melbury house is the psychological and economic hub of the story. Melbury is a timber merchant employed on the Hintock estate by Felice Charmond, and Marty South, who lives nearby supporting her ailing father, works for Melbury. She is in love with Giles Winterborne, a woodsman also working for Melbury but who, unfortunately for Marty, hopes to marry Melbury's daughter, Grace.

Above: The mainly seventeeth-century Melbury Bubb manor house.
Opposite: Initials carved in the stone door jamb of the manor house.

The significance of the manor house is that it defines the role and status of the Melbury family. It was, says Hardy, 'of no marked antiquity, yet of well-advanced age; older than a stale novelty, but no canonized antique; faded, not hoary; looking at you from the still distinct middle-distance of the early Georgian time, and awakening on that account the instincts of reminiscence more decidedly than the remoter and far grander memorials which have to speak from the misty reaches of mediaevalism.' In other words the house is old, but homely. Unlike more ancient buildings, remote and distant in time, this is not so antiquated as to be alien, and rather like the Three Mariners in *The Mayor of Casterbridge* it acts as an emblem of social continuity. Hardy stresses the unbroken link between past and present by suggesting that the building has become a kind of reservoir or container of memory where the faces, dress, passions, gratitudes, and revenges of the great-great-grandfathers and grandmothers who had been the first to gaze from those rectangular windows, and had stood under that key-stoned doorway, could be divined and measured by homely standards of to-day. It was a house in whose reverberations queer old personal tales were yet audible if properly listened for; and not, as with those of the castle and cloister, silent beyond the possibility of echo. (22)

The idea of cultural continuity was very dear to Hardy. For him, human identity was substantially defined by history and buildings played an important role as the custodians of historical memory. In *The Woodlanders* these sentiments are associated principally with the Melbury home, even down to some of its finest details. An incident early in the story brings this out.

Grace, who has been educationally hot-housed by her father, is returning from school. Giles Winterborne, having been commissioned to pick her up from the nearby station at Sherton-Abbas, has brought her to the house and stands deferentially at the front door. While he waits he finds himself 'mechanically tracing with his fingers certain time-worn letters carved in the jambs' which, Hardy tells us, are the 'initials of bygone generations of householders who had lived and died there'. (42) Lives come and go, but the letters in the stone remain, serving to link Grace and her family to previous generations of owners and occupiers. If we stand on the same spot occupied by Giles at the front door we can see what he saw. On the jambs there are some initials carved deep into the stone. Whether they are those of previous householders is uncertain, but at some point Hardy must have seen them, made a mental note of their significance and remembered them.

Not all the characters in *The Woodlanders* experience the past in this way and there is an important division between those who have the sense of being rooted in the land, the culture and the place and those who do not. When the novel opens, Winterborne, Melbury and Grace come into the first category and Hardy carefully enumerates their 'almost exhaustive biographical or historical acquaintance with every object, animate and inanimate' needed to produce the sense of belonging. Such a rooted individual, he says,

> must know all about those invisible ones of the days gone by, whose feet have traversed the fields which look so gray from his windows; recall whose creaking plough has turned those sods from time to time; whose hands planted the trees that form a crest to the opposite hill; whose horses and hounds have torn through that underwood; what birds affect that particular brake; what domestic dramas of love, jealousy, revenge, or disappointment have been enacted in the cottages, the mansion, the street, or on the green. The spot may have beauty, grandeur, salubrity, convenience; but if it lack memories it will ultimately pall upon him who settles there without opportunity of intercourse with his kind. (112)

The Melburys' house forms a nucleus for these associations and when Grace returns from the town where she has received her 'superior education' she realizes that she has begun to forget the 'good old Hintock ways'. (40) But once inside, the physical characteristics of the house with its low ceilings and worn surfaces serve to jog her memory, taking her back to her childhood. So, on her first evening, when dinner is over, she

> took a candle and began to ramble pleasurably through the rooms of her old home, from which she had latterly become well-nigh an alien. Each nook and each object revived a memory, and simultaneously modified it. The chambers seemed lower than they had appeared on any previous occasion of her return, the surfaces of both walls and ceilings standing in such relations to the eye that it could not avoid taking microscopic note of their irregularities and old fashion. (43)

The sitting room of Melbury Bubb manor.

The structure of the manor house at Melbury Bubb has changed very little over the years. The parlour is dominated by a vast open hearth, with a moulded oak frame that goes from floor to ceiling. The walls, here as in many other rooms, are lined with dark and mellow panelling, some of which originates in the seventeenth century. The beams supporting the ceilings are large and low and the mullioned windows admit only a limited amount of light. The parlour leads out to a warren of smaller rooms, all of them gracious, dignified but un-pretentious. The walls and floors are worn and in places the stonework exposed. Two staircases lead to a passage on the first floor dividing the house into two parts, north and south, and we can see that it would have been quite easy for Mr Melbury to create a separate living area for Grace and her husband when, after their marriage, they came to live there. Grace's bedroom was probably the one at the end of the passage in the south wing, spacious, lit by narrow windows and with a long window seat. When Grace went in, 'it wore a look at once more familiar than when she had left it, and yet a face estranged'. (43) Gradually, however, her old life comes back to her, and even the brown spot on the ceiling in her bedroom reminds her of the nights when she used to read in bed.

From that bedroom, Grace is able to look across the garden front, up the hill and towards Melbury Bubb woods and it is through this window on her first night at home that she sees strange lights in the trees. She learns later from Grammer Oliver that they radiated from the windows of a recent arrival in the village, Dr Edred Fitzpiers, as he worked on 'chemical experiments and anatomical projects'. (46) Fitzpiers is one of those who feels no real ties to land or culture. He is a newcomer to the region, bringing with him attitudes and values that are alien to this rural spot, and his house is one of the few in *The Woodlanders* for which we will look in vain for an original. It would have been located on Bubb Down just below the woodland belonging to the Earl of Ilchester, and today that woodland is still part of the Ilchester estates. Nevertheless the house is important in the novel because it expresses sensibilities that contrast with those of the manor house below. It was rented, not owned, and unlike the Melburys' house whose origins could be traced back to the Civil Wars and beyond, Fitzpiers's place was 'small, box-like, and comparatively modern'. Its most striking feature, however, was its garden, and like Fitzpiers himself it seemed strangely incongruous among the forests, woodlands and wildernesses of the Hintocks. Both cottage and garden, Hardy tells us,

> were so regular in their arrangement that they might have been laid out by a Dutch designer of the time of William and Mary. In a low, dense hedge was a door over which the hedge formed an arch; and from the inside of the door a straight path, bordered with clipped box, ran up the slope of the garden to the porch, which was exactly in the middle of the house front, with two windows on each side. Right and left of the path were first a bed of gooseberry bushes; next of currant; next of raspberry; next of strawberry; next of old-fashioned flowers; at the corners opposite the porch being spheres of box resembling a pair of school globes. (101–102)

Regular, rigid, symmetrical, balanced, this garden is an example of what the eighteenth-century poet Alexander Pope called 'nature methodized'. Everything is regimented into specifically designated areas, or forced by cutting and clipping into geometrical shapes, wedges and globes. It is not known whether Hardy had a specific cottage and garden in mind but there is one just outside Dorchester that fits the description. Hardy often walked the mile from Max Gate to Winterborne Came Rectory to visit the home of his friend the famous Dorset poet William Barnes. Like Fitzpiers's cottage Barnes's was relatively modern. It was built around 1813 by the Archdeacon of Dorset and former rector William England. Barnes's biographer, Alan Chedzoy, describes it as 'a symmetrical two storied box' about which 'nothing could be more rational'.[4] Even more significant is the unusual formal garden. Using nineteenth-century documents the present owner has established that Barnes had the rear garden laid out in a strictly formal grid not unlike the pattern of the beds that Hardy ascribes to Fitzpiers's cottage ('next of currant; next of raspberry; next of strawberry'). So Came Rectory also 'small [and] box like' looks over a garden that could have been laid out at 'the time of William and Mary' and now restored to how Barnes (and Hardy) knew it.

The 'symmetrical two-storied box' of Came Rectory and its formal garden.

Fitzpiers, of course, is not Barnes, and the reasonable, rational, controlled design of the cottage garden represents the way in which Fitzpiers (rather than Barnes) would have liked to organize his life. The scientist in him looks everywhere for reasonable explanations. His decision to live in Little Hintock was calculated not according to recommendation or sentiment, but simply by using a map and geometrical compass. His treatment of John South's totemic attachment to the tree outside South's window is rational but counter-intuitive and it precipitates the old man's death. Fitzpiers prefers the idea of a secular, state marriage to the rites of a religious one, and his dislike of travelling about the woods at night stems from his distrust of the wildness of nature. More broadly, his philosophical views and attitudes owe a great deal to seventeenth-century rationalism. While travelling through the night with Giles Winterborne he quotes Spinoza (1632–77) about the essentially subjective nature of love. He tells Giles that, irrespective of feelings and emotions, given the right time and place, a person will fall mechanically in love with whoever crosses their field of vision. One of those who crosses Fitzpiers's field of vision is, of course, the pretty Grace Melbury, but his initial attachment to her springs more from the need to counteract rural isolation than from strong passion. Given his temperament, then, it is not surprising that the cool geometrical design of the cottage and garden was very much to his taste.

There is, however, another side to Fitzpiers's character and one that seems very different from the rational and scientific part. It is the sentimental romantic in him. He reads 'rank literatures of emotion and passion' and has a liking for German idealist thinkers such as Schleiermacher, Schlegel and Schelling. At one point, like an armchair ruralist, he develops a fantasy about settling in the woodlands and 'sacrificing all practical aims to live in calm contentment'. (126) His marriage to Grace grows out of this pastoral sentimentalism, which rapidly evaporates in the face of economic reality. He then transfers his Quixotic emotions to a fantastic affair with Felice Charmond. Fitzpiers is a 'subtilist in emotions', he enjoys 'strange, mournful pleasures' (303), and when he is rejected by Grace for his infidelity with Felice his interest in her is considerably rekindled by the thought that she might have been sexually involved with Giles Winterborne. His own fantasies are promiscuous ones. They lead him into an impulsive liaison with the 'hoydenish maiden' Suke Damson, a bucolic infatuation with Grace and an operatic affair with Felice.

Fitzpiers, however, is not the only person in the novel to indulge in fantasy. Grace also has romantic notions, and these are directed at Fitzpiers himself. Encouraged by her father's foolishness she fixates on his aristocratic ancestry and his links to an ancient, decayed family from Oakbury-Fitzpiers. If she were to ally herself 'with such a romantical family', her father tells her, she would feel as though she had 'stepped into history'. (145) In order to substantiate this claim she visits Sherton Castle, 'the original stronghold of the Lords Baxby, Fitzpiers's maternal ancestors'. (145) In contrast to the Melbury house the ruins of the castle extend back in the 'misty reaches of mediaevalism'. Having no connection with contemporary life, they offer a remote and romantic stimulus to the imagination. Sherborne Old Castle (to distinguish it from the nearby Tudor building of Sherborne Castle) was built in the early eleventh century for Roger de Caen, Bishop of Salisbury. It remained as a fortified building until the mid-seventeenth century when after the Civil War its defences were dismantled. It stands on the outskirts of Sherborne on a well-manicured site under the protection of English Heritage. When Grace saw it, however, it was very different. It

consisted mostly of remnants of the lower vaulting, supported on low stout columns surmounted by the *crochet* capital of the period. The two or three arches of these vaults that were still in position were utilized by the adjoining farmer as shelter for his calves, the floor being spread with straw, amid which the young creatures rustled, cooling their thirsty tongues by licking the quaint Norman carving, which glistened with the moisture. It was a degradation of even such a rude form of art as this to be treated so grossly, she thought, and for the first time the aspect of Fitzpiers assumed in her imagination the hues of a melancholy romanticism. (145)

No doubt Hardy knew Sherborne Old Castle, but the view that he attributes to Grace was probably shaped by something other than his personal observation. Almost certainly this was an illustration of the castle in his own volume of Hutchins's *History of Dorset*. This is by an Irish artist, Philip Brannon (1817–90), which clearly shows the Norman vaulting, the capitals and the cattle grazing in the precincts. More importantly, Brannon's illustration is neither realist nor archaeological.

Philip Brannon's illustration of Sherborne Castle from *History and Antiquities of the County of Dorset* by John Hutchins.

Instead it is essentially picturesque. It is designed to create a certain atmosphere where the 'melancholy romanticism' of the ruins is intensified by stressing their neglect and by the way in which nature has begun to reclaim them. In Grace's mind these emotions are transferred by association to Fitzpiers, falsifying his real character and making him seem, like the castle, picturesque and slightly pathetic.

Grace may have been seduced by the stones of the castle, but she is not alone since the romantic in Fitzpiers is also susceptible to architectural sentiment. His rational side may have chosen the cottage with its formal garden, but his involvement with Grace owes something to the fact that he once believed her to be the owner of Hintock House. He admits this mistake when, after their engagement, the couple are walking in Hintock park near the house. "'This place would just do for us, would it not, dearest,'" said Fitzpiers, as they sit, looking at the facade. "'Oh yes,'" says Grace, plainly showing that no such fancy had ever crossed her mind.' '"Do you know, dear,"' he goes on, '"that at one time I thought you lived here."' (148) Though Grace may never have considered the possibility of living at Hintock House with Fitzpiers, when she is invited to visit Felice Charmond there for the first time she is considerably excited by the prospect of both the house and the exotic charms of the sophisticated owner. In the story, Felice has met Grace and her father in the woods. She notices that Grace is educated beyond most woodlanders and considers her as a possible travelling companion. An interview is proposed, and flattered by the prospect Grace dresses in her finest clothes to meet her.

To reach Hintock House, Grace would have left her own place in Little Hintock and taken the byway through the woods, crossed the main highway and then, using the footpath that led to the estate, arrived at Hintock House, taking (as Hardy suggests) about twenty minutes. If we followed her steps on that route, however, we would have a considerable surprise. As we approached Melbury Sampford House we would immediately realize that this is not the same building to which Grace made her pilgrimage in the novel, and Hintock House of *The Woodlanders* is certainly not the seat of the former Earls of Ilchester. The house that stands at the heart of the Ilchester estates rises bold and proud on a slight eminence surrounded by an expansive and graceful park. In contrast, Grace's walk 'brought her to the verge of a deep glen, at the bottom of which Hintock House appeared immediately beneath her eye'. Its most striking feature is its position. 'To describe it as standing in a hollow,' says Hardy,

> would not express the situation of the manor-house; it stood in a hole. But the hole was full of beauty. From the spot which Grace had reached a stone could easily have been thrown over or into the birds'-nested chimneys of the mansion. Its walls were surmounted by a battlemented parapet; but the gray lead roofs were quite visible behind it, with their gutters, laps, rolls, and skylights; together with letterings and shoe-patterns cut by idlers thereon. (53)

But if this is not Melbury Sampford House, what is it? Hardy himself admitted that he had used Turnworth House as his model, some twenty miles to the east of Melbury Sampford. This mock-Elizabethan mansion had been built around 1800 and Hardy had seen it when he first visited the area, probably in 1869. At the time he was working for G. R. Crickmay, who was rebuilding the nearby church of St Mary when Hardy was commissioned to design the capitals in the nave.[5] Unfortunately, we can no longer see the original house because it was burned down just after the First World War, but like Sherborne Castle it was illustrated in Hardy's edition of Hutchins's *History of Dorset*. Again the artist was Philip Brannon and his drawing of Turnworth House is very close in its detail to Hardy's account of Hintock House. With its raking perspective seen from above, it appears to be drawn from a spot identical to that of Hardy's desription. From there, the roof appears more clearly than the walls and the illustration gives the strong impression that the whole building stands in a 'hole'. In Hardy's account, however, the sense that Hintock House is rooted to the spot is strengthened by the way in which, with its covering of moss and lichen, it seems to merge with the ground:

> The front of the house exhibited an ordinary manorial presentation of Elizabethan windows, mullioned and hooded, worked in rich snuff-coloured freestone from Ham Hill quarries. The ashlar of the walls, where not overgrown with ivy and other creepers, was coated with lichen of every shade, intensifying its luxuriance with its nearness to the ground, till, below the plinth, it merged in moss.

Hardy's gaze then turns to the surroundings, and once again the details correspond closely with Brannon's illustration:

> Above the house to the back was a dense plantation, the roots of whose trees were above the level of the chimneys. The corresponding high ground on which Grace stood was richly grassed, with only an old tree here and there. A few sheep lay about, which, as they ruminated, looked quietly into the bedroom windows. (53)

Hardy, like Brannon, stresses the way in which the trees appear to grow above the roof and the sheep graze at a level higher the chimneys. This, says Hardy, is 'a spot to inspire the painter' and indeed there, in the illustration, sits an artist

Turnworth House (Hintock House), illustrated by Philip Brannon in John
Hutchins, *History and Antiquities of the County of Dorset.*

with a woman looking over his shoulder. But Hardy introduces sentiments that are not simply pictorial. Hintock House is what he calls 'vegetable nature's own home', whose 'hollow site was an ocular reminder', he says, of 'its unfitness for modern lives'. (53) But Felice Charmond is above all modern and consequently entirely out of place in this spot. She was an actress, a morally dubious occupation in the late nineteenth century, and a woman who had been plucked from the stage by a rich man thirty years her senior. He had retired from the iron trade in the north of England, bought the estate and died, leaving Felice, at the age of twenty-seven, with the burden of its management. Unable, as one of the rustics points out, to tell 'a beech from a woak', she hates everything about Hintock and its woods, loathing above all the loneliness and the damp. She longs for the south, and her very name, Charmond, suggests something demi-mondaine and French. In an attempt to make the house bearable and 'counteract the fine old-English gloom' of the place she fills it with 'Versailles furniture'. Curiously, however, she maintains the collection of man-traps placed on the walls by her metal-working husband, saying archly to Grace that 'man-traps are of rather ominous significance where a person of our sex lives, are they not?' (54) Grace is embarrassed by the sexual innuendo. Colloquially, a 'man-trap' means a vamp or femme fatale. Here it is an ironic reference to Felice herself, to her extensive romantic experience and to her numerous lovers. More than this, however, the man-trap suggests the mechanical sexual attitudes of both Felice and Fitzpiers, both of whom are able to change partners at will.

In the event, Grace's interview with Felice Charmond falls flat. When Felice catches sight of herself in a mirror beside the younger woman she sees that the comparison is not flattering, so however cultivated she may be, Grace's presence would do her no favours. It is not long, however, before Grace is noticed by Edred Fitzpiers. Though she was promised by her father to the humble Giles Winterborne, she has moved out of his sphere and is flattered by the attentions of the aristocratic doctor. She is a prosperous timber merchant's daughter and even though he is much her social superior, since there is money involved he courts her, and they marry. After an extended Continental honeymoon at Melbury's expense the couple make an autumn return to England, but before coming home to Little Hintock they pause in Sherton-Abbas. Predictably, Fitzpiers chooses 'the chief hotel' in the town, the Earl of Wessex. This Hardy tells us was a substantial inn of Ham-hill stone with a yawning back yard into which vehicles were driven by coachmen to stabling of wonderful commodiousness. The windows to the street were mullioned into narrow lights, and only commanded a view of the opposite houses; hence, perhaps, it arose that the best and most luxurious private sitting-room that the inn could afford over-looked the lateral parts of the establishment, where beyond the yard were to be seen gardens and orchards, now bossed, nay incrusted, with scarlet and gold fruit, stretching to infinite distance under a luminous lavender mist. (157)

The model for the Earl of Wessex was the Digby Hotel, in Digby Road, Sherborne, built in 1869 as a response to the new demand from travellers using the nearby railway station.[6] It is one of the grandest and most dignified nineteenth-century buildings in Sherborne, and a photograph, taken in 1896, shows that the area outside described by Hardy as a yard was by then a garden. It must have been from one of the large windows on the ground floor overlooking that garden that Grace Melbury catches sight of Giles Winterborne in the yard. Here, 'an apple-mill and press had been erected . . . to which some men were bringing fruit from divers points in mawn-baskets, while others were grinding them, and others wringing down the pomace, whose sweet juice gushed forth into tubs and pails'. (157) It is the cider-making season, and Giles is engaged in his customary autumn occupation. The apple harvest in the farms around Sherborn was not large enough to justify each farmer having his own press, so itinerant cider men like Giles made a good living by moving their portable press from location to location.[7] This is hard manual labour, but it has a profound attractiveness for Grace. Giles wears 'his shirt-sleeves rolled up beyond his elbows, to keep them unstained while he rammed the pomace into the bags of horse-hair'. Vigorous and sexually appealing, he has 'fragments of apple-rind . . . upon the brim of his hat – probably from the bursting of a bag – while brown pips of the same fruit were sticking among the down upon his fine, round arms'. (157–8) The contrast that Hardy establishes between the hotel interior and the activity in the yard is comparable to the sheep shearing supper in *Far from the Madding Crowd*. In the earlier novel, the socially inferior farm workers dine outside the window, while Bathsheba and Boldwood sit inside. Here, Grace is poised between her

Top: The Digby Hotel (Earl of Wessex) in 1896.
Above: A portable cider press working in the street near
Shaftesbury in the early twentieth century.

desire for the primitively energetic figure of Giles outside the casement and her sybaritic life inside with Fitzpiers, who, far from operating heavy machinery, had gone to experience romantic sentiments as the sun sets on Sherton Abbey. Grace's physical position, however, encapsulates her ambiguous social position. It was, as Fitzpiers was aware, 'a startling anomaly that this woman of the tribe without should be standing there beside him as his wife'. (161) Then using an appropriately Darwinian term, he tells Grace that he feels that he belongs to a 'different species' from the men in the yard. Grace, however, recognizes that her allegiances are divided between nature and culture. Genetically, or naturally, she is one of the 'tribe' outside; mentally, intellectually and culturally she has grown closer to her doctor husband inside.

Hardy's interest in what he called 'the deeper realities underlying the scenic' can be felt very strongly at this point in the novel. Here, Grace Melbury is divided between two impulses represented by rural labour in the yard outside the Earl of Wessex and the urban sophistication within. As the narrative progresses she becomes the pivotal figure between two sets of forces, forces that become more complicated and more polarized as the narrative unfolds. On the face of it this appears to be a contrast between those who are rooted in the soil and the place, notably Giles Winterborne and Marty South, and those who are alien to the natural environment, Edred Fitzpiers and Felice Charmond. Certainly the feeling of organic ripeness associated with Giles as he presses the apples in the yard of the Earl of Wessex has echoes elsewhere in the book. What Hardy calls his 'wonderful power of making trees grow' links him closely to the sylvan environment (58) where sometimes he seems like a 'wood god' (249) or 'Autumn's very brother'. (185) But his integration into the simple, primitive life of the world of the forest, which appears at first so strong and positive, when examined more closely is actually very precarious.

That precariousness becomes suddenly evident when Winterbourne is evicted from his house in Little Hintock. From that moment his commanding position in the woodlands begins to diminish. He loses the house because his tenure is lifehold, which means that his continued possession is tied to the life of Marty's father, John South. Because Giles's father had never put in place the necessary legal preparations for transfers, when South dies the property reverts to the landowner, Felice Charmond. She promptly and thoughtlessly pulls it down in an attempt to reduce her contribution to the poor rates.

After his eviction Giles withdraws to the margins of Hintock society, finding a 'mysterious hut' lying deep within the woods, even more remote than Little Hintock itself, and 'just beyond the boundary of Mrs Charmond's estate'. (202) It has long been thought that 'One Chimney Hut' as Hardy calls it was imaginary. Nevertheless, we can tentatively indentify its location. The forester of the Ilchester estates, Andy Poore, tells me that at Great Highwoods on the edge of the Ilchester estate towards Melbury Osmond there were once two cottages. One was called Flatman's after an old keeper and the other, Woods Cottage. Hardy suggests, however, that Winterbourne's once belonged to a charcoal burner and Andy Poore confirms that there is some evidence of charcoal burning in Highwoods. The design of this cottage is extremely primitive.

> The house was a square cot of one story only, sloping up on all sides to a chimney in the midst. It had formerly been the home of a charcoal-burner, in times when that fuel was still used in the county houses. Its only appurtenance was a paled enclosure, there being no garden, the shade of the trees preventing the growth of vegetables. She advanced to the window whence the rays of light proceeded, and the shutters being as yet unclosed, she could survey the whole interior through the panes. (269)

Though by the mid-nineteenth century charcoal burners continued to work in some parts of the country, the occupation had died out in Dorset. For this reason the place is abandoned, but its design is revealing. Charcoal burners' cottages were primitive in the extreme and, according to historians of the genre, had their origins back in the eighth century.[8] When they were active in this area the burners built small, temporary, conical huts on site and for a season. These were made out of a wigwam of wooden poles covered with turf or reed, and usually with a single door. Sometimes these were extended for more permanent residence, where two conical huts were built close together and joined by a ridge piece to create a single cottage. The roof of this type of cottage often reached down to the ground, though later builders introduced small sidewalls. Giles's cottage must have had such walls because it had overhanging eves from which he hung his lantern. Like the charcoal burners' huts, this one contained a single room 'that was kitchen, parlour, and scullery all in one' and inside the 'natural sandstone floor' was worn into ruts. (269)

Cottages like this represented the lowest level of rural dwelling. They were not, however, unusual, and contemporary reports on the state of the poor in the English countryside speak of their squalid living conditions. One artist, John Thomas Smith, recorded many such dwellings and his etching of one near Battle-Bridge (now Islington), for example, appears like Giles's to have just one room and a single chimney.[9] The figure in the foreground carries faggots for heating, and another, a woman, leans out of the only door. Unlike these people,

A pauper's cottage at Battle-Bridge, illustrated in John Thomas Smith, *Antiquities of London and its Environs* (1791).

Winterbourne, of course, is homeless rather than penniless. He still has employment in the woods and the cottage is well stocked with food. His plight focuses instead on the issue of housing and social exclusion, yet in Hardy's treatment of Giles's withdrawal into the forest we can detect the shadows of several problems that troubled Victorian reformers.

At the same time that Giles is moving into his primitive home, Fitzpiers and Felice Charmond run away to Germany in an attempt to relive their original fantasy romance. Grace remains with her family and adjusts to her solitary life there. While her father hopelessly and pathetically attempts to organize a divorce she tentatively renews her connection with Giles, only to be brutally admonished by her father, who has to recognize that divorce from Fitzpiers is impossible. On the Continent, Felice, after a disagreement with Fitzpiers, is murdered by a former lover and the doctor returns to England. As he re-enters Little Hintock one night, Grace takes flight and begins a difficult cross-country journey to catch a train at Ivel (Yeovil). She walks three or four miles westward towards Delborough (Chelborough) and towards the edge of Mrs Charmond's estate, where she stumbles across Winterborne's cottage. He offers to accompany her onwards. It begins to rain, and the journey becomes impossible. Returning to the hut, Giles coaxes her in, telling her that he has another for himself nearby. This, however, is not a cottage but a thatched hurdle and no real shelter from the storm that is now beginning to brew.

The dramatic climax of *The Woodlanders* hinges on Winterbourne's refusal to share the cottage for the night with Grace. In spite of her pleas for him to join her, his acute sense of propriety forces him to become exposed to the weather. Though Giles's self-sacrifice and concern for orthodox morality is debilitating to the point of self-harm, one of the anxieties of contemporary reformers was the lax moral standards in the cottages of the very poor. In these situations women, it was reported, lost 'all sense of modesty and decency' and 'men lost respect for the other sex'.[10]

Giles's moral conservatism identifies him with a simple rather naïve value system which, if old fashioned, is not to be disregarded. In the course of the narrative, his way of life is most closely bound up with the most bountiful aspects of the woods and above all with the ripeness and fertility of the cider orchards. As Grace and her father return from a spring journey to the woods, they see Giles leaning on a gate overlooking a wide valley, differing both in feature and atmosphere from that of the Hintock precincts. It was the cider country, which met the woodland district on the axis of this hill. Over the vale the air was blue as sapphire – such a blue as outside that apple-valley was never seen. Under the blue the orchards were in a blaze of bloom, some of the richly flowered trees running almost up to where they drove along. (125)

The clarity, intensity and luminosity of the colour here is a measure of the positive power of nature, a power that increases in autumn. Not long after Fitzpiers has begun his affair with Felice Charmond, he temporarily abandons Grace by riding off to see Felice at Middleton Abbey on the back of her own horse, Darling. As Grace watches her husband disappear into the landscape from the top of Bubb Down, Winterborne appears nearby climbing the hill, accompanied by his horse-drawn cider mill. He has about him the same sensuousness that he will have later in the courtyard of the Earl of Wessex. He is an icon of nature's bounty.

He looked and smelt like Autumn's very brother, his face being sunburnt to wheat-color, his eyes blue as corn-flowers, his boots and leggings dyed with fruit-stains, his hands clammy with the sweet juice of apples, his hat sprinkled with pips, and everywhere about him that atmosphere of cider which at its first return each season has such an indescribable fascination for those who have been born and bred among the orchards.

Giles's almost mythical role as 'Autumn's very brother' transforms him from a humble country worker into something almost mythological. In view of his prudery about sharing his hut with Grace, his physical presence temporarily awakens in Grace a primitive sexual desire that wells up from beneath her acquired conventionality.

Her heart rose from its late sadness like a released bough; her senses revelled in the sudden lapse back to nature unadorned. The consciousness of having to be genteel because of her husband's profession, the veneer of artificiality which she had acquired at the fashionable schools, were thrown off, and she became the crude, country girl of her latent, earliest instincts. (186)

Momentarily she luxuriates in the pleasure of the senses as the ripeness of the season and the appearance of the man fire her imagination: 'Her abandonment to the luscious time after her sense of ill-usage, her revolt for the nonce against social law, her passionate desire for primitive life, may have showed in her face.' (185–6)

But the positive, comforting, healing aspects of nature are brief and passing. It is as if Giles as representative of these qualities has lost his strength. Though he possesses a profound sympathy with the trees, he lacks the assertive power exemplified by the romanticized country dwellers of earlier years. He has little in him of the 'noble savage' of the eighteenth century, or the simple, strong shepherds, vagrants and country dwellers of, say, Wordsworth's *Lyrical Ballads*. Instead he seems to represent an aspect of nature that is passing or has passed away. It is one that has left only traces of its former existence, and has been superseded by another, very different in kind and quality. Critics have often noted that Giles persistently fails to assert himself. When, for example, under Fitzpiers's instructions, he is pollarding Mr South's tree, Grace passes beneath. She has been instructed to avoid him, but instead of calling out to her he withdraws upwards and vanishes eerily into the fog. Then, when he might have claimed her as she ran down the hill on midsummer's eve he steps aside and allows Fitzpiers to take precedence. His self abnegation is most graphically represented by his retreat to the remote and dilapidated 'One Chimney Cottage', and from there into a thatched hurdle. In his final moments, when Grace is searching for him in the woods near Delborough, he seems to have completed his passage from the animate world back into the inanimate world. She hears

low mutterings; at first like persons in conversation, but gradually resolving themselves into varieties of one voice. It was an endless monologue, like that we sometimes hear from inanimate nature in deep secret places where water flows, or where ivy leaves flap against stones; but by degrees she was convinced that the voice was Winterborne's. (281)

This raises the issue of the status of the woodland setting in this novel. In fact the word 'setting' is not quite the right one, because the woods are much more than a location for the story. They are more like a medium within which the narrative grows like a culture in a laboratory. On several occasions Hardy suggests that the remoteness of the Hintocks concentrates emotions in such a way that they can then be scientifically examined and analysed. In this experiment, people and trees persistently merge. On the very first page of the novel the 'extensive woodlands, interspersed with apple-orchards' are strongly anthropomorphized. The trees, like humans, stretch 'over the road with easeful horizontality, as if they found the un-substantial air an adequate support for their limbs', while the largest of the woods is 'bisected by the high-way, as the head of thick hair is bisected by the white line of its parting'. (3) When humans finally appear, stacking and sorting logs and making spas for thatching, it is clear that they are intimately dependent upon the woods, where they fell, strip, turn and fashion the trees.

Throughout the story, oak, ash, beech, fir and hazel are all identified for the different roles they play in the woodland economy, and specific trees, groups of trees, woodland areas and tree types map out the novel's topography. The elm tree standing outside the South's cottage precisely marks that spot; the hazels in a copse where Winterborne makes his hurdles 'returned purest tints of that hue' (203) and places it on the edge of Mrs Charmond's estate. Then there are the woods on Bubb Down, comprising beech, sycamore and conifers, where the girls of Little Hintock perform their midsummer marriage rites, and where Grace and Felice Charmond get lost after an acrimonious exchange about Fitzpiers. Finally, the early editions of the book mention the astonishing Great Willy or Billy Wilkins as marking the spot close to where George Melbury strikes Fitzpiers, who then falls concussed to the ground. This ancient oak stands today, to the south-west of Melbury Sampford House, in the same place that it has stood for a thousand years. Amusingly, in 1895 Hardy removed the reference to this famous tree for fear of placing the action firmly on the Ilchester estate.[11]

But the dominant relationship between man and his wooded environment in this novel is a fractious and uneasy one. The fleeting spring promise and the autumn harvest, both associated with Winterbourne, fail to counteract the more divisive forces operating in the natural world. Men persistently exploit the trees like predators, as exemplified most graphically by the process of oak-barking.

The ancient oak, Billy Wilkins, on the Ilchester estate.

The bark was used for its tannin in the leather industry and for nearly two hundred years oaks had been stripped on the Ilchester estates. But Hardy, who was clearly familiar with the process, describes it as a violation or assault. Each oak is 'doomed' to the 'flaying process', and the foresters prepare it 'like the executioner's victim'. When the tree is felled, the barkers attack it 'like locusts' until 'not a particle of rind was left on the trunk and larger limbs'. (122) But the trees have their revenge. Both Melbury and Winterborne, figures closest to the forest, suffer at their hands. Melbury is permanently injured by a falling elm, and the swaying boughs pound like an 'adversary' on Winterborne's cottage in the great storm.

In the exchange between the natural world and the human world the woods are often represented by similes and metaphors that connect them with the human body in pain or distress. When, for example, Melbury goes to find Winterborne to confide his anxiety about Grace, it is a 'rimy evening when the woods seemed to be in a cold sweat; beads of perspiration hung from each bare twig' (202) and as Grace flees from her house unable to face Fitzpiers on his return from the Continent, 'the smooth surfaces of glossy plants came out like weak, lidless eyes'.

(268–9) This merging of the vegetable and the human often involves disease and death. On one of his early visits to Felice Charmond, Fitzpiers 'went on foot across the wilder recesses of the park, where slimy streams of green moisture, exuding from decayed holes caused by old amputations, ran down the bark of the oaks and elms'. (177) On another occasion, Grace awaits the return of Fitzpiers on a spot 'beneath a half-dead oak, hollow, . . . disfigured with white tumours'. (191) This anthropomorphism with which Hardy first experimented in *The Return of the Native* reaches a climax in the autumn storm that precipitates Giles Winterborne's death. The aerial battle that takes place above his cottage is like an episode from Norse mythology: 'Sometimes a bough from an adjoining tree was swayed so low as to smite the roof in the manner of a gigantic hand smiting the mouth of an adversary, to be followed by a trickle of rain, as blood from the wound.' The following morning Grace looks out of her window, and the view that she has of the devastation of the previous night is a telling one.

> In front lay the brown leaves of last year, and upon them some yellowish-green ones of this season that had been prematurely blown down by the gale. Above stretched an old beech, with vast armpits, and great pocket-holes in its sides where branches had been amputated in past times; a black slug was trying to climb it. Dead boughs were scattered about like ichthyosauri in a museum, and beyond them were perishing woodbine stems resembling old ropes. (279–80)

With their armpits and amputations, the trees are again given human characteristics, but here is something new. The dead branches specifically invoke the world of palaeontology in a scene that looks like an illustration of evolutionary principles. This suspicion is supported by the view out of another window. Here there are 'more trees close together, wrestling for existence, their branches disfigured with wounds resulting from their mutual rubbings and blows. It was the struggle between these neighbours that [Grace] had heard in the night.' (280)

The struggle for existence in the tree world has its counterpart in the human world. When Hardy came to write *The Woodlanders* he seems to have shared the beliefs of Spencer and Huxley that Darwin's theories about struggle and wastage in the biological world might be applied to humans. Hardy explored this connection in a poem entitled 'In a Wood' that he wrote at the same time as the novel. Escaping from the cut and thrust of the city he speaks of how he came to the wood in search of Wordsworthian repose and retreat.

> Heart-halt and spirit-lame,
> City-opprest,
> Unto this wood I came
> As to a nest;
> Dreaming that sylvan peace
> Offered the harrowed ease –
> Nature a soft release
> From men's unrest.

But what he discovers instead is a struggle identical to the urban one he has left behind.

> But, having entered in,
> Great growths and small
> Show them to men akin –
> Combatants all!
> Sycamore shoulders oak,
> Bines the slim sapling yoke,
> Ivy-spun halters choke
> Elms stout and tall

'In a Wood' suggests that Darwinian laws of fight, survival and success are a feature of both rural and urban settings, and that the old idea of escape to a better world in nature is illusory. This is borne out in *The Woodlanders*. Giles, noble, honest, humble yet attractive, is close to the land and close to the trees, and his identity is most fully realized in the apple orchards with their brief but exquisite spring beauty and rich autumn. Yet the realities of the woodland world lie elsewhere, and where there is competition, strife or difficulty he is not a survivor. On his death he is re-assimilated into the old world. As he passes away 'the whole wood seemed to be a home of death, pervaded by loss to its uttermost length and breadth'. (293) Hardy is characteristically melancholy about the passing of beautiful things. The scientists of the nineteenth century had swept away the ancient spirit of nature to which, for hundreds of years, men had attributed the power of calming the mind and bringing peace.

When at the Earl of Wessex Fitzpiers identifies Winterbourne as someone from a different 'species', though he may not have known it he was borrowing the language of evolutionism and both men were acting out a struggle for survival. In that struggle, the weaker Giles is overcome by the more flexible, mobile and assertive representative of the new order in Fitzpiers. Fitzpiers is not an evil man but he is a post-Darwinian man. He is an opportunist. He takes chances and is competitive. He has no attachments to the Hintock woods or its people beyond sexual desire and the passing sentimental whim. But in *The Woodlanders* ideas about love, respect and fidelity are part of a passing world. Once the true dynamic of organic life was revealed, with its struggle and its ruthless craving for light and space, so the old values become obsolete. Giles's attitudes to propriety are as outmoded as the belief in the harmony of nature and by the end of the story it is impossible to go on clinging to them in the modern world.

At the end of Darwin's great work, he used the image of a web to explain the network of interactive events that went to make up the evolutionary process in nature. 'We can see clearly,' he said,

> how all living and extinct forms can be grouped together within a few great classes; and how the several members of each class are connected together by the most complex and radiating line of affinities. We shall probably never disentangle the inextricable web of the affinities between any one class; but when we have a distant object in view, and do not look to some unknown plan of creation, we may hope to make sure but slow progress.[12]

In the opening pages of Hardy's novel, he describes the way in which Marty South and Giles Winterbourne walk out in the dim morning air, and he, too, uses the image of the web. 'Hardly anything', he says, 'could be more isolated or more self-contained than the lives of these two . . . And yet, looked at in a certain way, their lonely courses formed no detached design at all, but were part of the pattern in the great web of human doings then weaving in both hemispheres, from the White Sea to Cape Horn.' (20)

In *The Woodlanders* Hardy explores the web of invisible and intangible natural forces that link man to man and man to nature. He said that he was keen to see 'the deeper realities under the scenic' and in representing the consonance between the human and the natural world he was doing something that the Darwinians were doing in a more abstract way. The sympathy that had once been thought to exist between man and nature had dissolved, and had been replaced by another relationship between man and nature that was competitive rather than sympathetic.

In the final scenes of the novel, Grace and Fitzpiers, tentatively reunited, leave the woods for a doubtful future in a medical practice in the Midlands. The last image of the book is a funereal one. It sees Marty South abandoned, standing beside Giles's grave in Great Hintock churchyard. Hardy writes:

> As this solitary and silent girl stood there in the moonlight, a straight slim figure, clothed in a plaitless gown, the contours of womanhood so undeveloped as to be scarcely perceptible, the marks of poverty and toil effaced by the misty hour, she touched sublimity at points, and looked almost like a being who had rejected with indifference the attribute of sex for the loftier quality of abstract humanism. (331)

Marty South inherits Winterborne's woodland values, but in this image she has become like an idealized funerary monument, a statue that might have been entitled 'Abstract Humanism'. She is silent, and her figure in its plain gown with no folds or decoration and her hands like smooth polished stone all have a marmoreal, sculpted quality about them. Her figure is sexless. She has renounced the struggle for survival but in doing so she has become a petrified memorial to a system that has become obsolete.

Chapter Five

Tess of the d'Urbervilles: The Return of the Pagan Gods

TESS OF THE D'URBERVILLES WAS and remains Hardy's most controversial novel. Many readers consider it to be his best and one of the greatest novels in English. Others struggle with the apparent inevitability of the plot and frequent awkwardness of the style. When it first appeared in serial form in 1891 it had to be carefully edited to avoid giving offence, but even then there was an outcry about its focus on the fleshly and the sensual. More recently it has been subjected to intense feminist scrutiny where Hardy has been accused of creating in Tess a sex object for the voyeuristic predilections not only of the male characters in the book but for the author himself. The debates continue and focus on such issues as whether Tess was seduced or raped by Alec d'Urberville, or what exactly Hardy means by words like 'nature' or 'purity'.

Like Hardy's previous novels this one is firmly rooted in the Dorset countryside. In September 1888 just before starting to write he took the short train journey from Dorchester to Evershot station and climbed to the top of Bubb-Down hill. Once again he was in the countryside of *The Woodlanders* but from this vantage point he could gaze across the valley to the country of his next novel. 'Looking east,' he wrote in his notebook, 'you see High Stoy and the escarpment below it.' From here, he said, 'the Valley of the Little Dairies is almost entirely green, every hedge being studded with trees.' And 'on the left you see to an immense distance, including Shaftesbury'.[1]

Though *Tess of the d'Urbervilles* was based on the traditional tale of the 'ruined maid' Hardy made it very much his own. Consequently when it was first published it was immediately recognized as something more than just a country story. Many readers interpreted the treatment of the central character as an attack on

Blackmoor Valley or the Valley of the Little Dairies from Bubb-Down, looking east towards Shaftesbury.

the 'double standard' of Victorian sexual morality, later critics read it as a record of the decline of agricultural communities, while others saw it as a critique of the detrimental influence of religious values on ethical ones. In terms of Hardy's method, however, many readers noticed, either with pleasure or disgust, how Hardy eroticized his heroine. He does this through his manipulation of the gaze, sometimes the narrator's gaze and sometimes the gaze of other characters. But Hardy never watches his heroine in isolation. She is always seen in the context of the landscape through which she passes. Of course landscape plays a central part in all Hardy's novels, but nowhere more so than in this one. Tess's world is an outdoor one, and the phases of her life are marked out and registered on the fields, hills, paths and woods around her. Hardy, of course, was personally familiar with all the settings that he chose for the novel, but they never appear as raw descriptive data. Whenever Hardy uses landscape he enhances, changes, manipulates and transforms it into something that transcends the material detail.

The opening account of the Blackmoor Valley provides a good example. The view that Hardy recorded from the top of Bubb-Down resembles the first sight of Tess's birthplace in the novel. 'It is a vale', Hardy writes, 'whose acquaintance is best made by viewing it from the summits of the hills that surround it.' It is, he continues, an 'engirdled and secluded region, for the most part untrodden as yet by tourist or landscape-painter'. (18) The words 'engirdled' and 'secluded' have strongly positive connotations. The nuetral prose of Hardy's original note to himself is transformed into a landscape that is benevolent and sheltering. Then there is the inclusion of the tourist and landscape painter. Though their presence in the valley is rare, it is not unknown, and using the special gaze of these two figures Hardy begins to shape how and what the reader might see in the valley. The tourist is interested in the local culture. The painter is concerned with the effects of light and colour, and it is his eye that takes precedence. Across the valley, Hardy writes,

the world seems to be constructed upon a smaller and more delicate scale; the fields are mere paddocks, so reduced that from this height their hedgerows appear a network of dark green threads overspreading the paler green of the grass. The atmosphere beneath is languorous, and is so tinged with azure that what artists call the middle-distance partakes also of that hue, while the horizon beyond is of the deepest ultramarine. (18)

Dark green, paler green, azure, deepest ultramarine – all these colours come straight from the artist's palette. But unlike landscape paintings the scenes in this novel are never quite empty of people. They always contain figures, and those figures are integral to the meaning of the scene. This is where the tourist comes in. Though tourists might be fascinated by views it is really the people who interest them: their attitudes, values and ways of life.

Hardy was not a tourist, but neither was he one of the local 'folk'. Living on the edge of rural culture he had always been fascinated by Dorset folklore. So, like the tourist, he was an observer of customs and manners. The mumming in *The Return of the Native*, the skimmity ride in *The Mayor of Casterbridge* and the midsummer festival in *The Woodlanders,* all these come to mind. In the nineteenth century new light had been shed on the significance of these traditions by early developments in anthropology and one of the concerns of this new science of human behaviour was the place of myth and mythology in ancient cultures and the links between folklore and pre-Christian religions. So, turning from the landscape to the culture in the Blackmoor Valley, Hardy points to the close relationship between the village communities and spirits that still seemed to haunt the natural environment. Tess's valley, he says, was once densely wooded, and 'though the forests have departed . . . some old customs of their shades remain. Many, however, linger only in a metamorphosed or disguised form.' (19) One of these customs was the May Day dance that took place in the meadow just outside Marlott.

Varieties of May Day dancing, or 'club walking' as it was called, were an exclusively female activity that still survive in many parts of the West Country. In 1876, Hardy was living in Sturminster Newton, just three miles from Marnhull, and from there he witnessed several of them. On one such occasion his eye briefly caught the sight of 'pretty girls, just before a dance stand[ing] in inviting positions on the grass',[2] but his account of a similar event at Marlott is much more extensive. The first appearance of the women, he says, was in a processional march, two by two around the parish. In this scene,

ideal and real clashed slightly as the sun lit up their figures against the green hedges and creeper-laced house-fronts; for, though the whole troop wore white garments, no two whites were alike among them . . . In addition to the distinction of a white frock, every woman and girl carried in her right hand a peeled willow wand, and in her left a bunch of white flowers. The peeling of the former, and the selection of the latter, had been an operation of personal care . . . The young girls formed, indeed, the majority of the band, and their heads of luxuriant hair reflected in the sunshine every tone of gold, and black, and brown. Some had beautiful eyes, others a beautiful nose, others a beautiful mouth and figure . . . And as each and all of them were warmed without by the sun, so each had a private little sun for her soul to bask in. (19–20)

The emphasis on the light and colour first suggests the painter's eye, but the intelligent onlooker in Hardy also watches and with anthropological insight, he hits upon a term that sums up this activity. It was, he said, a local 'Cerealia'. A Cerealia was an ancient spring ritual. It was performed in honour of the goddess Ceres to ensure the fertility of both land and people, and it welcomed in the spring, so essential to growth and fertility. As Hardy records it, the female dancers are infused with sunlight. It lights up their figures, illuminates their hair and metaphorically fills them with pleasure. Each girl, says Hardy, was 'warmed without by the sun, so each had a private little sun for her soul to bask in'. In Greco-Roman mythology the sun god was Apollo, who was a complex and ambiguous figure known for his positive and negative roles as healer and destroyer. His principal attributes were light and truth. But he was often held responsible for ill health and plague. The Marlott club walking may well have been a survival of a solar fertility rite, and as the novel unfolds fertility is double-edged. Tess's mother had been fertile, providing her daughter with the love and affection of a large family, but that same fertility leads to Tess's undoing. When she returns to her cottage, leaving the pleasure of 'the holiday gaieties of the field', the interior strikes her as unspeakable in its 'dreariness' (26) and the sight of her family makes her feel angry 'towards her mother for thoughtlessly giving her so many little sisters and brothers'. Providing food for all these mouths is hard enough but when Tess is responsible for the death of the family horse, Prince, economic disaster threatens. So it is fertility that indirectly drives Tess into the arms of Alec d'Urberville.

Today, from a distance, the Blackmoor Valley looks very much as it did in the nineteenth century with the ground divided into a patchwork of small fields separated by hedges and trees. Now, however, the dairy farms are few and far between and a farmer in Marnhull told me that he sold his last cow a few years ago. The reason was that modern agricultural practices demand at least two hundred animals to make dairying viable so that most of the land has now been given over to arable production. But the village of Marnhull (Marlott) is still much as Hardy describes it: 'long and broken' (31), shaped in this way because all the buildings were constructed on a dry ridge rising out of wet clay.[3]

It is striking, however, in light of Hardy's previous novels, how relatively little of the built environment features in *Tess of the d'Urbervilles*. It certainly exists, but in the main, cottages, huts and mansions serve like milestones in Tess's onward progress through the story. Instead, what we might call the symbolic centre of the novel has moved outdoors to the landscape. The early club-walking scene, the 'Cerealia', sets the tone for this. The simple procession is transformed by the light of the sun and the land is shaped by its association with ancient myths that once prevailed within it.

In the mid-nineteenth century scholars were beginning to look to myth to provide new sources of knowledge about religion and the growth of civilization. One of those was James Frazer and in 1890 he published the first two volumes of *The Golden Bough*, a book that would be one of the foundations of modern anthropology. Frazer controversially asserted that Christian beliefs were not the object of divine revelation. He believed, rather, that modern Christianity developed out of earlier primitive, natural religions and in his encyclopaedic study of ancient cults and rites one legend emerges most prominently, that of the sacred mistletoe or Golden Bough.

As Hardy was writing *Tess of the d'Urbervilles* in 1890 he read *The Golden Bough* and the question that Frazer poses in the first line of his book must have struck him with amazement: 'Who does not know Turner's picture of the Golden Bough?' he asks, continuing: 'The scene, suffused with the golden glow of imagination in which the divine mind of Turner steeped and transfigured even the fairest natural landscape, is a dream-like vision of the little woodland lake of Nemi...'[4] Ever since he first went to London in 1862, Hardy was an enthusiastic visitor to the National Gallery. One of the painters who attracted his attention was J. M. W. Turner, whose painting *The Golden Bough* (1834) hung prominently in the collection. But Turner was a controversial figure. His early work had been well received, but his later experiments with light and colour in a brilliant sometimes almost hallucinatory style puzzled an audience that preferred hard-headed realism and material accuracy. Hardy, however, hugely admired Turner, and late Turner in particular. In his landscapes, he said, Turner was able to express 'the tragical mysteries of life' by seeing 'the deeper reality underlying the scenic'.[5] In 1889, just as he was preparing to write *Tess of the d'Urbervilles*, Hardy's youthful enthusiasm was rekindled by an exhibition of Turner's watercolours at the Royal Academy. His excitement over these paintings matches Frazer's own. Every picture, said Hardy, was 'a landscape plus a man's soul'. Turner, he claimed, painted 'light as modified by objects' transfiguring, changing and distorting landscapes to create the illusion of something real by means of a 'pictorial drug'.[6]

In *The Golden Bough* Turner's imaginative treatment of composition, lighting and colour might well have inspired Hardy's own mythologizing of the ritual club walking at Marlott. In the painting the landscape is suffused with the glow of sunlight, and in that sunlight a group of figures is playing out a ritual dance. On the left stands the Cumaean Sibyl, one of the assistants of Apollo. In her right hand she holds a sickle with which she has cut the golden bough, or mistletoe, that she holds in her left. The mistletoe, which shone in the dark, giving Aenaeus access to the underworld, grew on sacred oaks and the oak was a powerful source of energy. Frazer goes so far as to say that for many people the sun's fire 'was regarded as an emanation of the mistletoe'.[7] Partly for this reason the mistletoe became a sexual symbol, bestowing on its worshipers both life and fertility, and when it was cut at the winter solstice by Druidic priests it became a powerful omen for loving couples.

Both Turner's picture *The Golden Bough* and Hardy's club-walking scene have strong solar associations and both are suffused by literal and metaphorical sunlight. At Marlott all the women 'were warmed without by the sun' and 'each had a private little sun for her soul to bask in'. Angel Clare, too, is drawn into the solarism of the episode. He is passing through the village with his brothers when he dances briefly with one of the girls. As evening draws on he runs off to the west, and Tess, who has not spoken to him, watches sadly as he goes. It is sunset, and the 'the rays of the sun . . . absorbed the young stranger's retreating figure on the hill'. (25) The moment remains in her memory, and returns much later when, after her marriage, Clare reappears in her imagination like Turner's *The Angel Standing in the Sun* (see p.167).

J. M. W. Turner, *The Golden Bough*, 1834, oil on canvas, 104.1 x 163.8 cm.

The landscape of the Blackmoor Valley defines the limits and the contours of Tess's early life. It 'was to her the world, and its inhabitants the races thereof' and the countryside around Marlott is the land of her innocence and her virginity. 'From the gates and stiles of Marlott she had looked down its length in the wondering days of infancy, and what had been mystery to her then was not much less than mystery to her now.' Though everyday she had seen the town of Shaston (Shaftesbury) 'standing majestically on its height' the adult world that this represented was strange to her. Her valley was a country that 'engirdled' her, and which, in its familiarity, resembles the family affection she experienced at home: 'Every contour of the surrounding hills', says Hardy, 'was as personal to her as that of her relatives' faces.' (42)

But childhood passes. The death of the horse Prince places the family income in jeopardy, and Tess feels the responsibility for setting matters right.

Boveridge House, built around 1808, was the model for Alec d'Urberville's country house, the Slopes, 'built for enjoyment pure and simple'.

She reluctantly volunteers to seek assistance from what her parents believe to be a rich branch of the d'Urbervilles living in the east of the county. She leaves Marlott and on the first significant journey of her life passes symbolically into a new world by walking to Shaston and catching the van that leads across the chalk country to Tantridge. Tantridge has long been identified with the village of Pentridge, but as Tony Fincham has shown, the only point of connection is the name.[8] In fact the village of Boveridge, a couple of miles to the north-east of Cranborne (or Chaseborough), qualifies in almost all respects as the original of Tantridge. Prominent in the village is the large and imposing Boveridge House that Hardy renames 'The Slopes'. It was built in the early nineteenth century and is now a private school. When Tess approaches it for the first time the sight fills her with amazement. She had been expecting a dignified pile worthy of the ancient name of d'Urberville, but what she finds 'was not a manorial home in the ordinary sense' but 'a country-house built for enjoyment pure and simple', where 'everything looked like money – like the last coin issued from the Mint'. (43) In 1887 the owner of Boveridge House, Francis Brouncker, undertook substantial restoration and rebuilding. For this he used red bricks from whose appearance Tess could be forgiven for thinking that the house was all 'new'. But the house, like the Slopes in the novel, is surrounded by parkland, lawns and gardens where 'everything . . . was bright, thriving, and well kept'. Nature is carefully regulated to produce fruit and flowers at all seasons from 'glass-houses [that] stretched down the inclines to the copses at their feet'. As Tess approaches the lawn she sees an 'ornamental tent' from which Alec d'Urberville emerges. Tents never bode well in Hardy. Frank Troy reappeared in Bathsheba's life in a tent set up at Greenhill Fair, Susan Henchard was sold in firmity tent, and Farfrae created a tent in the Casterbridge Walks for his one night's entertainment. Hardy seems to have associated all of them with the insubstantial, the showy and the temporary, and Alec's subsequent behaviour confirms his possession of all these qualities. But returning to the house, the brash newness of the building Alec inhabits is thrown into strong relief by its natural environment. 'Far behind the corner of the house, which rose like a geranium bloom against the subdued colours around,' Hardy writes, 'stretched the soft azure landscape of The Chase.' The alien brilliance of the building is set off against the sombre antiquity of the rural scene – 'a truly venerable tract of forest land, one of the few remaining woodlands in England of undoubted primaeval date'. (43–4) This ancient forest is Boulsbury Wood, part of Cranborne Chase, dense with oak and yew that forms a dark blue-green line across the ridge of the hill behind Boveridge House.

Boulsbury Wood, of course, is the wood of Tess's seduction, but Hardy prepares for that moment in the events of the preceding evening in Chaseborough. After several months working on the d'Urberville estate Tess decides to join her companions in the Saturday evening revels in the town. The area around Tantridge is characterized by hard drinking and loose morals, and it is clear from what follows that Alec has had sexual relations with many of the girls from the village before Tess's arrival. The whole tone of this part of the county, says Hardy, is determined by 'the choice spirit who ruled the Slopes', and that 'choice spirit' is, of course, Alec d'Urberville.

As Tess walks towards Chaseborough it is a fine September evening at the point 'when yellow lights struggle with blue shades in hair-like lines, and the atmosphere itself forms a prospect without aid from more solid objects'. (70–71) The idea that the atmosphere itself creates a picture closely resembles Hardy's remark that Turner painted 'light as modified by objects'.[9] So with Turner in mind, we are prepared for similar effects when Tess finds her companions in a nearby outhouse. Here she is greeted by a strange light from the open door, it is a 'mist of yellow radiance'. Inside the building, it becomes clear that the mist is generated by the visceral mixture of sweat and dust, 'vegeto-human pollen', as Hardy calls it, with candles lighting up an extraordinary scene. It is a wild and distracted bacchanal. The indistinct light transforms the country folk of Tantridge into characters from Greek and Roman myth and as they dance to fiddles they create a bizarre classical scene involving 'satyrs clasping nymphs – a multiplicity of Pans whirling a multiplicity of Syrinxes; Lotis attempting to elude Priapus, and always failing'. Each of the mythical figures that go to make up this transformation is involved in some kind of sexual engagement. The satyrs were the lecherous companions of Dionysius or Bacchus; Pan, a lustful fertility god, attempted to rape the chaste Syrinx and Priapus tried to violate Lotis in her sleep when she was attending a festivity given in honour of Dionysius. Enjoying the event at a distance are 'some Sileni' or satyrs, more drunken companions of Dionysus, sitting 'on benches and hay-trusses by the wall'. (72)

At first it seems that only Dionysus himself is absent, but in fact he is here, at the side, watching over this exhibition of drunken licence. It is of course Alec d'Urberville, 'the choice spirit' of the Slopes who, like the god of wine, presides over orgies of music and ecstatic dance. He even sports a 'thyrsus'. This is Bacchus's phallic staff tipped with a pinecone, symbol of his sexual vigour. Alec's is a prominent cigar, tipped with a 'red coal'.

At this point Hardy makes a remarkable transformation. Imprinted on the scene at Chaseborough emerges a representation of Bacchus with which he was very familiar. Once again, it came from the National Gallery. It was a version of the Bacchus and Ariadne story painted by Turner in 1840. This was a homage to Titian's more famous *Bacchus and Ariadne* (1523) hanging nearby, where Ariadne, who having been abandoned by Theseus on Naxos, is discovered by the priapic god. As the object of Alec's lust, Tess's vulnerability at Chaseborough resembles

J. M. W. Turner, *Bacchus and Ariadne* (detail), 1840, oil on canvas, 78.7 x 78.7 cm.

Ariadne's defencelessness. Like Ariadne, Tess is a spectator to the orgy, and like her, she is subject to male power. Turner, however, treats the figure of Ariadne very differently from Titian. Where in the Titian, she gazes fascinated into Bacchus' eyes, in the Turner she moves away from him in an attempt to flee, turning to the spectator as if appealing for help. The parallels between Tess's plight and Ariadne's are clear. Alec, the leader of the Chaseborough Bacchantes, having successfully conquered the other village girls is now determined to have Tess as his next partner while she, a spectator of the bacchanal, fears him and the shallowness of his motives. Tess, like Ariadne in Turner's picture, takes centre stage, and she, too, looks desperately for a way out. But events conspire to bring Alec and Tess together as they did Bacchus and Ariadne.

Tess's journey back from Chaseborough to the Slopes in the company of the revellers takes her out of the town by the road that on the map leads to Rockborne. After a while they leave the highway, and using a more direct footpath, begin crossing the fields towards Tantridge (Boveridge). An altercation breaks out between Tess and one of the other girls, Car Darch, who was the latest in the line of village women to have been taken up by d'Urberville and is jealous that he has now transferred his attention to the newcomer. Others confess to having once been preferred by Alec, and they all gang up against Tess. The situation begins to look ugly when the priapic d'Urberville appears and whisks Tess away on the back of his horse. The couple return to the road, continue up the hill, and, passing the junction for the village, turn into the Chase (Boulsbury Wood).

They now enter an ancient and dark landscape. It is a mysterious place. The trees around them are the primeval oaks and yews that could be seen from the Slopes. The oaks are hung with what Hardy calls 'Druidical mistletoe', the mystical golden bough, a symbol of fertility, while around them stand 'enormous yew-trees, not planted by the hand of man [that] grew as they had grown when they were pollarded for bows'. The September moon goes down, the forest fills with fog and they lose their way. Tess lies exhausted and motionless on the forest floor while Alec gropes blindly for the path home. To retrace his steps back to her he 'was obliged', like a sleep-walker, 'to advance with outstretched hands'. Again and again Hardy stresses the profundity of the gloom in the Chase. It 'was wrapped in thick darkness' where 'everything', he says, 'was blackness alike'. (82) The obscurity of the setting and its ancient associations reflect upon the issue of rape in this scene. In spite of the orgy over which Alec has recently presided, the implications here are that sex between Alec and Tess, though inappropriate, springs from primal, insistent, half-conscious urges. Both Tess and Alec are strongly sexed and the location on the forest floor in the company of 'gentle roosting birds' and 'hopping rabbits and hares' is significant. The couple become caught up in a natural cycle as old as the lusts of the classical gods. Here, sex is a matter of instinct not reason, and takes place in a realm that exists outside the sphere of conventional morality.

After several weeks as d'Urberville's mistress Tess returns to Marlott, pregnant with his child. Here she enters a new phase of life where she avoids village life and wanders the woods in the evening. Re-enacting the night in the Chase by

Map showing Boveridge House (the Slopes), Cranborne (Chaseborough) and Boulsbury Wood (the Chase), the scene of Tess's seduction.

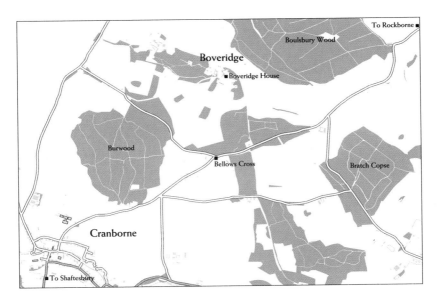

'walking among the sleeping birds in the hedges, watching the skipping rabbits on a moonlit warren, or standing under a pheasant-laden bough', she now 'looked upon herself as a figure of Guilt intruding into the haunts of Innocence'. (97) But, as Hardy makes clear, guilt and innocence play no part in her rite of passage. They carry no moral significance for the animals who share that experience, nor even for Tess's own mother, who claims that "Tis nater, after all.' (94) The guilt Tess experiences is entirely cultural in origin and the 'immeasurable social chasm' that divides her new self from her former self is the creation of imaginary moral 'hobgoblins'.

After the birth of her child Tess begins once again to turn back to society. As she had passed into the shades of uncertainty and night in the September sunset at Tantridge, her return from darkness is marked by the dawn breaking over Marlott. In Hardy's account of it the August sunrise becomes a metaphor for the struggle between darkness and light. He writes of how 'the denser nocturnal vapours, attacked by the warm beams, were dividing and shrinking into isolated fleeces within hollows and coverts'. The moving force in this drama is the sun, personified, gendered and deified. 'On account of the mist, [it] had a curious sentient, personal look, demanding the masculine pronoun for its adequate expression.' (99) 'His present aspect,' Hardy continues, 'coupled with the lack of all human forms in the scene, explained the old-time heliolatries in a moment. One could feel that a saner religion had never prevailed under the sky.' This 'golden-haired, beaming, mild-eyed, God-like creature, gazing down in the vigour and intentness of youth upon an earth that was brimming with interest for him' is surely the young Apollo, and where Bacchus or Dionysius had ruled over darkness at Chaseborough, it was now the turn of the sun god to bring back the light.

The sun that had warmed the spring club walking of Tess's childhood has now returned but is a more potent figure at the August harvest. As in ancient myth, he is an ambiguous god, energizing, yet imperious, comforting yet demanding. 'Awakening harvesters who were not already astir,' says Hardy, 'his light . . . broke through chinks of cottage shutters, throwing stripes like red-hot pokers upon cupboards'. (99) Outside the world is ablaze with energy and solar intensity. The arms of the reaping machine look as if they have been dipped in 'liquid fire', the brass star on the forehead of the working horse glistens, and the buttons of the male field workers 'twinkled and bristled with sunbeams at every movement'. (100) But the sun is amatory and violent by turns. He shines on Tess's erotically 'flexuous and finely-drawn figure' (101), lights up her 'deep dark eyes', and encourages her to gather the bundles of the corn 'in an embrace like that of a lover'. But there is something else lurking in his regnant power. On the one hand the sunshine allows the reaping machine to 'open' the field, a word that suggests sexual access; on the other hand, this 'opening' precipitates the unpleasant deaths of the small creatures that have their home in the wheat. At several points in the novel Tess herself is described as having a sympathetic affinity with small, vulnerable animals and it is her earlier sexual 'opening' that, in the fullness of time, precipitates her death.

The sun plays an integral part in the agricultural cycle of Marlott, and the study of sun worship was central to the research into myth amongst Hardy's contemporaries. One of them, Max Müller, whose work Hardy knew, was amongst the most prominent. Müller's study of Indian religions led him to the belief that the gods of primitive man were the personification of natural forces of which the dominant element was the sun. In his widely read book *Comparative Mythology* (1867), Müller stressed the importance of sunrise in terms very similar to Hardy's account of the August morning in Marlott. The dawn, he said, was 'the revelation of nature, awakening in the human mind that feeling of dependence of helplessness, of hope of joy, and faith in higher powers, which is the source of all wisdom, the spring of all religion'.[10] But Hardy goes further. In claiming that 'a saner religion had never prevailed under the sky', he is openly insinuating a contrast between sun worship and Christianity. Heliolatry, he implies, provided a more benevolent and humane set of religious beliefs than the harsh and draconian type of Christianity represented by the sign writer whom Tess came across on her return to Marlott writing in red letters the offensive words, 'THY, DAMNATION, SLUMBERETH, NOT', on country gates. (91) Hardy was far from alone in holding these views. The poet, historian and critic John Addington Symonds, for example, in his *Studies of the Greek Poets* (1873) praised the sanity of Greek religion in just these terms. Using sentiments that reflect back on the revels at Chaseborough and Tess's experience with Alec on the forest floor, Symonds contrasted the repressive morality of Victorian England with the 'animal unity' that existed among the Greeks. In the world of Dionysius and Pan, he said, 'the sensual impulses, like the intellectual and the moral, were . . . held void of crime and harmless.'

In the Chase, Tess and Alec found themselves among the wildlife of the forest and Symonds makes the point that the Greeks were also guided by animal impulses. 'Health and good taste controlled the physical appetites of man,' he said, 'just as the appetites of animals are regulated by unerring instinct.'[11]

Though Tess has returned to the Valley of the Little Dairies, and the land of her birth, her experiences have changed her. She is now 'living as a stranger and an alien' at Marlott (101), and her sense of alienation is made greater by the death of her child. So, in an attempt to obliterate the past, she decides to move elsewhere. She accepts a dairymaid's job in another valley, the valley of the Froom, and once again her psychological development is figured in the form of a journey. She travels southwards. Though the distance on the map from Marnhull to the Frome Valley is only about twenty-three miles the scenery is both beautiful and varied. After Stourcastle (Sturminster Newton) the road climbs steeply up to the summit of the chalk escarpment of Bulbarrow which, just under one thousand feet, provides spectacular views backwards over the Blackmoor Valley and onwards to southern Dorset. The last part of her route takes her from Weatherbury (Puddletown) across Egdon Heath of *The Return of the Native* as far as Rainbarrow, where she finds 'herself on a summit commanding the long-sought for vale', the object of her 'pilgrimage'. (118) This is the Valley of the Great Dairies, an almost mystical place, and replete with religious associations.

Tess's descent into the valley, in May, the month of the Virgin Mary, takes the form of an epiphany, or a visionary moment charged with a kind of ecstasy. This is a promised land flowing not with milk and honey but with milk and butter. (118) It is a land of plenty, 'drawn to a larger pattern' than the Valley of the Little Dairies, with 'myriads of cows stretching under her eyes'. (118) As with the Valley of the Little Dairies, however, we first see it in bird's eye perspective. It is fresh and clean, washed by the swift stream of 'the Froom waters . . . clear as the pure River of Life shown to the Evangelist, rapid as the shadow of a cloud, with pebbly shallows that prattled to the sky all day long'. The landscape here is sensuously suffused with light and colour as 'the ripe hue of the red and dun kine absorbed the evening sunlight, which the white-coated animals returned to the eye in rays almost dazzling'. Seeing all this Tess is filled with happiness. She is enveloped in a 'photosphere', or halo, where her powerful emotions merge with the details of the visionary landscape: 'Her hopes mingled with the sunshine in an ideal photosphere that surrounded her as she bounded along against the soft south wind. She heard a pleasant voice in every breeze, and in every bird's note seemed to lurk a joy.' She bursts into song, but finding country ballads inadequate to the occasion she chants from the Book of Common Prayer. Intuitively, however, she chooses a passage that personifies objects in nature: "'O ye Sun and Moon . . . O ye Stars . . . ye Green Things upon the Earth . . . bless ye the Lord, praise Him and magnify Him forever!'" This song, Hardy comments, 'was a Fetishistic (that is a pagan) utterance in a Monotheistic (or Christian) setting'. (119–20) With the use of these anthropological terms, the animism that has been lying just beneath the surface of the story becomes explicit.

Hardy, together with many of his contemporaries, was fascinated by the primitive roots of religious belief. The critic John Ruskin, for example, explained animism to his readers in 1866 by saying that the 'heathen concept of the deity' went through three phases: the physical, the ethical and the personal. In its first phase, the deity was associated with some of the great powers of nature such as the sun or the moon. Then the belief takes on an ethical character. 'Thus Apollo, in the first phase,' says Ruskin, is 'physically the sun contending with the darkness'. Then in the ethical phase he becomes 'the power of divine life contending with corruption'. Finally other gods take on personal characters as each is 'realised in the minds of its worshippers as a living spirit'.[12] The systematic study of animism began with the work of the famous nineteenth-century anthropologist Edward Tylor in his book *Primitive Culture* of 1873. Hardy read Tylor around 1884, was curious, and wondered how such ideas might relate to the survival of customs in Dorset. In 1890 he questioned his friend, the anthropologist Edward Clodd, about the subject. 'Mr Clodd this morning', he recorded in his notebook, 'gave an excellently neat answer to my question why the superstitions of a remote Asiatic and a Dorset labourer are the same: "The attitude of man", [Clodd] says, "at corresponding levels of culture, before like phenomena, is pretty much the same, your Dorset peasant representing the persistence of the barbaric idea which confuses persons and things . . .".'[13] Finally there was James Frazer to whose work Clodd

Lower Lewell Farm on the south side of the Frome, the farmhouse on the right, the dairy on the left.

---

first directed Hardy's attention. When he was writing *The Golden Bough*, Frazer realized that one of the themes that was emerging from his research involved 'the resemblance of savage customs and ideas to the fundamental doctrines of Christianity'.[14]

In *Tess of the d'Urbervilles* Hardy attributes the survival of ancient beliefs and customs of this kind to females rather than to males. It is women, he says, who 'retain in their souls far more of the Pagan fantasy of their remote forefathers than of the systematized religion taught their race at later date'. (120) In other words he claims that women in general, and Tess in particular, are closer to nature than men. As a result they preserve within them something of the 'saner' religions of heliolatry and sun worship, so when Tess was participating in the club walking at Marlott she was keeping alive this old solar fertility rite. Now, as she moves into the Valley of the Froom similar myths will mingle with her simple Christianity and come to shape her experience there.

There is some dispute as to whether Talbothays dairy, the object of Tess's journey, is modelled on Norris Mill Farm on the north side of the Frome and nearest to Puddletown Heath, or on Lower Lewell Farm on the south side of the Frome.[15] Both, however, are located in broad, lush, water meadows divided by the river. At a point on Puddletown Heath overlooking the valley is a signpost that directs the walker towards the Frome Valley. In following this we can trace the route taken by Tess down the hill and across the valley first to Norris Mill then across the valley to Lewell Farm. The difference between the steep, rough, wild land of the heath and the flat, loamy earth of the valley is striking. The path between the two farms crosses small bridges over clear, fast-flowing streams, and looking back Puddletown Heath, from where Tess had come, rises in the distance.

When Tess reaches the dairy she is greeted by the sight of an agricultural activity of great antiquity. 'Long thatched sheds stretched round the enclosure,' says Hardy, 'their slopes encrusted with vivid green moss, and their eaves supported by wooden posts rubbed to a glossy smoothness by the flanks of infinite cows and calves of bygone years, now passed to an oblivion almost inconceivable in its profundity.'

The record of this ancient way of life is preserved in a 'sun picture' almost like an early photograph. As the sun sinks in the west, it throws shadows of the cows on the wall 'with as much care over each contour as if it had been the profile of a court beauty on a palace wall; copied them as diligently as it had copied Olympian shapes on marble *façades* long ago'. (121) Here at Talbothays Tess's life also comes under the influence of the sun, and while she works at the dairy the stages of that life are marked out, not only by the rising and the setting of the sun, but by the seasons of the solar year. In addition to this each of these stages is punctuated by mesmeric, strangely visionary moments.

The first of these occurs a month after her arrival. She has already been attracted to Angel Clare, a clergyman's son who, temporarily abandoning his middle-class career, has taken on the role of dairyman to learn the skill. On a June evening of peculiarly silent intensity Tess hears the notes of a harp. It is Clare playing the instrument out of doors. She has heard it before when he practised in his attic room, but on this particular evening the notes seem to Tess to take on a new, almost corporeal, classical quality. They wander, says Hardy, in the perfectly still air with 'a stark quality like that of nudity'. Tess, like a 'fascinated bird', is drawn to the sound but in order to get nearer has to pass through the outskirts of an uncultivated garden. This, says Hardy,

> was now damp and rank with juicy grass which sent up mists of pollen at a touch; and with tall blooming weeds emitting offensive smells – weeds whose red and yellow and purple hues formed a polychrome as dazzling as that of cultivated flowers. She went stealthily as a cat through this profusion of growth, gathering cuckoo-spittle on her skirts, cracking snails that were underfoot, staining her hands with thistle-milk and slug-slime, and rubbing off upon her naked arms sticky blights which, though snow-white on the apple-tree trunks, made madder stains on her skin; thus she drew quite near to Clare, still unobserved of him. (138)

The critic David Lodge identifies the garden as an emblem of Tess's sensuous temperament.[16] Though it is wild and uncultivated it is as fertile and beautiful as gardens improved artificially. To refined and sophisticated people, the peculiar smells and the visceral sticky substances would be offensive. But Tess is as at home here as a cat. She moves through the luxuriant growth making no attempt to avoid the cuckoo-spittle, the thistle-milk or the slug-slime. When Angel, a little earlier in the novel, remarked that Tess was 'a fresh and virginal daughter of Nature' (136) he spoke truer than he realized. What he had in mind was the romantic idea of nature, with its purity and sanctity. Tess is indeed a 'child of Nature', but she is the offspring of another kind of nature than the one to which Clare refers. It is unregulated nature, the nature of Darwin's 'tangled bank'. When Hardy subtitled the novel 'a pure woman faithfully presented' he was referring ironically to this ambiguous view of nature where Tess was caught between conflicting attitudes to innocence and experience. In the wild garden that conflict finds an emblem in the 'sticky blights' on the trunks of the apple trees. Sticky blights are caused by woolly aphids, sap-eating insects whose name derives from the gluey white fluff they secrete. On the tree the 'wool', like Tess's illegitimate pregnancy, is simply a value-free biological fact, white and spotless. When it touches her skin, however, it becomes a mark on her flesh. So when her pregnancy is brought within the realm of culture, its natural innocence is transformed. It becomes a red 'blight' marking her out as a fallen woman.

Passing through the garden Tess gets much closer to Angel. The tune he plays is 'simple' but it creates in Tess a response resembling sexual ecstasy.

> She undulated upon the thin notes of the second-hand harp, and their harmonies passed like breezes through her, bringing tears into her eyes. The floating pollen seemed to be his notes made visible, and the dampness of the garden the weeping of the garden's sensibility. Though near nightfall, the rank-smelling weed-flowers glowed as if they would not close for intentness, and the waves of colour mixed with the waves of sound. (139)

This twilight event has parallels with the twilight bacchanal at Chaseborough. On both occasions pollen, an emblem of fertility, is stirred up by the presence of music. In Chaseborough the perspiration and warmth of the dancers created a 'vegeto-human' pollen through which the 'muted fiddles pushed their notes'. (72) Here Clare's playing materializes in the form of the rich mist of pollen sent up by the rank grass. But Chaseborough was presided over by the Bacchic figure of Alec d'Urberville.

At Talbothays we have a herdsman and harp player, so it is not difficult to identify his classical pedigree. The god Apollo was banished for a year when he served as shepherd to King Admetus of Pherae in Thessalay. Through this apprenticeship he became the protector of flocks. On another occasion, Hermes created a lyre for him and the instrument became one of his principle attributes. Above all he was recognized as the god of light and of the sun. Though Clare has some of the attributes of Apollo, in him they are muted and diminished. Like Apollo, he has temporarily become a herdsman in exile, but where Apollo was known for his magnificent playing on a lyre especially made in his honour, Clare's is just a second-hand instrument in which he lacks real proficiency. In the *Iliad*, Apollo was known as the physician of the gods for his power of healing. Tess hopes that Clare will bring healing to her, but fails to see that his powers are weak. Nevertheless, on hearing him play she tells him: '*you* sir can raise up dreams with your music and drive all horrid fancies away'. (140)

This visionary moment, like many such moments in *Tess of the d'Urbervilles*, takes place at twilight, and twilight was identified by nineteenth-century mythographers as the time of day most representative of the struggle between good and evil. The sun was setting over the club-walking episode at Marlott and then over the orgy at Chaseborough. It rose over the August harvest in Marlott and then set again during Angel Clare's harp playing near the wild garden at Talbothays. One of the most dreamlike sequences, however, takes place at dawn in the water meadows. It is late June. Angel and Tess rise at three in the morning before the other workers are up, and their regular meetings in the solitary beauty of the meadows mark an important moment in their developing mutual awareness. The episode is poised 'in that strange and solemn interval, the twilight of the morning, in the violet or pink dawn time at dawn' that Hardy anchors in carefully observed details of country life. Herons appear, 'with a great bold noise as of opening doors and shutters'. The summer fogs are spread 'in layers, woolly, level, and apparently no thicker than counterpanes' and the cows 'left dark-green islands of dry herbage on the grey moisture of the grass'. These subtle observations of natural events are accompanied by a meditation on the significance of the pre-dawn light. 'The gray half-tones of daybreak', Hardy says, 'are not the gray half-tones of the day's close though the degree of their shade may be the same.' The difference is that 'in the twilight of the morning light seems active, darkness passive; in the twilight of evening it is the darkness which is active and crescent, and the light which is the drowsy reverse'. (144–5)

The pre-dawn light of this preternatural interval invokes a whole series of mythological associations ranging from solarism to pastoralism, and from paganism to Christianity. The mythographer Max Müller claimed that in the early days of solar worship an emotion such as love 'was . . . like a morn radiating with heavenly splendour'. 'It was', he said, 'the blush of the day, the rising of the sun.' '"The sun has risen,"' said people in the dawn of civilization, where we say "I love"; "the sun has set", they said, where we say, "I have loved".'[17] At first Tess and Angel feel like the first couple in the world, discovering in 'the spectral, half-compounded aqueous light which pervaded the open mead . . . a feeling of isolation, as if they were Adam and Eve'. But the 'the mixed, singular luminous gloom' transforms Eden into another garden, Gethsemane, which in turn made Angel 'think of the Resurrection hour'. Though, as Hardy comments ironically, 'he little thought that the Magdalen might be at his side'. Finally, the Garden of the Resurrection modulates into the fields of Arcady as in this strange light Angel sees Tess as 'no longer the milkmaid, but as a visionary essence of woman'. (145)

As the season progresses the summer sun rises higher in the sky and the valley becomes torpid and lush. The sights and sensations of the vegetable world are transferred to the human realm through images of sexual desire, of penetration and conception: 'Amid the oozing fatness and warm ferments of the Froom Vale, at a season when the rush of juices could almost be heard below the hiss of fertilization, it was impossible that the most fanciful love should not grow passionate. The ready bosoms existing there were impregnated by their surroundings.' (164) Everywhere at Talbothays the power of the sun is felt as a sexually energizing agent. The air of the sleeping chamber of the dairy maids seems to palpitate with 'hopeless passion' as the girls 'writhed feverishly under the oppressiveness of an emotion thrust on them by cruel Nature's law – an emotion which they had neither expected nor desired'. It is the heat of a 'flame that was burning the inside of their hearts out'. (162) Meanwhile desire descends upon Clare 'like an excitation from the sky'. (166) His passion for Tess drives him to visit his parents in Emminster (Beaminster) to announce his feelings for her, and when the other love-sick dairymaids hear the news that their Apollo has temporarily departed, 'the sunshine of the morning went out at a stroke'. (173)

The visit is made, and from the bracing air of theological discussion with his father and brothers at Emminster, Angel returns to the 'green trough of sappiness and humidity' in the Froom. At this point the power of the sun reaches its zenith, raising the emotional temperature of the atmosphere of Talbothays to new levels of sensual intensity. On reaching the dairy Angel finds Tess, 'warm as a sunned cat', as she rises from a nap in the torrid afternoon. 'She had not heard him enter, and hardly realized his presence there. She was yawning, and he saw the red interior of her mouth as if it had been a snake's. She had stretched one arm so high above her coiled-up cable of hair that he could see its satin delicacy above the sunburn.'

Here, Tess appears at her most erotic. Her body is open and desirable, and in one secret part we can see the mark that the sun has left upon her. As Clare approaches she abandons her body to his and, simultaneously, gives herself both to him and to the phallic power of the sun. 'They stood upon the red-brick floor of the entry, the sun slanting in by the window upon his back, as he held her tightly to his breast; upon her inclining face, upon the blue veins of her temple, upon her naked arm, and her neck, and into the depths of her hair.' The innocent birth of love in the water meadows at sunrise has now, on this second encounter, given way to something more sensual, more passionate. In the fields they first woke to each other as Adam and Eve. Now with a neat erotic twist, Hardy says that Tess 'regarded him as Eve at her second waking might have regarded Adam'. (187)

This is in August; in September Tess agrees to marry, and her acceptance takes place on an unpropitious journey to the railway station to deliver the milk on an evening that is sunless and wet. In what Hardy implies is a retrograde step towards the institutionalization of affection, the power of the sun begins to decline. Their engagement marks a shift in Tess's attitude to Clare in which her love becomes a kind of veneration. As he had idealized her as Artemis and Demeter in the dawn light, she now idealizes him as a deity. She lifted 'up her heart to him in devotion'. 'There was', says Hardy, 'hardly a touch of earth in her love for Clare . . . She thought every line in the contour of his person the perfection of masculine beauty, his soul the soul of a saint, his intellect that of a seer.' (211) The splendid October weather provides the couple with a month of 'wonderful afternoons' in which the sun presides over their 'unreserved courtship' out of doors. During this period

> They roved along the meads by creeping paths which followed the brinks of trickling tributary brooks, hopping across by little wooden bridges to the other side, and back again . . . never out of the sound of some purling weir, whose buzz accompanied their own murmuring, while the beams of the sun, almost as horizontal as the mead itself, formed a pollen of radiance over the landscape. They saw tiny blue fogs in the shadows of trees and hedges, all the time that there was bright sunshine elsewhere. The sun was so near the ground, and the sward so flat, that the shadows of Clare and Tess would stretch a quarter of a mile ahead of them, like two long fingers pointing afar to where the green alluvial reaches abutted against the sloping sides of the vale. (212)

J. M. W. Turner, *Petworth Park: Tillington Church in the Distance*, c.1828.
Reproduced in *The Turner Gallery* (1859–61).

The intensely pictorial terms, dominated by the blue shadows and low rays
of the setting sun, in which Hardy chose to realize this phase of Tess's life may
well owe something to another picture by Turner. His *Petworth Park: Tillington
Church in the Distance* of 1828 had been in the National Gallery since 1856, but
Hardy could well have seen it in the form of an engraving in a splendid collection
called *The Turner Gallery* published in 1859. In a wide panorama of considerable
tranquillity, the sun sets over the lake at Petworth. The painting shows the pollen
of golden radiance suffusing the atmosphere and the engraving brings out the
immense shadows that fall across the flat grass of the park. In Hardy shadows
like this are not positive premonitory signs. One thinks of the 'mangled' shadows of Bathsheba and Troy projected by her lantern on to the trees of the fir
plantation, and of the shadows that stretch across the surface of Egdon Heath
at the time of Eustacia's acceptance of Clym Yeobright. Above all, the onset of
autumn heralds the waning of the power of the sun and its loss of strength as
the darkness begins to encroach.

J. M. W. Turner, *The Angel Standing in the Sun*, 1846, oil on canvas,
78.7 x 78.7 cm.

The struggle between solar light and nocturnal darkness, so prominent in this novel, becomes a central metaphor for Tess's consciousness. Her affection for Clare, writes Hardy,

> was now the breath and life of Tess's being; it enveloped her as a photosphere, irradiated her into forgetfulness of her past sorrows, keeping back the gloomy spectres that would persist in their attempts to touch her – doubt, fear, moodiness, care, shame. She knew that they were waiting like wolves just outside the circumscribing light, but she had long spells of power to keep them in hungry subjection there . . . She walked in brightness, but she knew that in the background those shapes of darkness were always spread. They might be receding, or they might be approaching, one or the other, a little every day. (213–4)

The solar 'photosphere' that was the expression of her original joy on entering the Valley of the Great Dairies has been focused on the joy she feels about Angel Clare and his power to save her from the ghosts of her past. But, as the sun loses its power and dies with the year, so those 'shapes of darkness' begin to intrude. Clare, however, remains 'godlike in her eyes' (199), and on her wedding day, 'she tried to pray to God, but it was her husband who really had her supplication'. 'Her idolatry of this man', says Hardy, 'was such that she herself almost feared it to be ill-omened,' (233) On the way to the church she thinks of him as 'a sort of celestial person' (231) and as she leaves the ceremony she feels 'glorified by an irradiation not her own, like the Angel who St John saw in the sun'. (232) Tess had already seen Angel standing in the sun as he left Marlott after the club walking (p.143), and in the Book of Revelation St John sees 'an angel standing in the sun' crying to all the fowls that fly to come to 'the supper of the great God'. Turner had interpreted this moment in a late work that Hardy knew well. *The Angel Standing in the Sun*, subtitled 'The Flight of the Angel of Darkness', hung in the National Gallery. In the original gospel, St John translated a spiritual drama into words. What attracted Hardy to these 'mad, late-Turner renderings', as he called them, was the way in which Turner transformed that same spiritual drama into visual terms and endowed the event with symbolical meaning. So, for Hardy, Turner's *The Angel Standing in the Sun* expressed visually something about Tess's hopes for her life with Angel Clare. In the painting, the Archangel Michael stands in a photosphere and, wielding his sword, drives away the terrible spectres of Darkness and Sin. Alas, in reality, Tess's Angel is not the Archangel Michael. He is the Apollo of solar myth and though for Tess he may be irradiated by the sun, she has forgotten that Apollo has two sides to him, two qualities, one as healer, the other as destroyer. This was encapsulated in the words of one of Hardy's favourite poets, Algernon Swinburne, who wrote in 'The Garden of Proserpine', 'Yea, is not even Apollo, with hair and harpstring of gold,/A bitter God to follow, a beautiful God to behold?'[18] So, though Tess does not recognize it, on her wedding-day, on the last day of December, the sun has effectively lost its power over the spectres of night, and by the time the couple reach Wellbridge Manor for their honeymoon its strength is almost extinguished. It is, Hardy writes, 'so low on that short last afternoon of the year that it shone in through a small opening and formed a golden staff which stretched across to her skirt, where it made a spot like a paint-mark set upon her'. (236) The golden staff may suggest potency, but the mark that it leaves on Tess is inauspiciously reminiscent of the vermillion letters painted by the evangelical sign writer defacing the countryside around Marlott. Finally, as the sunlight vanishes so does love. 'The sun has set', Müller claimed about early heliolators, where we say 'I have loved'; so at Wellbridge the change in season and weather is filled with unhappy omens. 'With the departure of the sun,' writes Hardy, 'the calm mood of the winter day changed. Out of doors there began noises as of silk smartly rubbed; the restful dead leaves of the preceding autumn were stirred to irritated resurrection, and whirled about unwillingly, and tapped against the shutters. It soon began to rain.' (236) The death of the sun and the death of the year foreshadow the death of love, and as Tess makes her confession to Angel about her previous sexual experience, the events of the past like the leaves outside, are stirred unwillingly back to life.

Following Tess's rejection by Angel things change. Sunlight largely disappears from the narrative, and appropriately for a solar deity, Angel Clare disappears westwards to Brazil in an attempt to set up a new life. Meanwhile Tess, after visiting her parents in Marlott, becomes nomadic and restless. First she seeks spring employment in dairies beyond Port-Bredy, far from both Marlott and Talbothays, then as winter approaches she goes to join her friend Marian in the upland chalk region of Flintcomb-Ash, where once again she seeks work. The village of Plush, the model for Flintcomb-Ash, has been considerably gentrified and is no longer the 'starve-acre place' (304) it was in Hardy's day. Nevertheless, though it is only twelve miles from the Frome dairies it still has about it a remote feel. It is situated in a deep valley between Plush Hill and West Hill on a very minor road branching from the B3143 northwards from Puddletown where the high fields are open and windswept. At the entrance to the village it is easy to locate the cottage that offers Tess the comfort of the warmth of its outer wall when she first arrives and in which she later takes lodgings.

On the way to Flintcomb-Ash Tess tried to change her appearance by cutting her eyebrows and putting on one of her oldest field gowns. The landscape around her, 'almost sublime in its dreariness', is similarly drained of identity. 'There was', Hardy continues, 'not a tree within sight; there was not, at this season, a green pasture – nothing but fallow and turnips everywhere, in large fields divided by hedges plashed to unrelieved levels.' (303) Tess and Marian are put to work grubbing up swedes in one such field that was 'in colour a desolate drab'.

> It was a complexion without features, as if a face, from chin to brow, should be only an expanse of skin. The sky wore, in another colour, the same likeness; a white vacuity of countenance with the lineaments gone. So these two upper and nether visages confronted each other all day long, the white face looking down on the brown face, and the brown face looking up at the white face, without anything standing between them but the two girls crawling over the surface of the former like flies. (304)

In contrast to the area around Marlott where 'every contour of the surrounding hills was as personal to her as that of her relatives' faces', the physiognomy of the fields at Flintcomb-Ash is large, featureless, friendless and impersonal, reducing the two girls to insects on its surface. If the Blackmoor Vale was the land of Tess's childhood innocence, and the Froom Valley the land of her fulfilment, Flintcomb-Ash is the lonely and sunless land of her exile. But a strange incident in the fields of Flintcomb-Ash suggests that her personal plight has a wider significance. It involves some migrating birds. 'After this season of congealed dampness,' says Hardy, 'came a spell of dry frost, when strange birds from behind the north pole began to arrive silently.' (307)

Associations of northernness had figured previously in Hardy's novels and in *The Return of the Native* a similar bird appears to Diggory Venn. On his way to see Eustacia Vye, Venn sees 'in front of him . . . a wild mallard – just arrived from the home of the north wind'. Its presence brings an Arctic bleakness to the surface of the moor, 'an amplitude of Northern knowledge. Glacial catastrophes, snowstorm episodes, glittering auroral effects, Polaris in the zenith, Franklin underfoot'. (86) The presence of the mallard hints at a modern version of the sublime, spectacular, yet desolate and lonely. In *The Return of the Native* Hardy argues that in the past, when the human race was young, it loved the warmth and colour of the Mediterranean and the south. Now, in its maturity, discoveries about the natural world and man's place there had changed this taste for warmer climates. Gone were all the old securities about Mother Nature and her bounty. Gone, too, was the comforting knowledge of a loving God working everywhere for the good of man. So the northern world, Hardy suggests, was the appropriate setting for the modern sensibility.

Nothing could be more northerly than the pole, and in the latter part of the nineteenth century polar exploration was very much in vogue. The name that towered over all others in this field was that of Sir John Franklin and the story of his legendary search for the Northwest Passage was widespread. Ever since his disappearance in 1847 Franklin had been a national hero and his name was synonymous with modern ideas of bravery in solitude, of isolation and loneliness in strange uncharted worlds.

The birds at Flintcomb-Ash, 'gaunt spectral creatures' with 'tragical eyes', resemble the mallard of Egdon Heath in that they, too, are familiar with 'scenes of cataclysmal horror in inaccessible polar regions', and they, too, introduce a chill to the already cold English landscape. As the silent companions of Tess and Marian in the inhospitable swede field they share something of the girls' loneliness and homelessness. But more broadly, they are also emblematic of the modern condition. Tess has been abandoned by her 'god', Angel Clare. So has modern man. And like her, modern man found himself in a sunless, lonely and cold world.

When the snow at Flintcomb-Ash is replaced by a hard frost Tess makes another journey, which corresponds with yet another phase of her life. She decides to seek help from Angel's parents in Emminster (Beaminster), some fifteen miles away across country. She leaves at dawn on the eve of the first anniversary of her wedding day. The dawns at Talbothays were mellow, soft and magical; this one is brittle with 'steely starlight' and Tess's footsteps can be 'heard on the hard road'. (315) Using Hardy's own map, her route is not difficult to trace. She would have left Plush climbing up the side of West Hill and on to the Wessex Ridgeway. She would have dropped into the valley, then climbed up to the ridge along Little Minterne Hill to Dogbury Gate. Here she would have walked a few yards south on what is now the A352, then turned right and up a narrow road that passes behind High Stoy and Telegraph Hills. This leads along the ridge of Batcombe Hill from which she would have been able to look across the Valley of the Great Dairies, 'now lying misty and still in the dawn'. (315) Hardy describes what she sees there in words very similar to those he used previously to introduce that same valley. 'Instead of the colourless air of the uplands,' Tess can see, 'the atmosphere down there was a deep blue. Instead of the great enclosures of a hundred acres in which she was now accustomed to toil, there were little fields below her of less than half-a-dozen acres, so numerous that they looked from

Hardy's copy of *Cruchley's Railway Map of Dorset* (1855) where he has traced Tess's route from Plush (Flintcomb-Ash) to Beaminster (Emminster) in red.

this height like the meshes of a net. Here the landscape was whitey-brown; down there, as in Froom Valley, it was always green.' (315–16) But there is a difference. The valley home that was once the land of her innocence she now sees with the eyes of experience. Like the artist she is an outsider, an observer, and she now perceives the valley through the eyes, as Hardy puts it, of 'one who has felt'. 'It was in that vale,' Hardy writes, 'that her sorrow had taken shape, and she did not love it as formerly. Beauty to her, as to all who have felt, lay not in the thing, but in what the thing symbolized.' (315–16)

Her arduous journey on foot to Emminster may have been sadly inconclusive since she never meets Angel's parents, but the return journey is traumatic. Passing once again through the village of Evershead (Evershot) where she had breakfasted that same morning she is startled by the sound of the voice of Alec d'Urberville preaching in a barn. His former Bacchic Paganism, it would seem, has passed into fervent Paulinism. Tess, 'her face fixed in painful suspense', comes round to the front of the barn, and passes before it: 'The low winter sun beamed directly upon the great double-doored entrance on this side; one of the doors being open, so that the rays stretched far in over the threshing-floor to the preacher and his audience, all snugly sheltered from the northern breeze.' (322) The listeners were entirely villagers, but her attention is given to the central figure, standing upon some sacks of corn and facing the people and the door. The accusing beams of the low winter sun mark him out, as they marked out Tess a year before at Wellbridge House. In a parodic version of the conversion of Paul of Tarsus by a great light from heaven, the sight of Tess in the sunlight brings Alec's newly won 'Paulinism' crashing down, returning him to his original 'Paganism'. (325)

He abandons his mission and pursues Tess on her journey back to Flintcomb-Ash. He overtakes her on Batcombe Hill at a point called the 'Cross-in-Hand'. The Cross-in-Hand, we learn, 'is a stone pillar [that] stands desolate and silent, to mark the site of a miracle, or murder, or both'. It can be found today (though protected by a small fence) as it was then on this high and open ground. For Tess it marks the onset of the last phase of her tragedy. The location is important. Shelterless and exposed to the elements the area is reminiscent of the open fields of Flintcomb-Ash. 'Of all spots on the bleached and desolate upland,' Hardy comments, 'this was the most forlorn. It was so far removed from the charm which is sought in landscape by artists and view-lovers as to reach a new kind of

The Cross-in-Hand on
Batcombe Down.

beauty, a negative beauty of tragic tone.'
(330) Both the Cross-in-Hand and the
field at Flintcomb-Ash, 'almost sublime
in its dreariness' (303), look back to the
brooding 'beauty in ugliness' of Egdon
Heath. Once again this is a landscape
that expresses the modern predica-
ment, cold, empty and colourless, and
it is here, at the Cross-in-Hand, that Alec, by placing Tess's hand on the sinister
monument, reasserts his physical possession of her.

Remaining at Flintcomb-Ash until March Tess undertakes yet another
journey, this time back to Marlott from where her sister came to tell her of her
parents' illness. The journey of fifteen miles on foot in the early hours of the
morning takes her first five miles across the chalk upland, followed by a plunge
down into the Blackmoor Valley. The difference between these two levels, says
Hardy, 'was perceptible to the tread and to the smell'. (365) The Valley of the
Little Dairies, however, has lost its former pastoral innocence and the earlier
hint of economic hardship and rural overpopulation has become its dominant
feature. Tess remains to help her family, but when her father dies they are all
forced out of their home. They become, like the northern birds at Flintcomb-
Ash, migrants. The arrival of the pathetic group, with all their belongings on
the back of a cart, at Kingsbere provides an ironic comment on the ineffectual
power of ancestral lineage. Kingsbere is modelled on Bere Regis, where, in the
church of St John the Baptist, the historical Turbervilles found their last resting
place. The family was at the height of its power in the fourteenth and fifteenth
centuries, during which they were responsible for changes in the fabric of the

One pane of the sixteenth-century Turberville window at St John's, Bere Regis, showing the Turberville coat of arms.

church including the burial vaults. In the sixteenth century John Turberville joined his ancestors with the dying request that a new window should be placed in the east wall. This resulted in the splendidly crimson stained glass bearing the coats of arms of the Turbervilles against which the Durbeyfield family camp for the night. Alone in the church, Tess is startled by the re-appearance of Alec, the mock d'Urberville, as he rises from one of the tombs. The obsession with her that had begun again at the Cross-in-Hand now bears fruit. Her family is homeless and destitute, and in exchange for their financial security he induces Tess into becoming his mistress.

Meanwhile, Angel, weakened, worn and altered in appearance by tropical disease, returns from Brazil and eventually tracks Tess down, now living with Alec in the seaside town of Sandbourne. Like its model, Bournemouth, it grew up in the middle of the nineteenth century and all the buildings, like the Slopes at Tantridge, appear to be new. It is 'a fairy place suddenly created by the stroke of a wand'. Just as the Slopes was set off against the primitive woods of the Chase, here in Sandbourne the town abuts 'an outlying eastern tract of the enormous Egdon Waste' where 'every irregularity of the soil was prehistoric'. (398) But something primeval lurks close beneath its nouveau riche appearance and at the Herons boarding house Tess murders Alec. As he dies it is as if the vitreous crimson from the Turberville window has deliquesced into the pool of blood that oozes through the floor of the bedroom and into the ceiling beneath.

Tess catches up with Angel on the outskirts of the town, where it becomes clear that her love for him is unchanged. In fact, her devotion is greater than ever, and for the first time Hardy names the god in him that she worships: 'Worn and unhandsome as he had become, it was plain that she did not discern the least fault in his appearance. To her he was, as of old, all that was perfection, personally and mentally. He was still her Antinous, her Apollo even.' (408)

Tess's belief in Angel Clare is both touching and pathetic, but even in the face of that love, he is unable to relinquish his blinkered, Victorian, middle-class morality. His godhead is skin deep and it fails utterly when put to the test. The reason for this is that Angel, like Alec, is not authentic. He is the pale survival of a pagan god that has long been exorcized by Christian belief, and Tess's mistake is to take him for the original. Because he is a survival, he possesses some attributes of his predecessor, including his harp. As an Apollonian figure he was able for a time to bring light and life to Tess, but like the original, healer and destroyer, he becomes her scourge. He may return to comfort her, but the damage is done.

The couple travel north through the New Forest, stopping at Bramshurst Court, wrapped in darkness and mist. Their furtive journey onward, the last that Tess makes in this novel, continues under the cover of darkness, and when they pass through Melchester (Salisbury), the 'graceful pile of the cathedral rose dimly on their left hand, but was lost to them now'. (414) Arriving on Salisbury Plain for the last act of the story, the 'night is as dark as a cave' and in that darkness they almost strike one of the standing stones of Stonehenge. As a result their first experience of the monument is not visual but auditory.

'What monstrous place is this?' said Angel.
'It hums,' said she. 'Hearken!'
He listened. The wind, playing upon the edifice, produced a
booming tune, like the note of some gigantic one-stringed harp. (415)

Hardy was, of course, familiar with Stonehenge, and he was familiar, too, with both the contemporary archaeological debate and the Druidic myths that surrounded it. When in 1899 it was briefly up for sale, a reporter in the *Daily*

Chronicle said that Hardy had often visited the site in preparation for this novel, and in the same interview said that Hardy claimed its most impressive feature was its sound. 'If a gale of wind is blowing,' said Hardy, 'the strange musical hum emitted by Stonehenge can never be forgotten.'[19] The suggestion of Stonehenge as a one-stringed harp conjures up Angel's harp playing, together with that of Apollo himself. But there is something about this episode that sets it apart from the other events of the book. There have been two previous moments when the sound of stringed instruments has played an important part in the narrative: the bacchanal at Chaseborough and the harp playing in the wild garden at Talbothays. Both were emotionally highly charged and each of them carried strong mythical overtones. But here at Stonehenge Hardy seems to have adopted a new register. The climactic nature of the event seems almost ritualized. Tess falls exhausted on the Stone of Sacrifice, speaks her last words to Angel Clare and then, just as the sun rises, is arrested by the police. The heightened emotion and the spoken dialogue accompanied by the humming music of Stonehenge are resolved visually into a tableau of the two figures surrounded by the ring of policeman. The moment aspires to the condition of opera.

Hardy had been passionate about opera from his first experience of it in the 1860s. As mentioned earlier, as a young man in London he attended performances of works by Rossini, Donizetti, Verdi, Meyerbeer and Bellini, and even patronized works by much lesser-known English composers.[20] Around 1886 he first heard the music of Richard Wagner and the experience might have influenced this scene in *Tess of the d'Urbervilles*. In the early days he thought that Wagner's music sounded like what he called the 'whistling of wind and storm',[21] and years later he tried to convince the composer Edvard Grieg that Wagner expressed emotion by means of sound that was like 'wind and rain' striking against solid objects.[22] The Wagner concerts that Hardy attended from the 1880s were probably those organized by the conductor and impresario Hans Richter. From 1877 Richter had been giving an annual series of concerts in London to promote the work of his countryman and, to great public acclaim, he specialized in staging extended sections from Wagner's operas.[23] Did Hardy have Wagner in mind when Angel described Stonehenge as a 'Temple of the Winds'? And when the couple 'listened a long time to the wind among the pillars' is it possible that Hardy had in mind one particular Wagnerian moment?

I think it is. In 1886 Richter conducted a performance of Wotan's farewell from the end of Wagner's late opera *Die Walküre* at the Royal Albert Hall. He put it on the programme again in 1889, when its 'intensity' and 'intelligence' were praised by the critic of *The Times*; Richter then staged it on a third occasion in 1890.[24] The opera ends in a scene of profound pathos. The deeply flawed god Wotan is obliged to leave his closest companion, his daughter Brünnhilde, on a rock, as punishment for her violation of the laws of the gods. He casts her into a deep sleep and surrounds her with a captive ring of fire. He knows she is doomed and he will never see her again. In *Tess of the d'Urbervilles* Angel Clare is a god in Tess's eyes, but he, too, is deeply flawed. Like Wotan he leaves her on a rock, the 'stone of sacrifice', where she begins to fall into sleep. As Angel 'knelt down beside her outstretched form, and put his lips upon hers,' the couple exchange their final farewells. "'Sleepy are you, dear? I think you are lying on an altar,'" says Clare. She replies: "'I like very much to be here . . . It is so solemn and lonely. . .'" (416) But Angel knows, as Wotan knew of Brünnhilde, that Tess will be punished and he will never see her again.

As Hardy was aware, Wagner put great stress on the production of his operas in an attempt to create the *kesamptkunstwerk* or 'complete artwork' involving music, singing, text and staging. In this climactic scene of the novel, in order to heighten its impact, Hardy invokes other arts too. In visual terms Stonehenge had enormous potential in terms of colour, scale and composition. Since the end of the eighteenth century the stones standing majestically alone on Salisbury Plain had been a favourite subject for landscape painters, including Turner (1828) and Constable (1836). In the 1889 Royal Academy exhibition Turner's version must have caught Hardy's eye. It depicts the stones in an apocalyptic moment when a great burst of sunlight descends from the sky during the aftermath of a storm.[25] In keeping with the solar theme of *Tess of the d'Urbervilles* Hardy sets his incident in the light of the dawn, though he follows Turner in his use of chiaroscuro, dark against light.

> In the far north-east sky he could see between the pillars a level streak
> of light. The uniform concavity of black cloud was lifting bodily like
> the lid of a pot, letting in at the earth's edge the coming day, against

which the towering monoliths and trilithons began to be blackly
defined.

One of the central thematic patterns of the novel, the drama of light bat-
tling with the dark, is now enacted for the last time:

> The band of silver paleness along the east horizon made even the
> distant parts of the Great Plain appear dark and near; and the whole
> enormous landscape bore that impress of reserve, taciturnity, and hes-
> itation which is usual just before day. The eastward pillars and their ar-
> chitraves stood up blackly against the light, and the great flame-shaped
> Sun-stone beyond them and the stone of sacrifice midway. (417)

The sun warmed Tess during the spring Cerelia at Marlott, and she is
warmed by it again as she lies on the stone of sacrifice. Her solarism never
seems to have wavered, and when she asks the question of Angel, "'Did they
sacrifice to God here?'" he replies, "'I believe to the sun.'" Ruskin claimed that
Turner was a 'Sun-worshipper of the old school'[26] and Tess, too, understands
that, for good or ill, in the sun's warmth she has arrived at her true pagan resting
place: "'You used to say at Talbothays I was a heathen. So now I am at home.'"
In the growing light of dawn the couple are entrapped by sixteen police officers.
Like Wagner's ring of fire around Brünnhilde, they encircle Tess, 'their faces and
hands as if they were silvered' (418), imprisoning her as securely as the flames
of the god Loge.

This is one of the most memorable scenes in a nineteenth-century novel,
and its power comes from Hardy's mythopoetic imagination. But he was not
alone in using myth as a way of adding a new dimension to his writing and he
admired both Turner and Wagner, each of whom had looked to myth, and in
Turner's case, solar myth, as a way of expressing something very elusive about
the human condition. When Hardy wrote *Tess of the d'Urbervilles* he already had
a long-standing admiration for Turner and more recently had come to admire
Richard Wagner. These were two artists whom one would not immediately think
of pairing, yet in 1906 Hardy made a connection that brought them together.
Having attended another Wagner concert in London he wrote in his notebook:

J. M. W. Turner, *Stonehenge*, 1827. Reproduced in *Turner's Picturesque Views of England and Wales* (1832–8).

'I prefer late Wagner, as I prefer late Turner,' adding, 'the idiosyncrasies of each master being more strongly shown in these strains.' In their late works, he said, each of them tried 'to achieve the impossible', by exhibiting the 'spectacle of the inside of a brain at work like the inside of a hive'.[27] Hardy knew that for him *Tess of the d'Urbervilles* was going to be a 'late work' in his novel-writing career. It was one in which he, too, attempted the 'impossible' by transforming, through the medium of painting, myth and opera, humble figures in a landscape. But before abandoning the novel forever, he would make one last attempt at the impossible. This would be *Jude the Obscure*.

Chapter Six

Jude the Obscure:
The Descent into Darkness

JUDE THE OBSCURE, LIKE MANY of Hardy's novels, is strongly rooted in his personal experience and in the life of his parents' family. Yet it has a very different quality from his previous novels. More than any other, the story is driven by arguments rather than impressions, and more than any other it is obviously polemical and controversial. The failure of Jude Fawley's plans for his own education and his rejection by the Oxford establishment contain echoes of Hardy's own frustrated ambitions, and just as Jude is driven into the artisan class of stonemason, so Hardy was propelled into an architectural career against the grain of his true talents. The bitter, sarcastic, authorial asides on marriage that punctuate *Jude the Obscure* reflect the disintegration of Hardy's own marriage, and Emma's intense dislike of the story is a confirmation of that unhappy fact.

Though the novel is much more than a personal statement, and Hardy was right to object to the way in which some people read it biographically, nevertheless the outlines of some of the people he knew or had known can be found in his characters. As a child he had seen a great deal of his uncle by marriage, the Puddletown cobbler John Antell. He was a maverick figure, an intelligent autodidact who had some knowledge of Latin, Greek and Hebrew, but his bitterness at having been denied a formal education erupted in violence and alcoholism. Though he died in 1878 he made a considerable impression on Hardy, who adopted something of his temperament for the character of Jude Fawley. As for Sue Bridehead, her physique and personality bear distant reminiscences of Hardy's cousin and possible childhood sweetheart, Tryphena Sparks, but have a closer connection to the soldier's wife Florence Henniker, whom he had met in Ireland in 1893. He was strongly attracted to her intelligence, responsiveness and sympathetic personality. For her part she offered him plenty of encouragement to the point of coquettishness but finally withdrew, leaving Hardy to chafe against the restrictions imposed by marriage. The pains and pleasures, hopes and fears of this affair were still fresh in Hardy's mind as he traced the flux and reflux of the relationship between Sue and Jude.

If the polemical element in *Jude the Obscure* sets the book apart from his other novels, so too does his treatment of the settings and locations. His early stories are located in the land of his childhood and youth, Stinsford, Puddletown Heath and Dorchester. In *The Woodlanders* he moved north to the land of his mother's family, Melbury Bubb and Bubb Down. *Tess of the d'Urbervilles* revolves around central Wessex, Marnhull, the Frome Valley, Plush and so on, but *Jude the Obscure* is focused on the most north-easterly part of Wessex on the border between Berkshire and Oxfordshire. Hardy's paternal grandmother, Mary Head, came from this region. She was born in 1772 in Great Fawley, just south of Wantage. By the mid-nineteenth century no members of the Head family remained in the village, though when Hardy's sister Mary visited the area in 1864 the local villagers told her stories about her ancestors. As for Hardy, though he had not yet begun his career as a novelist, it was not long before he travelled in her footsteps. In that same year he also went to Great Fawley, examined the parish records for signs of the Heads, and stayed long enough to do a drawing of the local church, St Mary's, which was about to be pulled down and replaced.[1]

The actual story for the novel came to him much later, in 1890, and in October 1892 he decided to go back and walk around the same area of north Berkshire. He left London, travelled to Oxford and continued on towards Great Fawley. Passing through the fields just outside the village he recorded how he 'entered a ploughed vale which might be called the Valley of Brown Melancholy'. Here, he said, 'the silence is remarkable'. It was a place that filled him with enormous sadness and he added the note: 'Though I am alive with the living I can only see the dead here, and am scarcely conscious of the happy children at play.'[2] In the novel Great Fawley becomes transposed into Marygreen, but it has one very significant difference from places that Hardy had previously used in his fiction: he had never known it as a child or as a young man. As a toddler he had played on the edge of Puddletown Heath; as a boy he had daily walked the streets of Dorchester and had been taken around the towns and villages of central Wessex. But when he came to write about north-east Wessex his familiarity with it was not much greater than that of the young Jude Fawley who, an orphan at the age of ten, arrived in Marygreen from Mellstock (Hardy's Stinsford) 'one dark evening'.

Jude's mother and father had long parted. His father had brought him up alone and when he died the boy was sent to his aunt, Drusilla Fawley, who reluctantly took him in at Marygreen. Though he is unwanted, friendless and rootless Jude is repeatedly drawn back to this windswept part of the downs. It is a point of departure and return, and as Hardy must have known when he visited, it would eventually become the central psychological node of the story. The north Berkshire Downs are high and open. The fields are large, the hedges are low, and clumps of trees dot the rise and fall of the hills. A footpath leads due north out of Great Fawley and dips down, crossing a deep hollow evocatively called Winterdown Bottom, almost certainly Hardy's 'Valley of Brown Melancholy'. Following the contour of the hill the path rises to join the road between Newbury and Wantage and its route is dense

Below: Winterdown Bottom, Hardy's Valley of Brown Melancholy, near Great Fawley, Berkshire. Opposite above: Map showing the position of the Red House (Brown House), the signpost and the milestone in relation to Great Fawley (Marygreen). Opposite below: The milestone on the road outside Wantage (Alfredston) on the back of which Jude carved his name.

with associations for this story. This is the path that Jude takes when he first goes to scare the rooks for farmer Troutham; he takes the same route when he is in search of a glimpse of Christminster; the path goes by the spot where he and Arabella pass their brief marriage together. Joining the main road, it brings the walker to the brow of the hill at the Ridgeway. To the left along the Ridgeway the 1880 Ordnance Survey map shows the Red House, now replaced by modern cottages. To the right is a building marked 'cottage barn' that corresponds with a red spot that Hardy marked on his own copy of the map of Berkshire.[3] This is the site of the Brown House and its adjacent barn from whose roof Jude believes he sees Christminster. A little further down the slope is a signpost pointing to Letcombe Regis. It was here, on this spot, that a gibbet once stood on which an ancestor of both Jude and Sue was hanged, and it was here that Jude's parents parted for the last time. A few yards before the signpost stands the milestone that features twice in the novel. On the first occasion it registers Jude's intellectual and clerical ambitions as it points the way to Alfredston (Wantage) and ultimately Christminster. On the back Jude, an apprentice stonemason, carves the letters 'Thither JF'. It features again at the end of the novel when, exhausted, wet and ill, Jude rests on his walk back to Alfredston after his last meeting with Sue Bridehead.

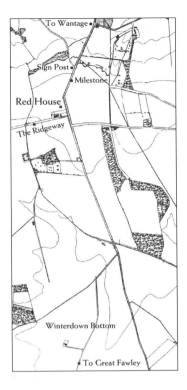

Above left: St Mary's church (1866) in Great Fawley by the Gothic revival architect G. E. Street. Above right: Cast-iron crosses in the former graveyard, now a small park.

The principal characteristic of this downland around Great Fawley is its lack of monuments, cottages, houses and churches. For Hardy these things were eminently important, and it was the impress of human life that made natural scenery valuable. He once wrote that 'an object or mark raised or made by man on a scene is worth ten times any such formed by unconscious Nature'. 'Clouds, mists, and mountains', he added, 'are unimportant beside the wear on a threshold, or the print of a hand.'[4] In Marygreen many of these prints have been obliterated. The majority of the thatched and dormered dwelling houses have been pulled down and the trees felled on the green. The twelfth- or thirteenth-century church of St Mary has been demolished and, with complete disregard for its venerable history, its stones used in a callously utilitarian way.[5] They were 'either cracked up into heaps of road-metal in the lane, or utilized as pig-sty walls, garden seats, guard-stones to fences, and rockeries'. (5) The new church, a 'tall . . . building of modern Gothic design, unfamiliar to English eyes, had been erected on a new piece of ground by a certain obliterator of historic records who had run down from London and back in a day'. (6) The 'obliterator of historic records' at Great Fawley was G. E. Street, a distinguished Gothic revival architect, famous for the Law Courts in London, and who had first apprenticed William Morris in the 1850s. When the church was moved to a new site to the west of the old one, the graveyard became a small public park and the abandoned graves commemorated by 'eighteen-penny cast-iron crosses warranted to last five years'. (6) Ironically, nearly one hundred and fifty years later those minimal signs of some ancient history still stand in the former graveyard.

If the built environment of Marygreen has been made featureless by human intervention the land around seems to be naturally bereft of human interest. Scaring crows in a 'wide and lonely depression', where 'the fresh harrow-lines lent a meanly utilitarian air to the expanse', it is not surprising that Jude thinks: 'How ugly it is here!' Had he living family bonds, had he been familiar with the area from childhood, he would know that the very path he was taking had been 'trodden once by many of his own dead family'. He would see that

> to every clod and stone there really attached associations enough and to spare – echoes of songs from ancient harvest-days, of spoken words, and of sturdy deeds. Every inch of ground had been the site, first or last, of energy, gaiety, horse-play, bickerings, weariness. Groups of gleaners had squatted in the sun on every square yard. Love-matches that had populated the adjoining hamlet had been made up there between reaping and carrying. Under the hedge which divided the field from a distant plantation girls had given themselves to lovers who would not turn their heads to look at them by the next harvest; and in that ancient cornfield many a man had made love-promises to a woman at whose voice he had trembled by the next seed-time after fulfilling them in the church adjoining. (8–9)

This attachment to a place, the significance of rootedness and belonging, is central to so many of Hardy's characters. Those who do not have it become unanchored and adrift. In *The Return of the Native* Eustacia Vye's romantic restlessness stems from her inability to appreciate the true beauty of Egdon Heath. In *The Woodlanders* Fitzpiers is blind to the rich life of the Hintock woods. Geographically rootless, he chooses Hintock more or less at random and possesses no sense of its local ways. But Jude's alienation is even more acute. At the age of ten he had lost his parents, and as the novel opens his one strong human bond with Richard Phillotson is about to be broken, as the schoolmaster is leaving Marygreen for Christminster. Without human associations, the village and its surroundings exist for Jude only as somewhere that can gratify immediate wants and needs: food, clothing and sexual pleasure. Having been denied love as a child, he mistakes the nature of his attraction to Arabella. She is just 'a complete and substantial female animal – no more no less', resembling the pigs she rears and hardly rising above her own fleshliness.

Jude's walk to the Brown House barn and his search for a view of Christminster are part of a desire to find something better than all this. The journey has all the marks of religious pilgrimage, and like all pilgrimages represents a hunger for something that transcends immediate experience. The details are significant. Asking in which direction Christminster lies he travels north; he walks across the field, on to the road and through a landscape bereft of human form, feature and almost of memory. 'Not a soul was visible on the hedgeless highway, or on either side of it, and the white road seemed to ascend and diminish till it joined the sky. At the very top it was crossed at right angles by a green 'ridgeway' – the Icknield Street and original Roman road through the district.' Though it is bare and featureless this ancient track at least seems to contain the residual traces of human activity. It runs, says Hardy, 'east and west for many miles, and down almost to within living memory had been used for driving flocks and herds to fairs and markets'. But that memory is immediately extinguished. The track, he adds, 'was now neglected and overgrown'. (14)

When he climbs to the roof, the scene that opens before him with its 'bluer, moister atmosphere' is reminiscent of Tess's view when she arrives at a spot on Rainbarrow and first sees the Valley of the Froom. Her view is figured by Hardy in terms of one of the visions of St John from the Book of Revelation. 'The Froom waters', he says, 'were clear as the pure River of Life shown to the Evangelist.'[6] In a similar way, the sight of Christminster for Jude is visionary. When Jude asks a tiler on the roof if he has ever seen the city from there, he says that he has noticed it 'when the sun is going down in a blaze of flame, and it looks like – I don't know what'. Jude is prompt with his suggestion: 'The heavenly Jerusalem.' (15) The heavenly Jerusalem is also described in Revelation: in the twenty-first chapter St John writes that one of the seven angels 'carried me away in the spirit to a great and high mountain, and shewed me that great city, the holy Jerusalem, descending out of heaven from God'.[7] Though St John's two visions appear in adjacent chapters of Revelation, Hardy's use of them in the two novels is very different. In the earlier story, it is not Tess who makes the comparison but Hardy, and the supernatural quality of the Froom Valley is endorsed by his authority. In the later novel, it is Jude himself who is anxious for a vision. He prays on the rungs of a ladder, and climbing again up to the roof, waits. 'In the course of ten or fifteen minutes the thinning mist dissolved altogether from the northern horizon,' says Hardy. Soon, 'the air increased in transparency with the lapse of minutes, till the topaz points showed themselves to be the vanes, windows, wet roof slates, and other shining spots upon the spires, domes, freestone-work'. (16) From this moment Jude becomes obsessed with an experience that exercises control over his whole life. Unlike the Valley of the Froom, Christminster is 'miraged' in Jude's mind, and in his mind alone, and it persists as an illusive alternative to the prosaic utilitarianism of daily life.

Jude's journey towards Christminster is driven by his rootlessness and his sense that life in Marygreen has nothing to offer. He teaches himself ancient languages and in order to make a living secures an apprenticeship as a stonemason. Though he is deflected from his ambitions into marriage with Arabella, once the couple have parted he returns to his intellectual and clerical ideals and travels onward towards the Promised Land. Hardy's choice of stonemason for Jude's trade was linked to his own experience of the architectural profession. Though Hardy was an architectural draughtsman and designer, not an artisan, he was familiar with all aspects of the trade. His own experience of that trade began in 1858 with his connection with John Hicks in Dorchester. Then in 1862 he went to join Arthur Blomfield's London firm. He probably first visited

Oxford between 1864 and 1865 when Blomfield was commissioned to design the Radcliffe Infirmary Chapel in the Woodstock Road.[8]

He would have arrived by train from the south; Jude came on foot from the west. But Jude, like Hardy, has first to consult a map to get his bearings; neither was familiar with the city or the layout of the colleges. Jude's first sight of Christminster, vague and nebulous, is made more mysterious by the darkness of the night and the absence of moonlight.

> After many turnings he came up to the first ancient medieval pile that he had encountered. It was a college, as he could see by the gateway. He entered it, walked round, and penetrated to dark corners which no lamplight reached. Close to this college was another; and a little further on another; and then he began to be encircled as it were with the breath and sentiment of the venerable city. (73)

Like Jude, Hardy would certainly have come with a sense of awe to Oxford, a place that he had heard much about but never seen. Jude, however, is so conditioned by his fantasy of Christminster that he sees only what he wants and 'when he passed objects out of harmony with its general expression he allowed his eyes to slip over them as if he did not see them'. (73)

During the day Oxford would have been bustling and lively. But Jude arrives in Christminster when the streets are empty, and that emptiness reflects 'the isolation of his own personality' in such a way that he feels 'like his own ghost'. In this condition he communes with other Christminster ghosts. Writers, poets and politicians, all former members of the university, jostle in his imagination, but they are dominated by the figures of Newman, Pusey and Keble, founders of the High Church medieval revival. These ghosts of the past move against the crumbling architecture with Jude stumbling about in the dark, fingering the mouldings. Most of all he is overwhelmed by the prevalent sense of decay. The porticoes and oriels have for him an 'extinct' air accentuated by the 'rottenness' of the stones; everything, he feels, is 'decrepit' and 'superseded'.

On the following morning the ghosts have fled and the actual has dispelled the ideal. Though Christminster remains for him dominantly an architectural complex, his perception of it is now more technical than emotional. At night the architectural details raised the famous dead; now he reads the numberless 'architectural pages' around him 'less as an artist-critic of their forms than as an artisan and comrade of the dead handicraftsmen'. Once again, he examines the mouldings and the sense of decay that he had detected on the previous evening is even greater. The buildings now appear to be 'maimed sentient beings' (78) eroded by the ravages of time and preserved only by the prosaic, mathematical precision of modern restoration. Everything in Christminster is 'copying, patching, and imitating'. Jude is a curious mixture of long-sighted but distorted idealism and selective myopia. What he fails to see is the connection between the architecture of Christminster and the culture at large. He is unable to recognize that the outmoded beliefs that this architecture represents have no real place in the modern world and Hardy interrupts to make that connection clear. Jude did not know, he says, that 'medievalism was as dead as a fern-leaf in a lump of coal' and 'other developments were shaping in the world around him, in which Gothic architecture and its associations had no place'. (79)

The new developments 'shaping the world' are introduced through Jude's cousin Sue Bridehead. She is an ecclesiastical illustrator in a High Church emporium, but with secret rebellious tastes suggestive of libertarianism and neo-paganism. Hardy illustrates the conflict between conservatism and liberalism in a significant, architectural metaphor. Just before her first meeting with Jude, Sue decides to use her day off work to walk into the countryside beyond the city limits. She probably travels in the direction of Boars Hill, because from this high spot she could see towers, domes and pinnacles in the distance. Towards her comes an itinerant salesman trading in plaster casts. In the late nineteenth century this was one of the occupations commonly taken up by immigrants, and this one, on seeing Sue, cries out 'I-i-i-mages' in an Italian accent.[9] For her part, Sue is very attracted to figures of Venus, Diana, Apollo, Bacchus and Mars. These 'reduced copies of ancient marbles' (87) are secured to a tray and though they are many yards away from her the sunlight coming from the south-west throws them into sharp relief against the church towers of the city. This strong chiaroscuro effect, the white of the plaster statuary contrasting with the dark ecclesiastical buildings of the city, is reminiscent of an experience Hardy once had as a young man in London. In 1865 he went to Covent Garden to hear the philosopher John Stuart Mill speaking in the open air in support of his candidacy for the borough of

Westminster. Mill's free-thinking, libertarian writings had had an explosive effect on Victorian intellectual life, and Hardy claimed to know his principal work, *On Liberty*, by heart (see p.15). On that afternoon Mill stood to speak to the crowd on a dais in front of St Paul's Church. Characteristically, Hardy's memory of the event was strongly visual. Mill, he said, 'stood bareheaded, and his vast pale brow . . . sloped back like a stretching upland'. But for Hardy, the piquancy of the scene lay in the way in which the visual contrast embodied a fundamental moral contrast; how 'the cameo clearness of [Mill's] face chanced to be in relief against the blue shadow of a church which, on its transcendental side, his doctrines antagonized'.[10] Mill was one of the late nineteenth-century antinomian writers who championed freedom for the individual and who objected to what he called 'the tyranny of the majority' and throughout his life he strongly supported the idea that men and women should exercise rational control over their lives. It is not difficult to see how Hardy, with the memory of this event in the back of his mind, has substituted the church towers of Christminster for the dark church of St Paul's and the white plaster casts of the pagan deities for the pale brow of J. S. Mill.

Sue decides to buy a Venus and an Apollo (probably Venus de Milo and the Apollo Belvedere) and embarrassed by their size and their nakedness, she is forced to conceal them from her High Church landlady, Miss Fontover. Back in her room, she unpacks them and, placing a 'Calvary print' between them, chooses to read two texts from her secret collection of books. One is Edward Gibbon's *Decline and Fall of the Roman Empire*, where Gibbon dealt with Julian the Apostate. Julian was regarded as an enemy of the Christian Church because in the fourth century he had attempted to re-establish pagan worship within the Roman Empire. The other text is the work of a contemporary, the poet Algernon Swinburne, and this, too, deals with Julian the Apostate. Sue reads Swinburne's 'Hymn to Proserpine', supposedly Julian's dying words in which the emperor laments the triumph of Christianity. It opens with the famous lines about Christ: 'Thou hast conquered, O pale Galilean: the world has grown grey from thy breath'. Significantly both Gibbon and Swinburne were Oxford students, albeit more than one hundred years apart. One attended Balliol, the other Magdalen, but both men came into conflict with the university authorities and had to be removed from their respective colleges.

This symbolic conflict between Christian and pagan comes to a head when Miss Fontover, finding the statues in Sue's room, falls into an iconoclastic fury and crushes them 'all to bits with her heel'. (97) Miss Fonthill's religious passion is fed by her attendance at the High Anglican church of St Silas and it is this church that Jude joins when he first arrives in the city. He may choose it because he heard a 'clever chap' (92), Sue Bridehead's father, did all the wrought-iron work there, since it was Sue's father's reputation that inspired Jude to take up ecclesiastical work in the first place. But, as Hardy made clear, St Silas was site specific. It was based on St Barnabas Jericho,[11] which held a special interest for Hardy. In 1867, just as he was leaving Arthur Blomfield's practice to return to Dorchester, Blomfield was negotiating with the Oxford printer Thomas Combe to design a new church in Jericho, for which the foundation stone was laid in 1868. St Barnabas is extremely unusual since its design, neither Gothic nor Classic, is based on the Byzantine, early Christian churches of Rome. Combe was a passionate Tractarian and wanted a building that would represent the High Anglican movement in Oxford. Consequently, the 'church of ceremonies' as Hardy calls it, was and has remained to this day, the local centre of Anglo-Catholicism. Sue might resent the narrowness of High Church dogmatism represented by Miss Fonthill, but her profession is closely associated with the Anglo-Catholic movement. The shop in which she works as an artist sells ritualist impedimenta that are almost indistinguishable from similar Catholic items of worship. There are 'ebony crosses that were almost crucifixes, prayer-books that were almost missals'. Unsurprisingly Jude's evangelical Aunt Drusilla fears that Sue might have become a Papist (82) and by meeting her Jude might be contaminated by her beliefs.

The lingering anxiety about the influence of Catholicism on the Anglican Church was not confined to Aunt Drusilla. The opening of St Barnabas was greeted with great suspicion by Oxford Protestants, and earlier in the century a specific monument had been dedicated to the early struggle between the faiths. This was the Martyrs' Memorial. For their first meeting Jude writes to Sue Bridehead suggesting a rendezvous at the Martyrs' Cross in Broad Street. In the sixteenth century, exactly on this spot just outside the town walls, the Protestant divines Thomas Cranmer, Nicholas Ridley and a little later Hugh Latimer were burnt at the stake for refusing to renounce their faith. The order for their execution had been given by the Catholic Queen Mary in an attempt to restore the Catholic faith to Britain and to eradicate Protestantism. Much later, in 1843 during a period of growing anxiety about the so-called Papal Aggression, Protestant fears throughout the country were fuelled by the popularity of the High Church Oxford Movement. So it was thought appropriate to erect, in Oxford itself, a monument to the Protestant martyrs. Since there was no room to build it on the spot in Broad Street, this was marked with a cross of stone embedded in the ground, while George Gilbert Scott was commissioned to build the memorial proper around the corner in St Giles. As the time approaches for Jude and Sue to meet, 'the broad street was silent, and almost deserted'. Suddenly, Jude 'saw a figure on the other side, which turned out to be hers'. But Sue is filled with trepidation, saying: '"I am not going to meet you just there, for the first time in my life! Come further on."' (94) She is of course right to be anxious about somewhere so 'inauspicious in its associations'. Though by the nineteenth

The cross placed in Broad Street, Oxford, to mark the spot where the Protestant martyrs were burned to death.

century people were no longer executed for their religious beliefs, another kind of martyrdom was taking place. As the story unfolds it becomes clear that both Sue and Jude are martyrs to repressive Victorian sexual conventions.

The Oxford martyrs flit once again through Jude's thoughts when, slightly drunk, and having received his famous letter of discouragement from the master of Bibliol College, he finds himself at Fourways (Carfax). This is another cross, and like the memorial in Broad Street, also provided a record of historical events. On this spot, says Hardy, 'men had stood and talked of Napoleon, the loss of America, the execution of King Charles, [and] the burning of the Martyrs'. It is also a memorial to domestic encounters. Like the country around Marygreen, Fourways retains the invisible record of suffering and pleasure of ordinary people, people who were the new martyrs of domestic life: 'Here the two sexes had met for loving, hating, coupling, parting; had waited, had suffered, for each other; had triumphed over each other; cursed each other in jealousy, blessed each other in forgiveness.' (111) The list of vicissitudes experienced within personal relations is later to be played out in its entirety between Jude and Sue, and when the first, Christminster phase of this relationship is complete, the location for the next phase moves to Melchester.

Jude introduces Sue to Phillotson, who falls in love with her and advises her to apply to a Teachers' Training School in Melchester, a thin disguise for Salisbury. Jude, who is also in love with her, is frustrated by his tie to Arabella, but decides, nevertheless, to follow Sue to Melchester. His Christminster experience grows out of his intellectual ambitions, his experience at Melchester is concerned with his ambition to train for the ministry, and both are expressed through architectural metaphors. At Christminster Jude climbs to the lantern of the Sheldonian Theatre, where he ritually abandons his academic aspirations in terms of the buildings that stand around him. He knows that 'those buildings and their associations and privileges were not for him. From the looming roof of the great library, into which he hardly ever had time to enter, his gaze travelled on to the varied spires, halls, gables, streets, chapels, gardens, quadrangles, which composed the *ensemble* of this unrivalled panorama.' (109)

His work as a stonemason in Christminster never permits him to enter its buildings and we, like Jude, are never permitted a glimpse of a college interior or any evidence of college life, teaching or scholarship. In the end Jude knows that 'only a wall divided him from those happy young contemporaries of his ... but what a wall!' (80) Travelling to Melchester he continues with his work as a stonemason, but now it is no longer clouded by illusions of scholarly advance. Arriving at the city, he

> looked about for a temperance hotel, and found a little establishment of that description in the street leading from the station. When he had had something to eat he walked out into the dull winter light over the town bridge, and turned the corner towards the Close. The day was foggy, and standing under the walls of the most graceful architectural pile in England he paused and looked up. The lofty building was visible as far as the roofridge; above, the dwindling spire rose more and more remotely, till its apex was quite lost in the mist drifting across it. (125)

It is significant that Jude on this foggy, cold and raw winter evening is denied the sight of the spire of the 'most graceful architectural pile in England'. Towards the conclusion of *Tess of the d'Urbervilles*, Tess and Angel Clare also fail to see the same cathedral as they pass it on their night-time, headlong dash to Stonehenge. They are driven by fear of capture; Jude is driven by something different, his need to find work, and his response to the cathedral is conditioned by utilitarian factors. Walking around to the west front, he 'took it as a good omen that numerous blocks of stone were lying about, which signified that the cathedral was undergoing restoration or repair to a considerable extent'. (125)

Jude probably arrives in the city around 1878, just when Gilbert Scott was completing the large project of restoring its crumbling fabric.[12] The architecture of Melchester, in contrast with that of Christminster, has no emotional charge for Jude; it is simply a necessary source of labour. Not so for Sue Bridehead, for whom the buildings of Melchester suggest outworn regimes, confinement and enclosure. The fifteenth-century windows of the training school are mullioned and transomed, the mullion dividing and narrowing the window space and the transom pushing down from above. Outside the courtyard at the front of the building is 'shut in from the road by a wall'. (125) If the oppressive nature of the training school regime finds expression in Hardy's representation of the architecture it is also expressed in Sue's body, again in terms of architectural design.

When Jude goes to meet her for the first time in Melchester she has the 'the air of a woman clipped and pruned by severe discipline' where her 'curves of motion had become subdued lines'. (126)

Hardy was familiar with Salisbury. His sister Mary attended the Salisbury Diocesan Training College for Schoolmistresses, and on a number of occasions in the early 1860s Hardy went to visit her. Seventeen years later, in 1877, she was followed by his sister Kate, who had already been working as a pupil teacher and went as a mature student. Though the concept of offering education to women was a pioneering one, the aims and methods of the college were both limited and draconian. The authorities were teaching young women to promulgate Christian principles, but doing so in an atmosphere of regimentation and suppression. Kate admitted that she was 'badly used'.[13] Sue, too, is 'badly used' and longs to break away. This desire to escape is expressed through her revulsion against ecclesiastical building in general and medieval architecture in particular. So when Jude suggests that they spend some time in the cathedral, she says that she would 'rather sit in the railway station'. '"The cathedral"', she says, '"has had its day!"' and the station now is '"centre of the town life"'. (128) Sue's preference for the railway station over the cathedral, for modern engineering over ancient architecture, is more than a belief in the superiority of secular reason over religious superstition. It also suggests a preference on Sue's part for movement over stasis, travel rather than meditation. So the choice of the railway station rather than cathedral marks a point in the novel when the railway itself will begin to play a progressively prominent part in shaping the narrative. In his preface to the novel Hardy claims that the story deals with the 'fret and fever' created by sexual relations. In the unfolding of the narrative that 'fret and fever' is specifically registered in the travel network, the trains, the lines, the railway companies and the various stations that now begin to determine the physical and psychological movement of characters. It begins with a journey to another architectural monument, Wardour Castle. Sue emerges from the training college for her day of leisure in a dress of regulation 'nunlike simplicity' that contrasts with the potential excitement of the day. She enjoys the vibrancy of rail travel in which 'the traipsing along to the station, the porters' "B'your leave!", the screaming of the trains', all form 'the basis of a beautiful crystallization', heightened in its intensity by the sexual innuendo of 'the guard of the train [who] thought they were lovers, and put them into a compartment all by themselves'. (130)

The journey to Wardour Castle on the London and South Western Railway takes about thirty minutes. At first Sue thinks Jude is proposing old Wardour Castle, a medieval monument (now in the care of British Heritage), objecting that she 'hates ruins'. Jude, however, knowing her tastes, intended the nearby new Wardour Castle, a classical, neo-Palladian country house. Both were once owned by the Catholic, Royalist Arundell family who, when the old castle was severely damaged during the Civil War had the new one built in the eighteenth century. The detail with which Hardy records their visit suggests that he had personal experience of the place and might have seen it in the company of his art-loving sister Mary when she was at the training college. Sue and Jude make a point of seeing the pictures, and though the Arundell Collection has long been dispersed, Hardy accurately records the names of the painters. Jude prefers the devotional pictures, virgins and saints, by Andrea Del Sarto, Guido Reni, Spagnoletto, Sassoferrato and Carlo Dolci, and Sue is drawn to the paintings by Lely and Reynolds that celebrate the wealth and secularism of the eighteenth century.[14]

For Sue, however, the whole trip has about it a break for freedom, and the novelty of the adventure is increased by Jude's proposal that they should not go straight back by train to Melchester, but instead walk north out of Tisbury and catch a train on another line seven miles away. The expedition is undertaken with renewed enthusiasm and Sue, who is inclined for any adventure, readily agrees. So, away they go, leaving behind the station from which they arrived and leaving behind, too, the exigencies of mechanical rail travel that force passengers into schedules determined by timetables, precise departures and destinations.

The walk, unclouded by controversy and guilt, is unusually energetic. The country is high, wide and open; they indulge in a pastoral fantasy with Jude cutting a walking stick for Sue 'with a great crook, which made her look like a shepherdess' and they talk freely. At one point they cross 'a main road running due east and west, the old road from London to Land's End', what is now the A303, and remark upon the desolation which has come over this 'once lively thoroughfare'. (131) As on the abandoned coach road at the opening of *The Woodlanders* here, too, the traffic has been taken over by the much faster railway. They pass through Fonthill Bishop, and make for (the now closed) Codford station on the Great Western Railway, but the route is far from direct and Sue grows tired. Looking for somewhere to stop they find a cottage four miles from the station where they can spend the night. The next day when Sue returns to the school she experiences a sense of imprisonment even greater than before. She is placed in solitary confinement for her misdemeanour and from this captivity she makes one last bid for freedom. She climbs through the window, fords the river and ends up in Jude's room, resembling one of the pagan sculptures she bought outside Christminster, her clothes clinging to her 'like the robes upon the figures in the Parthenon frieze'. (138)

Sue is expelled from the school and that expulsion accelerates her marriage to Phillotson. In his desperate passion for Sue, Jude now feels obliged to tell her about *his* marriage to Arabella. Unable to confess in the street or go to his place or hers, they enter the nearby Melchester market building. The market is over for the day, and the stalls and areas empty.

The interior of Salisbury (Melchester) market building in the late nineteenth century. It has now been demolished.

He would have preferred a more congenial spot, but, as usually happens, in place of a romantic field or solemn aisle for his tale, it was told while they walked up and down over a floor littered with rotten cabbage-leaves, and amid all the usual squalors of decayed vegetable matter and unsaleable refuse. He began and finished his brief narrative, which merely led up to the information that he had married a wife some years earlier, and that his wife was living still. (158)

The location is significant. Its bleak utilitarianism contains echoes of the field in which Jude as a child was forced to scare crows. Any suggestion of romance is dispelled by the squalid detritus that lies scattered around: 'decayed vegetable matter and unsaleable refuse'. The place contains echoes, too, of another moment when the ideal is undermined by the real. On his first outing with Arabella she and Jude had passed the Brown House from which Jude had earlier experienced his vision of Christminster and found themselves in a tavern. Here

they sat and looked round the room, and at the picture of Samson and Delilah which hung on the wall, and at the circular beer-stains on the table, and at the spittoons underfoot filled with sawdust. The whole aspect of the scene had that depressing effect on Jude which few places can produce like a tap-room on a Sunday evening . . . (41)

The nastiness of the ambience is reinforced by the proleptic image of emasculation and impotency in the story of Samson and Delilah displayed on the wall, foreshadowing Jude's confession in Melchester market hall where he is paralysed and defeated by his ignominious tie to Arabella. The harshly naturalistic detail of refuse scattered in the market also provides a reminder of the rubbish in Jude's life, acting as an emblem of what might be called the 'baggage' with which he is encumbered. Even the iron girders of the market building are starkly uncompromising. Like the railway station (and in contrast to the cathedral) the market hall is an example of utilitarian, mechanical engineering.

It is an interesting question as to how far Jude is consciously aware of the place, since, as we have already seen, his vision is highly selective and conditioned by his mental state. Hardy tells us that he would have preferred a more 'congenial' spot than the desolate hall, so he certainly has some peripheral awareness of the unpleasantness of the setting, but Sue's marriage to Philottson has such an impact on him that it induces in him a kind of sensory deprivation. As she leaves Melchester with her new husband, Hardy tells us that for Jude, the sunshine 'was as drab paint, and the blue sky as zinc'. (170) This state is not peculiar to Jude, and as the story unfolds the visual awareness of many of the other characters is changed or blotted out by unhappy mental states or psychological pressures. A dramatic example occurs in Christminster, when, restlessly, Jude moves back there to seek work. The city now wears an 'estranged look' for him and the many ghosts are replaced by the single phantom of his cousin. He comes to the street where he had first seen her, and finding her empty chair feels as 'if she were dead'. Arabella also thought that Jude was dead, but meets him by chance when she is serving in a Christminster tavern. On that same evening he had planned to join Sue in Alfredston, but Arabella persuades him that they must talk, and suggests that they take the train to Aldbrickham (Reading). They spend the night together in a seedy hotel. Returning next day to Christminster they part and Jude walks mechanically into the city as far as the Fourways. There,

> he stood as he had so often stood before, and surveyed Chief Street stretching ahead, with its college after college, in picturesqueness un-rivalled except by such Continental vistas as the Street of Palaces in Genoa; the lines of the buildings being as distinct in the morning air as in an architectural drawing. But Jude was far from seeing or criticiz-ing these things; they were hidden by an indescribable consciousness of Arabella's midnight contiguity [and] a sense of degradation at his revived experiences with her. (178)

The train, the mechanical movement, and above all the physical and psy-chological proximity of Arabella combine to create in Jude a kind of blindness. It is expressed through this architectural vision where Hardy presents the reader with a view of one of the most splendid architectural groupings in Europe. It is a view that almost certainly derives from the reminiscence of a picture of

Oxford High Street by J. M. W. Turner, though, curiously, it is one from which Jude is explicitly excluded.

In 1810 the Oxford bookseller James Wyatt commissioned from Turner two views of Oxford, one of the city from the Abingdon Road, the other of the High Street.[15] His plan was to have them engraved and sell the prints in his High Street shop. Though the painting (now in the Ashmolean Museum, Oxford) was privately owned, in January 1889 it was shown as part of an exhibition called 'A Century of British Painting' at the Grosvenor Gallery in Bond Street.[16] At almost the same time the Royal Academy put on a special exhibition of Turner's water-colours about which Hardy was enormously enthusiastic. Turner, like Hardy, had trained as an architectural draughtsman and was particularly sensitive to architectural form. For the view of the High Street he positioned himself at the east end of the road looking back to St Michael's Church and Carfax, the point where, in the novel, Jude is standing. In Turner's painting the morning is similarly clear and bright and the light falling from the south brings the buildings into sharp relief, creating an effect that is almost visionary in its compositional clarity.

This was not the first time that Hardy had used Turner's painting as a point of reference for the use of light and colour. In *Tess of the d'Urbervilles*, immediately after Tess's marriage, Hardy seems to have connected her joy and freedom with the energetic radiance of Turner's painting *The Angel Standing in the Sun* (see p.166). Though Tess would not have understood the connection, for the reader it lends, almost subliminally, a transcendent dimension to her feelings. Hardy's use of the Turner in *Jude the Obscure* has points of similarity. Once again the reader shares with Hardy a sense of the great beauty of the scene, and one that transcends the naturalistic and the commonplace. The difference, however, is that in this novel, Jude is not associated with the experience. He is 'far from seeing or criticizing these things' and is deprived of a powerful source of positive pleasure.[17]

With Arabella's departure from Christminster and temporarily from the narrative, Jude returns to Melchester in order to be close to Sue's new home with Phillotson in Shaston (Shaftesbury). In mid-September 1894 Hardy visited Shaftesbury and amongst his drawings in the Dorset County Museum is one of Old Grove Place, the house in which he locates Phillotson, a native of Shaston, and his new bride. Hardy, of course, knew Shaftesbury well and he liked it; he

liked the spectacular views it offered of south-west Wessex, and he recommend-
ed the purity of the air to friends. Shaftesbury had an ancient and dignified history, but it was largely an ecclesiastical history and one that had been obliterated
by the Reformation. 'Its castle,' Hardy writes, 'its three mints, its magnificent
apsidal abbey, the chief glory of South Wessex, its twelve churches, its shrines,
chantries, hospitals, its gabled freestone mansions [are] all now ruthlessly swept
away', and this sense of destruction and of loss, he adds, 'throw the visitor,
even against his will, into a pensive melancholy, which the stimulating atmosphere and limitless landscape around him can scarcely dispel'. (191) For these
details of Shaston's history Hardy turned to his copy of Hutchins's *History of
Dorset*, but uncharacteristically, he took them up in a curiously detached manner.
Like Hutchins's, Hardy's language resembles that of the historian or guide-book
writer. The prevailing atmosphere of loss denies the visitor (and the reader) any
sense of Hardy's characteristic visual pleasure in the landscape, and though not
all the ancient buildings have gone, those that remain have about them an oppressive air. Old Grove Place is a case in point. Jude goes looking for it and 'soon
discovered [it] from [Sue's] description of its antiquity'. From outside he could

> see the interior clearly – the floor sinking a couple of steps below the
> road without, which had become raised during the centuries since the
> house was built. Sue, evidently just come in, was standing with her
> hat on in this front parlour or sitting-room, whose walls were lined
> with wainscoting of panelled oak reaching from floor to ceiling, the
> latter being crossed by huge moulded beams only a little way above her
> head. The mantelpiece was of the same heavy description, carved with
> Jacobean pilasters and scroll-work. The centuries did, indeed, ponder-
> ously overhang a young wife who passed her time here. (197–8)

History, even obliterated history, serves to crush Sue. The heavy mantel-
piece and moulded beams of the house bear down upon her like the matrimonial
conventions with which she is in conflict and that symbolic sense of oppressiveness is felt even more strongly in the bedroom. Here, 'the heavy, gloomy
oak wainscot, which extended over the walls upstairs and down . . . and the
massive chimney-piece reaching to the ceiling, stood in odd contrast to the new

and shining brass bedstead, and the new suite of birch furniture'. (211) It is out of the window of this room that Sue famously throws herself, creating a 'white heap' on the gravel outside.

High, remote and relatively featureless, Shaston is a kind of aerie or cage for Sue and in the course of the novel she is frequently compared with a bird. Reluctantly agreeing to marry Jude, she says of herself that 'the little bird is caught at last' and when she comes to move from Aldbrickham she feels impelled to release her pet birds from their cage. But she is not the only bird at Shaston. The members of the strange sub-culture who live on the margins of orthodoxy, the 'proprietors of wandering vans, shows, shooting-galleries and other itinerant concerns, whose business lay largely at fairs and markets', make their seasonal home at Shaston and are compared to 'strange wild birds [that] are seen assembled on some lofty promontory, meditatively pausing for longer flights'. (192) Migrant birds have played a part in previous novels where they have come as outsiders into the main action. The wild mallard on Egdon Heath with its 'Northern knowledge' appears to Diggory Venn, and 'strange birds from behind the North Pole' are seen in Flintcomb-Ash. The Shaston migrants also stand outside society and its conventions. Their lone voices in support of Phillotson's allowing his wife to join her lover are voices of sympathy, because, says Hardy, their own domestic experiences have been 'not without vicissitude'. (239)

When Sue physically leaves Phillotson and journeys away from Shaston she thinks that she is going to meet Jude at Melchester. Instead, however, he joins the train as it pulls into the station and they go on together to Aldbrickham (Reading). In contrast to the antiquity of Christminster, the crumbling decay of Melchester and the ruins of Shaston, Aldbrickham is a place that has no history and the couple's descent into withdrawal and sensory deprivation intensifies. This becomes clear soon after they arrive in the town. Jude and Sue independently secure divorces from their respective spouses and they decide to celebrate:

> By degrees Sue acquired her lover's cheerfulness at the sense of freedom, and proposed that they should take a walk in the fields, even if they had to put up with a cold dinner on account of it. Jude agreed, and Sue went up-stairs and prepared to start, putting on a joyful coloured gown in observance of her liberty; seeing which Jude put on

a lighter tie. 'Now we'll strut arm and arm,' he said, 'like any other engaged couple. We've a legal right to.'

The situation seems unexceptional, but when they set out for their walk, things change:

> They rambled out of the town, and along a path over the low-lying lands that bordered it, though these were frosty now, and the extensive seed-fields were bare of colour and produce. The pair, however, were so absorbed in their own situation that their surroundings were little in their consciousness. (248)

Jude and Sue suffer what might be called double-deprivation. The landscape around Aldbrickham is as raw and unfriendly as the swede field at Flintcomb-Ash or the field of Brown Melancholy outside Marygreen, but Jude and Sue are excluded even from that dreary world because their surroundings are 'little in their consciousness'. Just as the architectural beauty of Chief Street was obscured from Jude by his mental state, so the unorthodox situation in which Sue and Jude find themselves denies them any possible solace in the natural world.

Though displacement and deprivation are experienced by most of the central characters in this novel none suffers more than the strange child of Jude and Arabella, Little Father Time. He exhibits many of the symptoms of what we would now identify as autism. He arrives one night in Aldbrickham by train. His 'large frightened eyes' never turn to the window but stare straight ahead at the back of the seat opposite. Lonely and isolated, he has to make his own way to Jude and Sue's house in Spring Street to which he walks with a 'steady mechanical creep [and] without an enquiring gaze at anything'. Jude saw nothing in the fields outside Marygreen and Sue and Jude nothing when they walked the fields around Aldbrickham. For Little Father Time as he travels to Aldbrickham the blankness is even greater. For him, 'the houses, the willows, the obscure fields beyond, were apparently regarded not as brick residences, pollards, meadows; but as human dwellings in the abstract, vegetation, and the wide dark world'. (267)

With the arrival of the child, marriage for Sue and Jude becomes a pressing necessity so, girding themselves for a civil ceremony, the couple set out for the office accompanied by their only witness, Widow Edlin. The weather is unpropitious, 'chilly and dull . . . a clammy fog blew through the town from "Royal-tower'd Thame"'. What they find at the office is even more dispiriting. On the steps 'there were the muddy foot-marks of people who had entered, and in the entry were damp umbrellas'. Soon they find themselves in a room that is 'a dreary place to two of their temperament'. The details of transactions between marrying couples are reduced to 'law-books in musty calf . . . Post-Office directories, and other books of reference' together with 'papers in packets tied with red tape', while the anonymous procession through the building of grotesque couples is signified by 'the bare wood floor [which] was, like the door-step, stained by previous visitors'. (273) All this, says Sue, 'seems so unnatural as the climax of our love!' (274)

Writing to his friend Edmund Gosse, Hardy said that the 'grimy' features of the story 'go to show the contrast between the ideal life a man wished to lead, & the squalid real life he was fated to lead', adding that 'the throwing of the pizzle, at the supreme moment of his dream, is to sharply initiate this contrast'.[18] In *Jude the Obscure* the whole trajectory of love and affection is marked by a series of squalid details. Sexual attraction is emblematically represented by the pig's penis that Arabella throws at Jude; courtship takes place in the unpleasant interior of the tavern near Marygreen where Jude and Arabella have their first drink; the violence of emotion within marriage is represented by the pig-sticking episode, and marital failure by the detritus of Melchester market. In each case the vulgar and coarse aspects of commonplace life undermine romance, tenderness and idealism, adding to the sense of divided sensibilities and alienation from sensory pleasure.

By the time that Jude, Sue and Little Father Time arrive at the Great Wessex Agricultural Show at Stoke Barehills (Basingstoke), the sense of alienation and deprivation has expanded to encompass the population at large. The town itself is bereft of visual interest with 'its gaunt, unattractive, ancient church, and its new red brick suburb, amid the open, chalk-soiled cornlands'. (278) Its most prominent monument is its cemetery, placed 'among some picturesque medieval ruins beside the railway; the modern chapels, modern tombs'. The importance of the railway is enhanced by the demise of slower-paced methods of transport and at Stoke Barehills, the inhabitants have lost any connection with the ancient system of roads. The highway from London passes through the town, divides and comes together at Lopcombe Corner some eight miles to the east of Salisbury. At one time, Hardy tells us, the townsfolk debated the 'endless questions of choice between the respective ways', but now, 'not a single inhabitant of Stoke-Barehills is . . . even aware that the two roads which part in his town ever meet again; for nobody now drives up and down the great western highway'. (278) Instead they come by railway and at Stoke Barehills there is not one but two stations standing side by side.[19] The first serves London and brings Arabella and her Australian husband, Cartlett, to the town; the other, travelling cross country, serves Aldbrickham and brings Jude and Sue. As the critic Charles Lock notes, in Hardy's fiction the railway transforms landscapes into networks and changes geography into systems.[20] He points out how, in *Jude the Obscure*, this finds expression in the chapter headings: 'At Christminster', 'At Melchester', 'At Aldbrickham and elsewhere' where the preposition 'at' gives precedence to place over narrative. Sue is correct when she says that the station is the centre of modern town life. Ever since the couple's escape to Wardour Castle the train has transported passive characters across the country without any reference to the places through which they pass. For example, Phillotson's parting words to his wife when she leaves Shaston to join Jude are:

'You go by the six-thirty train, don't you? It is now a quarter to six,'
'You . . . You don't seem very sorry I am going, Richard!'
'O no – perhaps not.' (225)

At the request stop at the station near Shaston, Sue is amazed that her simple gesture can bring to a halt 'such a powerful organization as a railway-train'. (228) Railway travel becomes more and more prominent as the story develops.

When the couple are dismissed as morally unsuitable for restoring the Ten Commandments in a church just outside the town they leave Aldbrickham and, for a period of two years, move from place to place. The fret and the fever mentioned by Hardy in his preface takes over the narrative. The nomadic pair go from Sandbourne to Casterbridge, Exonbury to Stoke-Barehills, Stoke-Barehills to Quatershot, finally pausing in Kennetbridge (Newbury). The last phase of the novel brings the family to 'Christminster Again' where, appropriately, they all arrive by train. Leaving their bags at the station, their journey into town matches very precisely one that Hardy must have taken in early June 1893. He was researching for the novel and came specifically to witness the events of the annual Oxford Commemoration Day or Encaenia. His aim was to be there anonymously, or, as he put it, 'entirely as a stranger'.[21] Jude also comes as an observer, and in order to feed his passion for Christminster ceremony, instead of finding lodgings immediately, the whole group walk to Fourways, down Chief Street and past the University Church of St Mary's with its 'Italian porch' and 'helical columns' (314), features that are all clearly visible in Turner's painting. Turning left they go towards Christopher Wren's Sheldonian Theatre, pausing opposite Hertford College, where they wait with the crowd for the dons to emerge and process to the theatre. As Hardy records in the novel, the weather on the day of his visit was threatening and showery. The thundery downpour mentioned in *The Times* the next day[22] reappears in the novel and makes Little Father Time think that it must be 'Judgement Day', and the rain soaks the family as they stand outside the theatre to hear the degree awarding ceremony with its shouting and singing. Hardy himself witnessed the ceremony from inside the undergraduates' gallery and afterwards retired to the Wilberforce Temperance Hotel at 34 Queen Street. Sue and Jude, however, go to look for accommodation closer to hand. Jude's sentiments as 'an outsider to the end of [his] days' (318) are probably Hardy's. In spite of all the bravura enthusiasm, Jude's feelings were shared by many of other well-known nineteenth-century figures who found Oxford undergraduate life alienating. Some had fallen foul of the university regime; others had felt that they were out of place in a world of privilege and orthodoxy. Algernon Swinburne, William Morris and Edward Burne-Jones had struggled to survive in Oxford, with only Morris completing his degree. John Ruskin, who attended Christ Church between 1837 and 1840, also failed to complete the course. He expressed his unease with the rough and tumble of bawdy student life in specifically architectural terms.

> From many a mouldering oriel, as to flout,
> Its pale, grave brow of ivy-tressed stone,
> Comes the incongruous laugh, and revel shout –
> Above, some solitary casement, thrown
> Wide open to the wavering night wind,

Admits its chill, so deathful, yet so kind,
Unto the fevered brow and fiery eye
Of one, whose night hour passeth sleeplessly.[23]

When Sue later tells Jude 'Gothic is barbaric art, after all. Pugin was wrong, and Wren was right', she is making a point about the Christminster ethos as it is embodied in its architecture. Ruskin interpreted the oriel windows of Christ Church as the 'pale, grave brow of ivy-tressed stone'; windows that for Jude become 'lifted eyebrows, representing the polite surprise of the university at the efforts of such as I'. (381)

Suddenly remembering that they have no lodgings, Sue, Jude and the children turn up the nearby Mildew Lane (Queen's Lane and New College Lane). This is a narrow road 'close to the back of a college, but having no communication with it'. The houses, dwarfed, darkened and overshadowed by the 'high collegiate buildings', are separated from college life by just the 'thickness of wall', though that life might as well have been 'on opposite sides of the globe'. (319) They are repeatedly rejected by landlords because of the children; the only place that will accept them is too small to accommodate Jude who looks for lodgings elsewhere, probably the nearby Turf Tavern. Almost immediately, Sue, because of her unmarried state, is asked to leave the next day. Now the mother is rejected by the town much as the father had been rejected by the university, and her plight is reflected back to her in the details of her architectural environment. She

> sat looking at the bare floor of the room, the house being little more
> than an old intramural cottage, and then she regarded the scene out-
> side the uncurtained window. At some distance opposite, the outer
> walls of Sarcophagus College [All Souls] – silent, black, and window-
> less – threw their four centuries of gloom, bigotry, and decay into the
> little room she occupied, shutting out the moonlight by night and the
> sun by day. The outlines of Rubric College [Brasenose College] also
> were discernible beyond the other, and the tower of a third farther off
> still. (322)

She puzzles over Jude's persistent idealism and how he is unable to read the architectural message. Why, she wonders, could he not hear 'the freezing negative that those scholared walls had echoed to his desire'? (322)

With the death of the children the story descends into its blackest phase. Sue retreats into self-laceration. Her belief that their deaths were divine judgement on her unacceptable sexual behaviour drives her back to religious belief, and back, too, to the high church 'of ceremonies', St Silas. When Jude goes to find her there, its neo-Byzantine interior is in darkness, and he can hear sobbing on the ground.

> High overhead, above the chancel steps, Jude could discern a huge, solidly constructed Latin cross – as large, probably, as the original it was designed to commemorate. It seemed to be suspended in the air by invisible wires; it was set with large jewels, which faintly glimmered in some weak ray caught from outside, as the cross swayed to and fro in a silent and scarcely perceptible motion. Underneath, upon the floor, lay what appeared to be a heap of black clothes, and from this was repeated the sobbing that he had heard before. It was his Sue's form, prostrate on the paving. (338)

The cross must have been made by the man who first inspired Jude, Sue's father, who had designed the wrought-iron work when the church was first built. Now, its physical weight seems to push downwards and crush the frail form of the daughter beneath. Under the weight of that cross she appears as a black heap of clothes, in an image that provides a visual and emotional counterpart to her prostrate form in white on the gravel outside Old Grove Place in Shaston when she made a leap for freedom.

Convinced that she should return to Phillotson and remarry him, she now begins to share the blindness and sensory deprivation already experienced by Jude and Little Father Time. Her mind is filled with dutiful dread and the impending ceremony. Phillotson has moved back to the schoolmaster's cottage in Marygreen and when Sue arrives there her mental state drives out any response to visual stimuli. She 'seemed to see nothing of the room they were in, or any detail of her environment'. (352) It is here in Marygreen that Jude,

'A huge, solidly constructed Latin cross' that hangs over the nave in St Barnabas, Oxford.

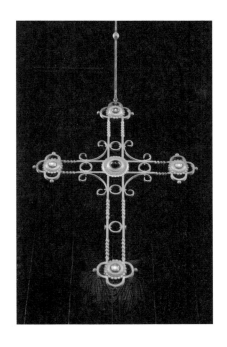

weak and dying, goes to visit her for the last time. He takes the train to Alfredston, climbs the hill to the village and on his return journey crosses the same field where he had once attempted to scare crows for farmer Troutham. This journey brings him back, too, to the central node of the story, the spot where he had his first vision of Christminster. There are, says Hardy, 'cold spots up and down Wessex in autumn and winter weather; but the coldest of all when a north or east wind is blowing is the crest of the down by the Brown House, where the road to Alfredston crosses the old Ridgeway'. Here, 'in the teeth of the north-east wind and rain Jude now pursued his way, wet through'. (378–9) Like Egdon Heath in the November storm, like the Schwartzwasser of Casterbridge behind the prison, like the fields above Flintcomb-Ash, and like the area around the Cross-in-Hand, the crest of the down is one of those places that Hardy seems to associate with the 'northern sublime'. It is a location that is marked by execution, parting and failed ambition, and like those other places, its bleak featurelessness is a reminder of the loneliness and desolation of the modern condition. This is a world from which God has departed and nature is featureless and hostile. In his exhaustion Jude comes to the milestone that had been a waypoint on his journey to Christminster, and, 'raining

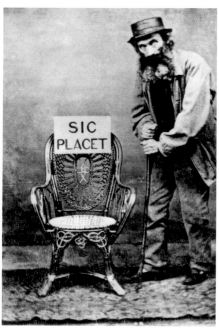

Above: Jude at the
milestone, illustration
by William Hatherall for
the serialization of *Jude
the Obscure* in *Harper's New
Monthly Magazine* (1894).
Left: John Antell,
Puddletown shoemaker,
1816–78.

as it was, spread his blanket and lay down there to rest'. When the novel was serialized in *Harper's New Monthly Magazine* the artist William Hatherall chose to illustrate this moment and the drawing so impressed Hardy that he wrote to congratulate him. It undoubtedly reminded him of the curious affinity it had with a grotesquely macabre photograph of his uncle, John Antell, entitled *Sic Placet*, 'Thus it Pleaseth Him', taken when he was dying of cancer. Hardy told Hatherall that his picture was 'a tragedy in itself' and so pleased was the artist that he gave him the original. Hardy hung it in his study, where it remained until his death.[24]

When *Jude the Obscure* appeared in 1895 it was either loved or hated, and the 'grossness, indecency and horror'[25] that many critics found in it was balanced by admiration for the classic nature of its tragedy. 'Jude the Obscene' and 'Hardy the Degenerate' were the headlines for reviews that represented him as attacking the fundamentals of sexual orthodoxy and Christian marriage. Hardy was plunged into despair, despair about novel writing and about friends and foes alike. One of his friends, Edmund Gosse, wrote a long account in the magazine *Cosmopolis*. It was appreciative but it was also critical. Gosse perceptively recognized that Hardy had made Wessex his own, and that he was 'happiest at the heart of it'. 'Wherever', Gosse said, 'the wind blows freshly off Egdon Heath, he is absolute master and king.' Moving away from that centre was a risky activity, and choosing a location as far removed as north Berkshire and Oxford even riskier, and he put his finger on one of the central elements at work in this book. 'Berkshire', said Gosse, 'is an unpoetical county, "meanly utilitarian" as Mr Hardy confesses; the imagination hates its concave, loamy cornfields and dreary, hedgeless highways.' In addition to its natural featurelessness, the area is bereft of another element that resonated so powerfully in Hardy's mind. 'The local history', Gosse continued, 'has been singularly tampered with in Berkshire; it is useless to speak to us of ancient records where the past is all obliterated, and the thatched and dormered house replaced by modern cottages.' Alienation, obliteration and denial, all these are prominent features of *Jude the Obscure*. There is no pastoral here, and in choosing north Wessex 'Mr Hardy wilfully deprives himself of a great element of his strength.' Unwittingly identifying Hardy with his own hero, Gosse linked the two by unconscious reference to the picture that hung on the wall of the Sunday tavern where Jude and Arabella had their first drink:

'Where there are no prehistoric monuments, no ancient buildings, no mossed and immemorial woodlands, he [i.e. Hardy] is Samson shorn.'[26]

What Gosse has missed here is that the Wessex to which he urged Hardy to return was in fact Hardy's own creation. Had Hardy possessed the same empathy with north Berkshire that he had for Stinsford and Dorchester, had he been born there and grown up there, then he might well have drawn all his imaginative power from that area. Furthermore, in choosing to move away from the certainties and securities of central Wessex Hardy was deliberately creating a novel full of unease, anxiety and rootlessness. When he worked for Blomfield in Oxford, and when he went to visit Great Fawley he, like Jude, was an outsider and he saw that the usual channels of delight, pleasure, ease and familiarity would be closed to him. He knew that *Jude the Obscure* would be challenging, controversial, edgy and filled with a darkness that he saw as characteristic of the modern condition. The 'mossed woodlands' and the prehistoric monuments of his previous novels express feelings of continuity and permanence. The sunlight and colour of central Wessex were sources of visual pleasure, and in Hardy, visual pleasure is always life-enhancing. There is very little pleasure in *Jude the Obscure*. Hardy's characters exist in a largely featureless world in which the sun offers neither warmth nor light but is instead 'as drab paint, and the blue sky as zinc'. (170)

Chapter Seven

The Poems

HARDY WAS COMPOSING POETRY before he thought of becoming a novelist, and after the appearance of *Jude the Obscure* in 1895 and its intensely hostile reception, he abandoned the writing of fiction. By 1898 with enough verse to make up his first publication, *Wessex Poems*, he had thrown himself into poetry so that when he died in 1928 he had established an extraordinary double reputation as one of the greatest British novelists and one of its finest poets. There are many factors that make his poetry so inimitable, but dominant amongst them is its conscious provinciality. Nearly all his best poems are set in the West Country. Many of them draw on a particular Dorset use of words and language; some derive from Dorset myths, legends and tales; but a very large number of them are rooted in the country that Hardy created for himself, Wessex.

The break between Hardy's novel-writing career and his career as a poet is often exaggerated. The shift to poetry was more a change of focus than a radical upheaval. Despairing at the abuse heaped on *Tess of the d'Urbervilles* and *Jude the Obscure*, then hurt by loss of support from his wife, Emma, and hostility from some of his friends, he turned inward and away from public scrutiny. As a result his perspective shifted from 'out there' in the wider world of farms, villages and forests, to 'inside' and to the subjective world of personal emotional impulses. He moved away from a panoramic view of the wider world and towards closely observed details and subtle mental events. In doing so, however, he retained his genius for narrative, for storytelling and for creating figures in specific and sharply defined settings.

This change of direction is exemplified by a small group of poems that relates directly to the novels. One of them, 'In a Wood', has already been mentioned (see p.136), but there is also 'The Pine Planters', 'Tess's Lament' and, subtlest of all, 'The Moth Signal', poems which are adjuncts to earlier stories. 'The Moth Signal' draws on an event in *The Return of the Native*. It is set in the cottage rented by Clym and Eustacia soon after their marriage and comprises a story in miniature set on Egdon Heath, where the landscape supplies the necessary, sympathetic context. The same narrative impulse lies behind the many ballads in Hardy's work. Thom Gunn has pointed out that several of Hardy's novels – he mentions *Far from the Madding Crowd* and *Tess of the d'Urbervilles* – have their roots in West Country ballads,[1] and in poems like 'During Wind and Rain' or 'The Trampwoman's Tragedy' Hardy used the repetitive ballad form in an almost incantatory way.

Some of Hardy's finest and best-known poems were written after the death of his wife. In fact he wrote some hundred and fifty about her in all, but the small collection entitled 'Poems 1912–13' have found a place as the most intense elegiac writing in English. Here you would expect to find the expression of strong feeling, but on closer inspection these poems often owe their originality and power to Hardy's ability to express that feeling in terms of action and place. In almost every poem, his personal sentiments about some special location are identified. Then the narrative element is developed swiftly and economically, and, in a sudden and unexpected twist, the full emotional impact is delivered.

The poem that opens the sequence, 'The Going', is characteristic in this respect. It records the first shock of surprised anguish that Hardy felt at Emma's death. Like many of the others it is a poem about mourning. Hardy grieves for Emma's unexpected departure but he also mourns the slow disintegration of his marriage, simultaneously expressing grief for something that has died within him. But the emotions here are neither abstract nor disembodied. They have a visceral immediacy that is lent credibility by identifying his grief with specific locations. In the poem Emma's spirit appears and re-appears, sometimes in places with which both she and Hardy were familiar and sometimes as a ghost in places that Hardy remembered from the distant past. But the point of departure is Max Gate, the house where Emma and he spent the largest part of their married life and where Emma died. The poem begins:

Why did you give no hint that night
That quickly after the morrow's dawn,
And calmly, as if indifferent quite,
You would close your term here, up and be gone
Where I could not follow
With wing of swallow
To gain one glimpse of you ever anon.

Hardy is numbed by Emma's sudden death and his shocked and puzzled re-alization is expressed in three questions addressed to his wife. Stanzas one, three and five each begin with word 'Why?': 'Why did you give no hint?'; 'Why do you make me leave the house?'; 'Why . . . did we not speak?' And each question takes him to a new location: first, the interior of the house, then the garden, and finally the north Cornwall coast. The first question is asked abruptly, almost imperi-ously. It reads as though it were addressed to a casual traveller who, on leaving, had forgotten to say goodbye: 'Why did you give no hint that night?' Only in the second part of the stanza does it become clear that this journey is not, after all, a casual one. Instead, in Hamlet's words, it is to 'the undiscover'd country from whose bourn/No traveller returns'.

Never to bid good-bye,
Or give me the softest call,
Or utter a wish for a word, while I
Saw morning harden upon the wall,
Unmoved, unknowing
That your great going
Had place that moment, and altered all.

'Never', the first word of the second stanza, drives home the sense of the finality of Emma's departure. She said nothing on leaving and will never greet Hardy again. The affectionate gentleness expressed in the 'softest call', the call that he failed to hear and will never hear again, jars against the word with which it rhymes, 'wall'. But the soft 'call' resonating against the hard 'wall' precisely identifies the location. It is the wall of Hardy's bedroom in Max Gate.

The second question serves to introduce another location. Hardy asks his wife why, as a ghostly presence, she entices him into the garden around their house.

Why do you make me leave the house
And think for a breath it is you I see
At the end of the alley of bending boughs
Where so often at dusk you used to be;
Till in darkening dankness
The yawning blankness
Of the perspective sickens me!

At first this seems to be a reassuring, domestic place where Emma appears in Hardy's mind at 'the end of an alley of bending boughs'. The alley that forms the perimeter of the garden at Max Gate is still partly in place and it was one that both he and she often walked at evening. Hardy wrote to Florence Henniker in 1912 that he would go into the 'long straight walk' at the top of the garden, where Emma 'used to walk every evening just before dusk, the cat trotting faithfully behind her', and 'expect to see her as usual coming in from the flower-beds with a trowel in her hand'.[2] But in the poem he sees her for only a fleeting moment, a 'breath', and its brevity contrasts with the 'yawning blankness' of reality that follows. The experience of her 'going' has been repeated. She has vanished for a second time, and the comforting evening garden has turned into a 'darkening dankness'. The receding pastoral 'alley' of trees has changed, too. Now it is diagrammatic, an empty, cold 'perspective', leading off, as perspectives do, into the blankness of infinity.

The third location in the fourth stanza, Cornwall, springs not out of a question but spontaneously from Hardy's memories of his courtship days.

You were she who abode
By those red-veined rocks far West,
You were the swan-necked one who rode
Along the beetling Beeny Crest,
And, reining nigh me,
Would muse and eye me,
While Life unrolled us its very best.

In this stanza Emma's identity has changed. Previously, she was 'you'; now she has become a younger version of herself, 'she'. 'You were she', he says, and 'she' is rediscovered in association with living, red-veined rocks near St Juliot, rocks that reflect metaphorically her pulsating full-blooded character. The idealized image of her as 'swan-necked' is further romanticized by her adventurous, daring spirit as she rides along the edge of the dangerously high 'beetling cliffs'. The verse, no longer halting and clogged, unrolls in Hardy's memory as life also 'unrolled us its very best'.

A third question prompts a recollection of the same places imagined in the recent past.

> Why, then, latterly did we not speak,
> Did we not think of those days long dead,
> And ere your vanishing strive to seek
> That time's renewal? We might have said,
> 'In this bright spring weather
> We'll visit together
> Those places that once we visited.'

The chattering suggestion of what the silent couple might have said with its inconsequential nursery rhyme rhythm, 'In this bright spring weather/We'll visit together/Those places that once we visited', is a passing wishful impulse. It could never have happened and its flow is immediately halted with the fragmented, end-stopped finality of:

> O you could not know
> That such swift fleeing
> No soul foreseeing –
> Not even I – would undo me so!

Locations and places in this poem are hinted at in small but telling details, but they are details that make them entirely recognizable. The wall, the alley and the rocks of the Cornish coast each provide an anchor for the vision of the woman who passes through. Each sighting involves both Hardy and Emma in a new place, and the emotional strength of the event stems from the vivid nature of the recall. In the poetry, albeit on a smaller, subtler and more concentrated scale, Hardy was doing something he had already achieved in the novels. In the novels Hardy was the narrator, an outsider and an observer; in the poetry he has stepped into the scene of his own narrative.

The sense of loss is perhaps even more graphically expressed in 'The Voice', where Hardy seems to be attempting, but failing, to adjust to his new state. In this poem he moves from Max Gate, outwards to Cornwall and back to Dorchester again. His journey is prompted by an echoing voice that seems to speak to him from beyond the grave.

> Woman much missed, how you call to me, call to me,
> Saying that now you are not as you were
> When you had changed from the one who was all to me,
> But as at first, when our day was fair.

The opening lines are what the critic Phillip Mallet aptly calls 'at once desolate and intimate'[3] and what the woman tells the poet when eventually he catches her words is that she is not the unhappy, querulous person she was in the last years of their marriage, but has returned to become the young woman he knew in his youth. Still not certain that it really is her voice, he asks to see her.

> Can it be you that I hear? Let me view you, then,
> Standing as when I drew near to the town
> Where you would wait for me: yes, as I knew you then,
> Even to the original air-blue gown!

Characteristically Hardy's memory places her precisely: 'standing when I drew near to the town'. The date is August 1870, when Hardy returned to Boscastle to see the young Emma Gifford whom he had met for the first time in the previous March.[4] He recognizes her from a distance by her clothing, her 'original air-blue gown'. The word 'original' suggests that Emma is wearing the very same dress that she wore on that day over forty years ago and has put it on to convince Hardy of the truth of his vision. But what about the colour, 'air-blue'? Sky-blue is what we expect and it hovers in our minds, producing the sense of a bright summer's day. But 'air-blue' is different. Air has no colour; it is light, almost weightless. Placed next to blue, this weightless substance is gently suffused with the colour of the sky, creating an image of semi-transparent evanescence subtly introducing into the poem a single note of sensuous pleasure.

The air-blue gown also provides the emotional pivot of the poem. It guarantees that Hardy's vision is authentic, that this really is Emma. Or is it? The next phrase introduces lingering doubt: 'Or is it only the breeze?' Slowly, as the imagined figure vanishes, Hardy is transported from summer at Boscastle back to the present. Back presumably to Dorchester and the water meadows of Fordington fields, open land outside Max Gate.

> Or is it only the breeze, in its listlessness
> Travelling across the wet mead to me here,
> You being ever dissolved to wan wistlessness,
> Heard no more again far or near?

The original scene comes back into focus. The verse loses its energy and becomes as listless as the breeze we hear for the first time crossing the unpleasant 'wet mead'. The blue gown fades and becomes wan, and the figure is dissolved into the air as easily as the word 'listless' dissolves into 'wistless'. Emma's death, and her wistless or unconscious state, is reaffirmed.

But Hardy, unconvinced that she has disappeared, continues his search, staggering, like the verse itself, into a landscape that is autumnal, harsh, hostile and cold. The breeze is now no longer 'travelling' but unpleasantly 'oozing thinly', and as it does so its northerly direction through the thorn gives it a sharp, biting edge. Suddenly the poem falls into a condition of stasis or paralysis.

> Thus I; faltering forward,
> Leaves around me falling,
> Wind oozing thin through the thorn from norward,
> And the woman calling.

The living questions and answers have stopped, the interaction has come to an end, and Hardy creates a tableau comprising three elements – the poet appearing to move forward, the autumn landscape and the 'woman calling'.

Almost immediately after Emma's death Hardy discovered two personal documents she had written. One, 'What I think of my Husband', was a diatribe against Hardy and what she considered to be his cruelty to her, the other, an account of her life as a young girl in Devon and Cornwall. Both must have had a traumatic effect on Hardy, and though the first was destroyed possibly in a conflagration organized by his second wife, Florence, the second was published under the title *Some Recollections by Emma Hardy*. They are both objects of considerable curiosity. We shall never know the full story of Emma's grievances against Hardy. The two substantial accounts of his married life, one by Denys Kay-Robinson and the other by Robert Gittings and Jo Manton, make it clear that the early attraction between the couple was strong and mutual.[5] Hardy admired Emma's energetic, daredevil girlishness as she rode unchaperoned over the cliffs of Cornwall. She loved his retiring, bookish, thoughtful nature. They shared enthusiasms for art, poetry, novels and music. Almost immediately, however, their relationship was overshadowed by domestic problems. Neither family liked the other and long-standing mutual hostility between the two groups set in. As Hardy's career as a novelist flourished and Emma's did not she, living in his shadow, became restless and unhappy. But greater difficulties lay ahead. Emma's religious orthodoxy strengthened while Hardy's waned to scepticism and she was embarrassed by what she considered his godless public pronouncements. Worse still was his attitude to marriage. Even before he met her he had been distrustful of the institution. As time past this distrust developed into a cynicism that was often, to her disgust, expressed in his novels. Eventually he became cold towards her, and she antagonistic towards him. He was drawn to admiring, younger, intellectual women; she was left alone to find her own company. They grew apart mentally and physically and her profound unease with the publication of *Jude the Obscure* marked the beginning of the last sad phase of pain and anguish on both sides. His earlier bookishness turned into withdrawal; her early childlikeness became eccentric childishness.

Some Recollections was composed just before her death, but it reads like the work of a young girl. It is a tender, naïve series of fragments about her early years in Plymouth with a romantic account of the way in which Hardy's visit to restore the church in St Juliot brought him into in her life on the north Cornwall coast. She writes with great affection of her childhood and adolescence, of her homes and gardens in Plymouth, of excursions on the river Tamar, and later around Tintagel and Boscastle. She had always wanted to go back to these places with Hardy, but he had refused. When he read about them in this touching manuscript he must have been overcome by remorse. Emma died in November 1912 and in March 1913 Hardy made a melancholy pilgrimage back to St Juliot, the north Cornwall coast and all the places he had failed to revisit with her. There was something very important in this ritual but painful journey because, paradoxically, it brought him closer to Emma than they had been in life. He needed to see these locations, and to re-envisage himself and her in them, before he could effectively express the precise nature of his feelings for her or come to an understanding of their time together. Before he wrote each novel Hardy insistently researched its setting. He needed to see and feel his characters moving in the places he had chosen for them. Now he was a character in his own story and viewing the scene was even more important for him.

In one of Hardy's most evocative poems, 'Beeny Cliff', there is a persistent exchange between the place itself, the object of the poem, the 'woman' and the first person of the poet.

O the opal and the sapphire of that wandering western sea,
And the woman riding high above with bright hair flapping free –
The woman whom I loved so, and who loyally loved me.

The pale mews plained below us, and the waves seemed far away
In a nether sky, engrossed in saying their ceaseless babbling say,
As we laughed light-heartedly aloft in that clear-sunned March day.

A little cloud then cloaked us, and there flew an irised rain,
And the Atlantic dyed its levels with a dull misfeatured stain,
And then the sun burst out again, and purples prinked the main.

Still in all its chasmal beauty bulks old Beeny to the sky,
And shall she and I not go there once again now March is nigh,
And the sweet things said in that March say anew there by and by?

What if still in chasmal beauty looms that wild weird western shore,
The woman now is – elsewhere – whom the ambling pony bore,
And nor knows nor cares for Beeny, and will laugh there nevermore.

Reading the opening of this poem is like putting a shell to your ear. In the movement of the first line you are transported to the sea shore and can hear the rise and fall of the waves. The colours, 'opal and sapphire', are those of the water, but they reflect, metaphorically, the early mutual love of the couple. But the whole tenor of the first two lines communicates the excitement that Hardy felt in the company of this energetic, vital young woman, an excitement that he characteristically expresses in terms of visual pleasure. The ecstasy of the second stanza is positively aerodynamic where emotion is communicated in the manipulation of space. The couple seem to be flying like kites, 'light-heartedly aloft', above the waves, above the birds even. In the third stanza a shower runs in from the sea. Though for them, like a many-coloured cloak, it is light and almost comforting, it casts, nonetheless, an ominous shadow across the sea, marking it with a 'dull misfeatured stain'. This one hint of future trouble is rapidly dispelled, however, and the joy of the moment is restored with the sun bursting out, and dressing up or 'prinking' the sea in purple. The fourth stanza brings the poem into the present and takes the form of a question. Though the cliff remains in all its ancient grandeur, shall the couple go there again? The answer comes only indirectly. The adjective 'chasmal' to describe Beeny cliff takes on a mournful quality when it is repeated, and the same shore that in the first stanza was home to the exotic 'wandering western sea' has now become 'wild' and 'weird'. In the first stanza the alliterative 'w' links the sea with the woman; in the fourth stanza the link is broken by the half spoken, hesitant 'elsewhere'. The woman has been torn from her habitat, and in the euphemistic, understated 'elsewhere' Hardy dramatizes the pain of bereavement. The Beeny of 1913 is physically unchanged from the Beeny of 1870, but since Emma has lost all consciousness of the place it has, for Hardy, lost its earlier beauty.

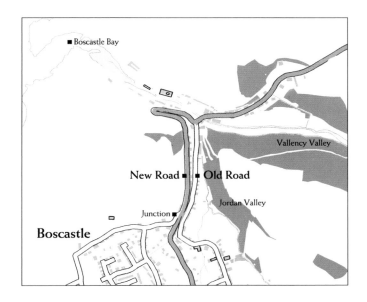

Map showing the relationship of Old Road to New Road in Boscastle, Cornwall.

Many of the other poems that Hardy wrote at this time compare the richness of his life with Emma in 1870 with the bleakness of the present, but none more movingly than 'At Castle Boterel'. The drizzling wet March day of 1913 contrasts with the dry March weather of 1870. Once Emma had shown Hardy the local sites; now he journeys alone. One of the places they both visited was the small town of Boscastle on a hill overlooking Boscastle Bay. The couple were travelling in a light, two-seater chaise when they began to climb from the bay. Two roads, New Road and Old Road, connect the bay with the town. Though both are narrow the newer road winds around the hill and is more accessible, whereas Old Road rises steeply up the valley of the River Jordan. The poem opens in the present when Hardy is revisiting Boscastle. He

'The junction of lane and highway', Boscastle. New Road is on the left and Old Road goes down the Jordan Valley.

has come up from the bay in a heavier 'wagonette' or public vehicle using New Road. When he comes to the junction with Old Road at the top of the hill he turns and looks down the byway.

> As I drive to the junction of lane and highway,
> And the drizzle bedrenches the waggonette,
> I look behind at the fading byway,
> And see on its slope, now glistening wet,
> Distinctly yet
>
> Myself and a girlish form benighted
> In dry March weather. We climb the road
> Beside a chaise. We had just alighted
> To ease the sturdy pony's load
> When he sighed and slowed.

As the first stanza runs on, unstopped, into the second so the place remains but the image dissolves from present into past. He sees himself and Emma walking beside the chaise as the gradient becomes steeper. The verse slackens and as the horse 'sighed and slowed' so the poem arrives at its first full stop. The pause is a meditative one and the poem shifts from its first theme, place, to its second theme, time. Unusually, Hardy dismisses the narrative element in this encounter, suggesting that the actual events and their consequences are not his principal concern.

> What we did as we climbed, and what we talked of
> Matters not much, nor to what it led,
> Something that life will not be balked of
> Without rude reason till hope is dead,
> And feeling fled.

Suddenly and unexpectedly, however, the poem's second subject, time, changes in scale.

> It filled but a minute. But was there ever
> A time of such quality, since or before,
> In that hill's story? To one mind never,
> Though it has been climbed, foot-swift, foot-sore,
> By thousands more.

On the one hand, in historical time, thousands of people endlessly tramping 'foot-swift, foot-sore', had passed this very spot on the hill in the Jordan Valley. On the other, Hardy's experience on that same spot in 1870 'filled but a minute', but it was one so intense and concentrated that it stands out as singular and precious. In stanza five the temporal scale changes yet again, moving from historical time to pre-historical or geological time.

> Primaeval rocks form the road's steep border,
> And much have they faced there, first and last,
> Of the transitory in Earth's long order;
> But what they record in colour and cast
> Is – that we two passed.

The 'primaeval rocks' that form the border of Old Road, Jordan Valley.

The valley, up which the narrow road ascends, has just the steep borders described in this stanza and in some places the strata of the rock are exposed. Geology tells us that these strata provide a record of the earth's history. Theoretically, or perhaps fancifully, they provide a record of everything that has taken place on earth including the crucial moment that Emma and Hardy passed. If the enormous spans of historical and geological time endow Hardy's moment on the hill with precious intensity, in the sixth stanza everything collapses.

> And to me, though Time's unflinching rigour,
> In mindless rote, has ruled from sight
> The substance now, one phantom figure
> Remains on the slope, as when that night
> Saw us alight.

Here time is given another face, and instead of helping to memorialize Hardy's special minute, it acts to destroy it, and the meditative, philosophical tone of the previous stanzas gives way to something more personal and rancorous. The hard, mechanical 'r's – 'rigour', 'rote', 'ruled' – and sibilant, hissing 's's – 'sight', 'substance' – express Hardy's resentment of Emma's removal from the scene by the harsh passage of time. In the final stanza time reasserts itself as 1870 dissolves back into 1913.

I look and see it there, shrinking, shrinking,
I look back at it amid the rain
For the very last time; for my sand is sinking,
And I shall traverse old love's domain
Never again.

Time took away his wife and now the shrinking of his younger self is caused by the 'sinking' of the sand in his hourglass. Loss of memory is slowly obliterating them both. Again, time and place intersect as Hardy is returned from past to present, from the dry March weather and back to the rain. The two two-syllable words with which the poem ends, 'never again', have about them a sense of absloute finality. The situation is irreversible; the clock cannot be put back and however intense that minute in Old Road might have been the place as it was cannot be revisited or the minute relived.

In no other poem is place so important in Hardy's grieving process as 'After a Journey'. The journey of the title is one that Hardy took to Pentaragan Bay, a few miles north of Boscastle, in 1913, four months after Emma's death. The 'whim' that drew him there was, of course, Emma's. In her *Recollections* she recalled how, 'I rode my pretty mare Fanny and he [i.e. Hardy] walked by my side, and I showed him . . . the cliffs. . . sometimes gazing down at the solemn small shores [below] where the seals lived, coming out of great caverns very occasionally.'[6]

I come to view a voiceless ghost;
Whither, O whither will its whim now draw me?
Up the cliff, down, till I'm lonely, lost,
And the unseen waters' ejaculations awe me.
Where you will next be there's no knowing,
Facing round about me everywhere,
With your nut-coloured hair,
And gray eyes, and rose-flush coming and going.

The details of the 'unseen' waters and the seals are Emma's and though Hardy describes her as a 'voiceless ghost' the dead woman was, in her *Recollections,* far from inarticulate. As the critic Barbara Hardy points out, the poem is strongly sensual.[7] Emma first appears as a young girl in her sexual prime, with 'gray eyes, and rose-flush coming and going', and what follows is a narrative of pursuit which plays, as Barbara Hardy suggests, on a double entendre of dangerous haunting and wanton allure. This is a quest narrative. Re-entering Emma's old haunts is, for Hardy, both an act of contrition and communion. He is willing to be seduced and coming to the place of his original seduction is important for both of them. He asks rhetorically if she, like him, feels pained about the 'division' between them. But returning to Pentaragan, seeing it through her eyes, and expressing it in his words acts as a positive link between them. Even though she is a ghost the journey serves to empower her, and she achieves in death what she was unable to in life. Looking once again at the beauty of the place offers them both a kind of ghostly second honeymoon where the scenic details exist not for their picturesque value but to express their mutual, romantic pleasure.

> I see what you are doing: you are leading me on
> To the spots we knew when we haunted here together,
> The waterfall, above which the mist-bow shone
> At the then fair hour in the then fair weather,
> And the cave just under, with a voice still so hollow
> That it seems to call out to me from forty years ago,
> When you were all aglow,
> And not the thin ghost that I now frailly follow!

In 'Beeny Cliff', 'At Castle Boterel', 'After a Journey' and many other poems written at this time, place is central to their meaning. Through the locations Hardy re-enacts various states of feeling, and in each case the physical details of landscape, sea or coastline provide a context for that feeling. Stimulated first by reading about these places in Emma's *Recollections*, then visiting them after a lapse of forty years, revivified Hardy's memory in such a way that they become filled with memories and charged with emotion. The two roads and the rocks that feature in 'At Castle Boterel' release feelings of loss and dismay at the passing of time; the mist bow and the caves in 'After a Journey' express former feelings of mutual affection. The humans in the landscape, 'the girlish form', the girl with 'gray eyes' and 'one phantom figure' of Hardy himself, are essential to the narrative but it is as if the emotions between poet and lover have been implicitly transferred to the objects and places within which they are rediscovered.

In a significant number of poems outside the group of 1912–13, 'place' is represented in a non-verbal way as the subject of Hardy's own drawing and painting. In August 1870 he and Emma set out together with sketchbooks and drawing materials to record some of the details of the coast near St Juliot. At one point it came on to rain and in the poem 'The Figure in the Scene' Hardy describes the way, as he was drawing it, Emma stepped in front of the drizzly 'cragged slope'. A sketch, dated 22 August 1870, shows Beeny Cliff in the rain with a hooded female figure in the foreground.

> And thus I drew her there alone,
> Seated amid the gauze
> Of moisture, hooded, only her outline shown,
> With rainfall marked across.

Though 'only her outline' can be seen her presence is crucial because, he tells us, she is 'the Genius of the spot'. Emma died without ever returning, but her image in the sketch remains 'immutable', forever printed on the landscape, and by extension forever printed on Hardy's mind. A second poem, 'Why did I Sketch', enlarges on the relationship between figure and landscape. In it Hardy warns: 'If you go drawing on down and cliff'/Let no soft curves intrude/Of a woman's silhouette . . .' Why? Because you may have created a hostage to fortune. The drawing may outlive the figure and become a kind of *memento mori*. In these sketching poems Hardy explains how the landscape and the figure within it become bonded in the act of representation.

After Emma's death the area around St Juliot took on such a quality for Hardy that it hardly existed independent of her presence for him. A powerful, but less despondent version of this connection between person and place figures prominently in 'Under the Waterfall'. In *Some Recollections* Emma mentioned how when Hardy visited her at St Juliot in August 1870 the couple 'sketched and talked of books', often walking 'down the beautiful Valency Valley', and on one occasion, she says, 'we . . . lost a tiny picnic tumbler . . . between two

Top: Hardy's drawing of Beeny Cliff, 22 August 1870. Pencil on paper, 11 x 17 cm. Above: Emma searching for the lost drinking glass in the Valency river, 19 August 1870. Pencil on paper, 8.5 x 13 cm.

of the boulders'.[8] While Emma was searching in the stream for the glass Hardy made a drawing of her. As a figure study it is not especially competent, but the emotional intensity of the moment is subtly revealed in the way in which Hardy has stressed Emma's secondary sexual characteristics, her breasts, her buttocks and her loose hair. The poem, however, is considerably less personal than many Hardy wrote about his courtship. The emotional charge of the event is distanced by placing the whole experience in the mouth of a female whose reminiscence of it is triggered by placing her arms in a basin of cold water.

> Whenever I plunge my arm, like this,
> In a basin of water, I never miss
> The sweet sharp sense of a fugitive day
> Fetched back from the thickening shroud of grey.
> Hence the only prime
> And real love-rhyme
> That I know by heart
> And that leaves no smart,
> Is the purl of a little valley fall
> About three spans wide and two spans tall . . .

For her, the sound of the river and the waterfall is like a 'rhyme of love' and the only one that, for her, (significantly) 'leaves no smart'. The rhyming couplets and the long sentences vividly represent the 'cascade's rhyme', as it tumbles perpetually over the rocks. When asked by her friendly companion why this movement of the water is for her a 'love rhyme' she replies by explaining the circumstances of the lost glass, but she does so in strongly visual terms – terms that probably have their roots in the drawings the couple did that day.

> For, down that pass,
> My love and I
> Walked under a sky
> Of blue with a leaf-wove awning of green,
> In the burn of August, to paint the scene . . .

This is unusual amongst the Cornish poems. Usually the 'scenes' are less detailed, more starkly economical, and leave little opportunity to luxuriate in their sensuousness. But this one is turned into a carefully organized pictorial composition. There is a still life of fruit and wine placed by 'the runlet's rim' in which the *dejeuner sur l'herbe* is completed by the two figures who sit and drink 'arched by the oak copse'. As the speaker goes to rinse the glass in the waterfall it drops into the water and in the last section of the poem the wider significance of the event unfolds.

> By night, by day, when it shines or lours,
> There lies intact that chalice of ours,
> And its presence adds to the rhyme of love
> Persistently sung by the fall above.
> No lip has touched it since his and mine
> In turn there from sipped lovers' wine.

The glass becomes a religious 'chalice', a holy grail of love, a unique symbol of their affection. In falling into the water it unites with the love rhyme of the river itself and its 'persistent' song. In this way, the spot by the waterfall is a shrine to their love. Whatever may happen in the future, whether it 'shines or lours', whether their affection comes or goes, the glass will remain as an emblem, unchanging, like the everlasting flow of the river. The poem endows the Valency river with special meaning. It is infused with the romantic presence of the two lovers whose mutual affection fills the carefully composed space.

Even in this small selection of poems that deal with Hardy's relationship with Emma it is clear that he figures his emotions in terms of place. But the habit began early in his writing career when he was writing poetry as a young architect in London and he soon adopted it for his first novels. It was strengthened by his development of the concept of a geographical Wessex where author and creation became closely identified. A poem that he composed on the cusp of abandoning novel writing expands on his deeply seated commitment to place. 'Wessex Heights' is an intimately personal work in which the loneliness of the Wessex hills offers peace and consolation to Hardy's troubled mind. It was written in 1896 after the appearance of *Jude the Obscure* at a point in his life when he was being reviled for immorality, irreverence and indecency and when his marriage was going into sharp decline. In the poem, the Wessex world is divided into two topographical levels, the lonely heights with which the poem both opens and closes, and in between, the populated lowlands.

> There are some heights in Wessex, shaped as if by a kindly hand
> For thinking, dreaming, dying on, and at crises when I stand,
> Say, on Ingpen Beacon eastward, or on Wylls-Neck westwardly,
> I seem where I was before my birth, and after death may be.

> In the lowlands I have no comrade, not even the lone man's friend –
> Her who suffereth long and is kind; accepts what he is too weak to mend:
> Down there they are dubious and askance; there nobody thinks as I,
> But mind-chains do not clank where one's next neighbour is the sky.

The heights are places of meditation and calm. Hardy has a sense that he knew them before his birth and will return to them after his death. Shaped by a 'kindly hand' there is something hauntingly numinous about them. In contrast, the lowlands offer nothing but distress, social friction and rejection. The critic and scholar Tom Paulin points out how 'the enormous iambic couplets create a terrifying monotony'[9] – monotony that reflects the depressingly mechanical nature of the lower land with its clanking 'mind chains'. 'Down there' Hardy is a pariah. He is pursued by ghosts from the past including himself as a 'young and promising man'. His 'chrysalis', as he calls him, accuses him of being his 'strange continuator', a figure simultaneously connected and alien. Then there are the ghosts 'with weird detective ways', journalists who pursued him in the wake of the publication of his last novel. But he nominates four people in particular who contribute most to his misery. Though he has concealed their identities the detective ways of modern scholars have helped to name them.[10] It has been reasonably suggested that 'her who suffereth long and is kind' is his wife, Emma. 'The figure against the moon' who makes his 'breast beat out of tune' is his mother, Jemima, and the ghost that inhabits Yell'ham bottom and the Froom-side-Vale might well be Tryphena Sparks. The 'one rare fair woman' is almost certainly Frances Henniker, but by 1896 she had pained him by her final rejection.

The last section of the poem finds him once again in meditative isolation on the heights, Ingpen Beacon and Wylls-Neck, to which the 'homely Bulbarrow' and the familiar 'little Pilsdon Crest' are added.

So I am found on Ingpen Beacon, or on Wylls-Neck to the west,
Or else on homely Bulbarrow, or little Pilsdon Crest,
Where men have never cared to haunt, nor women have walked with me,
And ghosts then keep their distance; and I know some liberty.

These hills mark out an approximate rectangle around central Dorset, and correspond to the heart of the Wessex world Hardy had himself created. They are places to which he can withdraw, familiar, homely, but solitary. Beneath him on the lowlands where he had written his novels he was forced to negotiate the opinions of critics, journalists and friends. On the heights, alone with himself, he can think and dream without the oppressive mind-chains of the valleys below. The shift here, surely, is from writing novels to writing poetry. Throughout his life he had turned to the solace of writing poetry in the intervals between writing novels. Novels are very public, poetry is very private, and Hardy was a shy, private man. The crisis over *Jude the Obscure* brought matters to a head, and in 1895 he decided to abandon the lowlands forever. Escaping the fever and fret of earning a living he turned to the meditative world of poetry because there he could find, as he says in the last line of 'Wessex Heights', 'some liberty'.

Afterword

AS A YOUNG MAN in the 1860s Hardy made a rather startling statement. 'The poetry of a scene', he wrote, 'varies with the minds of the perceivers.' 'Indeed,' he added, 'it does not lie in the scene at all.'[1] When, fifty years later in 1910, he thanked the town council for granting him the Freedom of Dorchester, he expressed a similar idea in a different way. He admitted that in *The Mayor of Casterbridge* his account of Casterbridge was 'more Dorchester than Dorchester itself', confessing that he had changed and intensified the urban 'scene' that lay before him according to a personal vision of his own. Throughout his novels and poetry Hardy often expressed ideas that suggested writing, painting and music were essentially subjective activities. Art, he said, was a 'changing of the actual proportions and order of things' to reflect the 'idiosyncrasy of the artist'.[2] Realism, he said, was not art because true art manipulated, distorted or saw 'round corners' to create its effect. The phrase about seeing round corners was one he used when comparing his own work with the paintings of Turner,[3] because for him, Turner, like Richard Wagner in music, communicated the 'deeper reality underlying the scenic'.[4] Both of them transformed the material world to express the poetry that lay in the artist's mind.

But none of these, the musician, painter or writer, was working in a vacuum. Wagner's point of departure for *Die Walküre* was the forests of northern Germany; Turner transformed the landscapes of Italy, and Hardy looked outward from the rolling countryside of Dorset. For each of them 'poetry' had to be discovered in the scene, and in Hardy's case the starting point held special significance. For him, the scene had to be first observed and recorded in all its physical details before its poetry could be identified and this process is one of the most intriguing aspects of his writing. On the one hand Hardy was a sharp observer. He understood country ways, the barking of trees, the construction of hurdles or the making of cider, and he was alive to the sound of the wind through the forest and the feel of the earth under foot. Again and again his novels document rural cultures that were slipping into historical oblivion. But Hardy was not just a social historian. He was also a writer who was emotionally and psychologically alert, who adopted the lanes and byways of the West Country for compelling stories of joy, pleasure, pathos and tragedy. Beyond that he had a wider vision where the same villages, towns, landscapes and characters were employed to express what he called the Victorian, intellectual 'ache of modernism'.

This rich yet paradoxical aspect of Hardy's work is summed up in his creation of 'Wessex'. In one sense it is a 'dream place', a tessellation of locations varying from novel to novel, rarely overlapping, and where the parts, though close geographically, are remote in terms of atmosphere, climate and ethos. On the Ordnance Survey map Puddletown is no more than three miles from Puddletown Heath, whereas Weatherbury in *Far from the Madding Crowd* is psychologically and culturally very remote from Egdon Heath of *The Return of the Native*. In another aspect, however, Hardy created a Wessex that was a matter-of-fact place, where, as he realized, you could 'take a house in and write to the papers from'.[5] Just as he made people believe that Henchard might have lived at 10 South Street, Dorchester, so he succeeded in creating a plausible fiction with its roots in geographic Dorset. When the dust had settled around the controversies of his later novels, he began to realize that not only had his readers been captivated by the stories, but many of them wanted to visit the places in which those stories were set.

Foremost among these were his birthplace in Higher Bockhampton and the parish of Stinsford which together served as the imaginative centre of Wessex. Not all Hardy's writing draws upon this part real, part imaginary location. Several novels, and some of his finest poems, 'The Convergence of the Twain' or 'Beyond the Last Lamp', for example, are neither rural nor West Country in origin. But so much of Hardy's mental energy had as its centre Puddletown Heath and radiated out into Dorset and beyond. Letters and requests for information grew, so, around 1912, together with his friend the photographer Herman Lea, Hardy set off, sometimes by bicycle, later by car, to record those places. As a result Hardy, beyond any other English novelist, has been powerfully identified with a single region.

Since then many have followed in his footsteps. The most distinguished was Denys Kay-Robinson, the most recent Tony Fincham, and between them scores of writers, photographers and artists, amateur and professional, have gone off in search of more and more accurate details, hoping to pin down the topography of Wessex. But this passion for location is much more than simple curiosity. Though Hardy knew that his 'dream country [had] solidified by degrees into a utilitarian region' and that people wanted to visit, the question has never been asked as to why exactly we want to see Tess's cottage in Marnhull or the Melburys' house in Melbury Bubb or stand on the Bronze Age tumulus at Rainbarrow. There is no simple answer to this. Certainly the experience of 'being there' vividly brings the narratives to mind or adds a new pleasure to the poems or the stories. But how does this happen? Hardy's statement about the 'poetry of the scene' may help. He claimed the poetry did not lie in the scene at all but in the mind of the perceiver. In other words had Hardy been born and grown up in East Anglia we might now be celebrating his 'Mercian' novels with conferences in Aldeburgh. Or to put it another way, it was historical accident that Dorset provided the location for Hardy's 'dream country'. He carefully observed the villages, buildings and landscapes to create an expressive relationship between those places and the fictional characters who inhabited them. When we read Hardy's work he communicates that relationship sometimes overtly, sometimes subliminally. For example, in *Far from the Madding Crowd*, by framing the sheep-shearing scene in the ancient barn he explicitly stresses the sympathetic link between the community of Weatherbury and the barn, whereas in *The Woodlanders* the elision between the characters and the forest world of the Hintocks is more shifting and elusive. But in both cases Hardy's genius was to translate the prose of Puddletown and Melbury Bubb into the 'poetry' of Weatherbury and Little Hintock.

In this interaction between time and place, Hardy often plays off the permanence of place against the passing of life in the context of what the poet Thom Gunn called Hardy's 'mastering obsession' – his sense of regret for the past.[6] Even as Hardy takes a delight in things, says Gunn, he mourns their passing or their loss. Places remain, people come and go. A good example is to be found in the poem 'In a Eweleaze near Weatherbury'. Weatherbury was Hardy's fictional name for Puddletown, and its use in this poem places the events just

Hardy's vignette accompanying 'In a Eweleaze near Wetherbury' for *Wessex Poems* (1898).

---

one step away from autobiography. By general consent, the poem written in 1890 relates to the death of Hardy's youthful Puddletown sweetheart Tryphena Sparks.[7] Hardy was then fifty and the 'leaze' or meadow that frames the poem in the second and the last lines is located a mile or two to the west of the village near Coombe farm.

> The years have gathered grayly
> Since I danced upon this leaze
> With one who kindled gaily
> Love's fitful ecstasies!

In the rhythm of the opening stanza the phrase 'this leaze' suggests that Hardy perceives it in the immediate present, a fact corroborated by the rather curious illustration he drew for the first edition of *Wessex Poems*. This shows a pair of spectacles in close-up hanging in mid-air before a rural landscape, including the leaze. The presence of the spectacles gives us two points of view. One is the meadow seen directly, the other is the meadow seen through the spectacles. Presumably, the landscape seen through the spectacles is what Hardy perceives as a middle-aged man. The landscape outside the spectacles is the one that exists today and as it did when, as a young man, he pursued Tryphena Sparks. In the drawing both versions of the landscape are quiet and pastoral, with sheep grazing in fields enclosed by hedge, wood and a clump of trees. But in the past, as Hardy remembers it, this place was occasionally turned into an erotic location, a field of sexual fantasies. Temporarily the sheep would have been cleared away and the flat area of land turned into an open-air dancing space, perhaps the same one in East Egdon on which Eustacia Vye danced with Damon Wildeve.

But the passing years have 'grayly gathered'. Time has sculpted away Hardy's youthful features, introduced the aches and pains of old age, and as the presence of the spectacles testifies, weakened his eyesight. Yet in spite of this Hardy claims that his essential spirit is unchanged and even now he would still risk all for the pleasure of a passionate affair.

> Still, I'd go the world with Beauty,
> I would laugh with her and sing,
> I would shun divinest duty
> To resume her worshipping.
> But she'd scorn my brave endeavour,
> She would not balm the breeze
> By murmuring, 'Thine for ever!'
> As she did upon this leaze.

The 'one' who kindled love in him has passed away, and in the poem has been replaced by a generic young woman, 'Beauty'. But here is a dilemma. Though he might be able to throw everything over for pleasure, 'laugh with her and sing', a stark realization brings him abruptly back to the present and the leaze in which he is stands. *He* might be willing, but would she? Would her modern equivalent be prepared to indulge in the youthful fantasy and whisper 'thine for ever', formerly spoken on the leaze?

Throughout his life Hardy was inspired to express his visionary experience of places in words, and we, as readers, are delighted to share it. So, with this in mind, if we travel to the locations that triggered his imagination, if we stand, for example, by the tithe barn at Cerne Abbas, or in the 'eweleaze' just outside Puddletown, something remarkable takes place. As a place, the barn is simply an extremely ancient building, and the field, just a dip in the hills surrounded by trees. In both the novel and the poem, however, those places are transformed into something visionary and through Hardy's language we can participate in the experience of that transformation. Through Hardy's words, we are privileged to see and feel what he felt and through those same words places and locations become infused by the poetry that Hardy himself perceived in the scene.

Notes

INTRODUCTION

1 Michael Millgate, ed., *The Life and Works of Thomas Hardy* (London & Basingstoke: Macmillan, 1984), p.158.

2 Ibid., p.355.

3 *Far from the Madding Crowd*, pp.3–4.

CHAPTER ONE: *FAR FROM THE MADDING CROWD*

1 These are now in Dorset County Museum.

2 John Newman and Nikolaus Pevnser, *The Buildings of England: Dorset* (Harmonds-worth: Penguin Books, 1972), pp.441–2.

3 Hardy went with Sidney Cockerell to visit the barn at Cerne Abbas on 27 June 1915 and later sent him a copy of *Far from the Madding Crowd* indicating the description of the great barn that they visited together. See Richard Purdy and Michael Millgate, eds., *The Collected Letters of Thomas Hardy* (Oxford: Clarendon Press, 1978–2012), v, p.123 note.

4 Michael Millgate, ed., *Thomas Hardy's Public Voice: The Essays, Speeches and Miscellaneous Prose* (Oxford: Clarendon Press, 2001), p.253.

CHAPTER TWO: *THE RETURN OF THE NATIVE*

1 Hardy first gave the fictional name 'Blackbarrow' to the tumulus, later identifying it by its geographical name 'Rainbarrow'. I adopt Rainbarrow here.

2 'Domicilium' from James Gibson, ed., *The Complete Poems of Thomas Hardy* (London: Macmillan, 1976).

3 Richard H. Taylor, ed., *Emma Hardy Diaries*, (Northumberland: Mid Northumberland Arts Group and Carcarnet New Press, 1985), p.103.

4 William Wordsworth, 'Lines Composed above Tintern Abbey' (1798).

5 Charles Darwin, *The Origin of Species* (1859) (Oxford: Clarendon Press, 1998), pp.52–3.

6 Millgate (1984), p.124.

7 *Handbook for Travellers in Holland and Belgium* (London: John Murray, 1868), p.36.

8 William Stevenson, *General view of the agriculture of the county of Dorset; with observations on the means of its improvement* (London: G. & W. Nicol, 1815), p.332.

9 Tony Fincham, *Hardy's Wessex Revisited*, (London: Robert Hale, 2010), p.25.

10 Darwin (1998), p.176.

11 Ibid., p.56.

CHAPTER THREE: *THE MAYOR OF CASTERBRIDGE*

1 Thomas Hardy, 'Speech on Receiving the Freedom of the Borough' (1910), in Millgate (2001), p.320.

2 Thomas Hardy, 'Memories of Church Restoration' (1906) in Millgate (2001), p.251.

3 Thomas Hardy, 'Some Romano-British Relics Found at Max Gate, Dorchester' (1884) in Millgate (2001), p.62.

4 *Proceedings of the Dorset Natural History and Antiquarian Field Club*, xiv (1884), p.xiv.

5 This refers to an incident that took place in 1839. When a road was being cut through Fordington Hill some fifty bodies were found in a second-century graveyard. At the time Henry Moule's father, the vicar of Fordington, came across two coins (now in Dorset County Museum) lodged in an ancient skull, placed there, it was said, to pay the ferryman Charon when the dead reached the banks of the Styx.

6 Kevin O'Brien, 'The House Beautiful: A

Reconstruction of Oscar Wilde's American Lecture', *Victorian Studies*, 17:4 (1974), pp.395–418.

7 Claudius J. P. Beatty, *The Part Played by Architecture in the Life and Work of Thomas Hardy* (Dorchester: Plush Publishing, 2004), p.305.

8 Hutchins (1863), vol. ii, p.796, now in Dorset County Museum.

CHAPTER FOUR: *THE WOODLANDERS*

1 Hardy's own copy of Hutchins, *History and Antiquities of the County of Dorset*, 3rd edition, augmented by William Shipp and James Whitworth Hodson (London, 1861–70), is heavily annotated by him in the entries that deal with Melbury Sampford and Melbury Bubb in volume II.

2 Hardy, letters to Edmund Gosse, 31 March 1887 and 5 April 1887 in Purdy and Millgate (1978–2012), i, p.163–4.

3 Millgate (1984), p.192.

4 Alan Chedzoy, 'Winterborne Came Rectory: The Home of William Barnes', *Proceedings of the Dorset Natural History and Archaeological Society* 123 (2001), p.2.

5 While he was there he struck up a friendship with the local vicar but never seems to have met the owner of Turnworth House.

6 Paid for by George Wynfield Digby, the owner of Sherborne Castle, it provided the venue for the first meeting in 1877 of the Dorset Natural History and Antiquarian Field Club, of which Hardy was a member. It is now a school.

7 The box on the left is being fed with whole apples that are being ground by the man using the large wheel in the foreground. To the left are two presses. The first has just finished its task of squeezing the apples, and the juice has run into the containers on the ground; the second is full of apple pieces, and the man on the far right is about to begin compression by moving the lever up and down.

8 C. F. Innocent, *The Development of English Building Construction* (Cambridge: Cambridge University Press, 1916), p.13.

9 John Thomas Smith, *Remarks on Rural Scenery with Twenty Etchings of Cottages from Nature* (London: Joseph Downes, 1797), plate 6.

10 These are the words of Alfred Austin, who in 1843 submitted a report to Parliament about the conditions of agricultural workers in Dorset and elsewhere, quoted in Karen Sayer, *Country Cottages: A Cultural History* (Manchester: Manchester University Press, 2000), p.56. Giles has also been suffering from a mysterious disease. The infection seems to pass, but leaves him weak. When eventually Fitzpiers is summoned he is quick to diagnose his disease as typhus, another shadow that hung over the rural poor. The same report that invoked lowered moral standards amongst the poor also highlighted the insanitary living conditions of 'old and decaying' cottages in the West Country, where 'malignant typhus' was identified at Blandford and Stourpain in Dorset.

11 The forester of the Ilchester estate, Andy Poore, tells me that the tree, which is 39 feet in diameter, is certainly alive but in a state of suspended animation. In the Middle Ages, together with a number of oaks in this part of the estate it was 'worked', that is shredded for animal food and pollarded for firewood. This stopped around 1547, but the estate still contains a number of these biologically valuable 'veteran' trees.

12 Darwin (1998), p.351.

1 Millgate (1984), pp.223–4.

2 Ibid., p.118.

3 Unlike *The Mayor of Casterbridge* and *The Woodlanders*, few buildings are endowed with social or psychological resonance. In *Tess of the d'Urbervilles* Hardy's treatment of building has little of the resonance that he had given it before. Literary detectives have worked hard to place the locations that Hardy mentions in the novel. The Dew Drop Inn can be linked to the Crown near the village church, and Rollivers to a former tavern called the Lamb, now a private house at the southern end of the village.

4 James Frazer and Robert Fraser, *The Golden Bough: A Study in Magic and Religion* (Oxford: Oxford University Press, 2009), p.9. Hardy used the first, two-volume, edition of *The Golden Bough* published in 1890.

5 Millgate (1984), p.192.

6 Ibid., pp.225–6.

7 Frazer (2009), p.798.

8 Fincham (2010), p.209.

9 Millgate (1984), p.283.

10 Friedrich Max Müller, 'Comparative Mythology' (1858), *Chips from a German Workshop* (London: Longmans, Green, 1867–75), ii, pp.99–100.

11 John Addington Symonds, *Studies of the Greek Poets* (London: Smith Elder & Co., 1873), p.419.

12 E. T. Cook and Alexander Wedderburn, eds., *The Works of John Ruskin*, 39 vols. (London, G. Allen, 1903–12), xviii, pp.347–8.

13 To which Hardy added the comment: 'This "barbaric idea" . . . is, by the way, also common to the highest imaginative genius – that of the poet.' Hardy felt that one of his strengths as a writer was the possession of a primitive mythopoetic faculty, and he felt that there were similarities between his own mental processes as a writer of fiction and the myth-making propensities of the savage mind.

14 Frazer and Fraser (2009), p.xx.

15 Though Fincham (2010), pp.46–8, argues cogently for Norris Mill Farm, Hardy on his own copy of Cruchley's *Railway and Telegraphic Map of Dorset* (1855) in Dorset County Museum marked 'Tess's tracks' showing clearly that Talbothays was located on the spot occupied by Lower Lewell Farm.

16 David Lodge, 'Tess, Nature, and the Voices of Hardy', *Language of Fiction* (London: Routledge, 1966), pp.190–96 passim.

17 Müller (1867–75), ii, p.132.

18 In *Jude the Obscure* Sue Bridehead reads this same poem by Swinburne. See p.89.

19 Harold Orel, ed., *Thomas Hardy's Personal Writings* (London: Macmillan, 1967), p.200.

20 Millgate (1984), p.45.

21 Ibid., pp.187–8.

22 Ibid., p.355.

23 *The Times*, 10 June 1886, p.4.

24 *The Times*, 17 June 1886, p.10; 19 June 1889, p.15 and again on 22 April 1890, p.4.

25 Turner engraved a sunrise picture for his *Liber Studiorum*.

26 Ruskin, *Fors Clavigera* (1874), in Cook and Wedderburn (1903–12), xxviii, p.147.

27 Millgate (1984), p.354.

CHAPTER SIX: JUDE THE OBSCURE

1 This is now in Dorset County Museum, Dorchester.

2 Millgate (1984), p.265.

3 Hardy's copy of *Cruchley's Railway and Station Map of Berkshire* (n.d.) is in the British Library [c.134.bb.1/40] where Great Fawley is marked with a similar dot and the road from the 'Brown Barn' to Oxford is traced with a red line.

4 Millgate (1984), p.120.

5 The church of St Mary replaces an older structure which stood further to the east, the graveyard of which remains. The new church was erected in 1865–6 and the old building was taken down in the latter year. No record of its plan or appearance seems to have been kept, but some fragments which have been used in the new structure show that some parts, at least, were late twelfth or early thirteenth century. The new church, which was consecrated on 12 April 1866, was designed by George Edmund Street. See William Page and P. H. Ditchfield, eds., *Victoria County History: A History of the County of Berkshire* (London, 1924), p.174. http://www.british-history.ac.uk/report.aspx?compid=62698

6 Rev. 22:1.

7 Rev. 21:10.

8 Beatty (2004), pp.488–9. It was while he was on this architectural project that he probably made his first visit to Great Fawley.

9 Lucio Sponza, *Italian Immigrants in Nineteenth-Century Britain: Realities and Images* (Leicester: Leicester University Press, 1988), p.71 et seq. says that image makers came mainly from the Valtaro and Lucca.

10 Millgate (1984), p.355.

11 Both St Barnabas and St Silas were saints who accompanied St Paul on his missionary journeys.

12 St Barnabas in Oxford was completed in 1869 and Sue's father, according to a stonemason called Uncle Joe, worked on the church 'ten years ago'.

13 Millgate (2004), p.323.

14 Richard Colt Hoare and James Everard Arundell, *The History of Modern Wiltshire* (London: J. Nichols, 1822–44), pp.170–71.

15 Colin Harrison, *Turner's Oxford* (Oxford: Ashmolean Museum, 2000), p.76 ff.

16 *The Times*, 21 January and 1 February 1889.

17 Giles Winterborne has a similar experience when he goes to pick up Grace Melbury on her arrival from school in Sherton Abbas. He 'drove . . . into the streets – the churches, the abbey, and other medieval buildings on this clear bright morning having the liny distinctness of architectural drawings, as if the original dream and vision of the conceiving master-mason, some mediaeval Villas or other unknown to fame, were for a few minutes flashed down through the centuries to an unappreciative age. Giles saw their eloquent look on this day of transparency, but could not construe it'. (33) Giles sees, but cannot appreciate because he is unlearned in the language of architectural form.

18 Letter to Edmund Gosse, 10 November 1895, in Purdy and Millgate (1978–2012), ii, p.93.

19 The London and South Western Railway ran one station, with the Great Western Railway opening a second competing station to the north in 1848.

20 Charles Lock, 'Hardy and the Railway', *Essays in Criticism* 50:1 (2000), 44–66. p.44.

21 Millgate (1984), p.272.

22 *The Times*, 22 June 1893, p.10.

23 John Ruskin, 'Christ Church, Oxford: Night' (1837).

24 Millgate (2004), pp.319–20.

25 Margaret Oliphant, 'The Anti-Marriage League', *Blackwood's Magazine*, January 1896, reprinted in R. G. Cox, *Thomas Hardy: The Critical Heritage* (London: Routledge & Kegan Paul 1970), p.257.

26 Cox (1970), pp.264–5.

CHAPTER SEVEN: THE POEMS

1 Thom Gunn, 'The Influence of the Ballad Forms', in James Gibson and Trevor Johnson, eds., *Thomas Hardy Poems: A Casebook* (London: Macmillan, 1979), p.226.

2 Purdy and Millgate (1978–2012), iv, p.243, letter dated 13 December 1912.

3 Phillip Mallett, 'You Were She: Emma Hardy and the Poems 1912–13', *The Thomas Hardy Journal* 20:3 (2004), pp.54–75.

4 Millgate (1984), p.81.

5 Denys Kay-Robinson, *The First Mrs Thomas Hardy* (New York: St Martin's Press, 1979), and Robert Gittings and Jo Manton, *The Second Mrs Hardy* (Oxford: Oxford University Press, 1981).

6 Evelyn Hardy and Robert Gittings, eds., *Some Recollections by Emma Hardy* (Oxford: Oxford University Press, 1979), p.35.

7 Barbara Hardy, *Thomas Hardy: Imagining Imagination, Hardy's Poetry and Fiction* (London and New Brunswick: Athlone Press, 2000), pp.148–9.

8 Hardy and Gittings (1979), p.35. Hardy includes an almost identical incident in his early novel *A Pair of Blue Eyes* (1873).

9 Paulin (1975), p.128.

10 J. O. Bailey, *The Poetry of Thomas Hardy: A Handbook and Commentary* (Chapel Hill: University of North Carolina Press, 1970), p.275.

AFTERWORD

1 Millgate (1984), p.52.

2 Ibid., p.239.

3 Purdy and Millgate (1978–2012), vi, p.161.

4 Millgate (1984), p.192.

5 *Far from the Madding Crowd*, p.4.

6 Gunn in Gibson and Johnson (1979), p.226.

7 The part played by Tryphena Sparks, Hardy's young cousin from Puddletown, in his life is unclear. In the absence of very positive evidence some biographers dismiss it as insignificant. Others, notably Ralph Pite, suggests that it was highly significant, but deliberately obscured by Hardy. See Ralph Pite, *Thomas Hardy: The Guarded Live* (Basingstoke & Oxford: Pan Picador, 2006), pp.215–224.

Bibliography

Bailey, J. O., *The Poetry of Thomas Hardy: A Handbook and Commentary* (Chapel Hill: University of North Carolina Press, 1970).

Beatty, Claudius J. P., *The Part Played by Architecture in the Life and Work of Thomas Hardy* (Dorchester: Plush Publishing, 2004).

Chedzoy, Alan, 'Winterborne Came Rectory: The Home of William Barnes', *Proceedings of the Dorset Natural History and Archaeological Society* 123 (2001), pp.1–6.

Cook, E. T. and Wedderburn, Alexander Dundas Ogilvy, eds., *The Works of John Ruskin*, 39 vols (London: G. Allen, 1903–12).

Cox, R. G., *Thomas Hardy: The Critical Heritage* (London: Routledge & Kegan Paul, 1970).

Darwin, Charles, *The Origin of Species* (Oxford: Oxford University Press, 1998).

Davie, Donald, *Thomas Hardy and British Poetry* (London: Routledge and Kegan Paul, 1979).

Fincham, Tony, *Hardy's Landscape Revisited* (London: Robert Hale, 2010).

Frazer, James George Sir, and Fraser, Robert, *The Golden Bough: A Study in Magic and Religion* (Oxford: Oxford University Press, 2009).

Gatrell, Simon, *Thomas Hardy's Vision of Wessex* (Basingstoke: Palgrave Macmillan, 2003).

Gibson, James, and Johnson, Trevor, *Thomas Hardy Poems: A Casebook* (London: Macmillan, 1979).

Gibson, James, ed., *Thomas Hardy: The Complete Poems* (Basingstoke: Palgrave, 2001).

Gittings, Robert, *Young Thomas Hardy*, Harmondsworth: Penguin, 1978).

——, *The Older Hardy* (Harmondsworth: Penguin, 1980).

——, and Manton, Jo, *The Second Mrs Hardy* (Oxford: Oxford University Press, 1981).

Hardy, Barbara Nathan, *Thomas Hardy: Imaging Imagination, Hardy's Poetry and Fiction* (London: Athlone Press, 2000).

Hardy, Emma Lavinia Gifford, *Some Recollections*, ed. Evelyn Hardy and Robert Gittings (Oxford: Oxford University Press, 1979).

Harrison, Colin, *Turner's Oxford* (Oxford: Ashmolean Museum, 2000).

Hoare, Richard Colt, and Arundell, James Everard, *The History of Modern Wiltshire.* (London: J. Nichols, 1822–44).

Hutchins, John, Hodson, James Whitworth, and Shipp, William, *The History and Antiquities of the County of Dorset*, 3rd edition, corrected, augmented and improved by William Shipp and James Whitworth Hodson, 4 vols (London: J. B. Nichols & Sons, 1861).

Innocent, C. F., *The Development of English Building Construction* (Cambridge: Cambridge University Press, 1916).

John, Murray, *A Hand-Book for Travellers on the Continent: Being a Guide through Holland, Belgium, Prussia, and Northern Germany, and Along the Rhine, from Holland to Switzerland* (London: John Murray, 1868).

Lock, Charles, 'Hardy and the Railway', *Essays in Criticism* (2000), pp.44–66.

Lodge, David, *Language of Fiction: Essays in Criticism and Verbal Analysis of the English Novel* (London: Routledge & Kegan Paul, 1966).

Millgate, Michael, ed., *The Life and Works of Thomas Hardy*, (London & Basingstoke: Macmillan, 1984).

———, *Thomas Hardy's Public Voice: The Essays, Speeches and Miscellaneous Prose* (Oxford: Clarendon Press, 2001).

———, *Thomas Hardy: A Biography Revisited* (Oxford: Oxford University Press, 2004).

Müller, Friedrich Max, *Chips from a German Workshop*, 4 vols (London: Longmans, Green, 1867–75).

Newman, John, and Pevsner, Nikolaus, *The Buildings of England: Dorset* (Harmondsworth: Penguin Books, 1972)

O'Brian, Kevin, 'The House Beautiful: A Reconstruction of Oscar Wilde's American Lecture', *Victorian Studies,* 14 (1974), pp.395–418.

Orel, Harold, ed., *Thomas Hardy's Personal Writings: Prefaces, Literary Opinions, Reminiscences* (London: Macmillan, 1967).

Paulin, Tom, *Thomas Hardy: The Poetry of Perception* (London: Macmillan, 1975).

Purdy, Richard Little, and Millgate, Michael, eds., *The Collected Letters of Thomas Hardy*, 8 vols (Oxford: Clarendon, 1978–2012).

Sacks, Peter M., *The English Elegy: Studies in the Genre from Spenser to Yeats* (Baltimore & London: Johns Hopkins University Press, 1985).

Sayer, Karen, *Country Cottages: A Cultural History* (Manchester: Manchester University Press, 2000).

Smith, John Thomas, *Remarks on Rural Scenery with Twenty Etchings of Cottages from Nature* (London: Joseph Downes, 1797).

Sponza, Lucio, *Italian Immigrants in Nineteenth-Century Britain: Realities and Images* (Leicester: Leicester University Press, 1988).

Stevenson, William, *General View of the Agriculture of the County of Dorset* (London: G & W Nicol, 1815).

Symonds, John Addington, *Studies of the Greek Poets* (London: Smith Elder & Co., 1873).

Taylor, Richard, ed., *Emma Hardy Diaries* (Ashington: Mid Northumberland Arts Group, 1985).

Wilson, Keith, *A Companion to Thomas Hardy* (Oxford: Wiley-Blackwell, 2009).

Further Reading

Bullen, J. B., *The Expressive Eye: Fiction and Perception in the Work of Thomas Hardy* (Oxford: Clarendon, 1986).

———, 'The Gods in Wessex Exile', *The Sun is God: Painting, Literature, and Mythology in the Nineteenth Century*, ed. J. B. Bullen (Oxford: Clarendon Press, 1989).

Kay-Robinson, Denys, *The Landscape of Thomas Hardy* (Exeter: Webb & Bower, 1984).

Lea, Hermann, *Thomas Hardy's Wessex* (London: Macmillan, 1977).

Mallett, Phillip, *The Achievement of Thomas Hardy* (Basingstoke: Macmillan Press, 2000).

Pite, Ralph, *Hardy's Geography: Wessex and the Regional Novel* (Basingstoke: Palgrave Macmillan, 2002).

Index

Page numbers in *italic* refer to illustrations.

Acknowledgments

My greatest debt in writing this book is first to Helen Gibson whose help and inspiration at the Dorset County Museum was invaluable, and then to Jane Thomas who by asking me to speak at the biannual Thomas Hardy Society conference, Dorchester, stimulated me to think of Hardy's work in this way. I am grateful also to Tony Fincham who was so willing to share his detailed knowledge of Wessex topography, and to Alistair Tearne, Stuart Ackland and Michael Athanson for help with the maps and their design. Katharine Butler was kind enough to allow me to photograph Waterston Manor, John and Lindsey Pedder to spend time at the tithe barn in Cerne Abbas, Warren Davies who showed me round Came Rectory and Amanda Blaine who introduced me to Melbury Bubb manor house. Andy Poore's combination of warmth and expertise at the Ilchester Estates was indispensible for the book, and so was the advice, opinions and guidance of many others including Matthew Beckett, Alan Chedzoy, Julie Davis, Jane Dennison, Mark Forrest, Jennifer Glanville, Colin Harrison, Stephanie Jenkins, Vera Jesty, Scotford Lawrence, Andrew Leah, Simon McBride, Peter McSweeney, Charles Pettit, Danae Tankard, Emma Tomlin, David Tuffin and George Wickham. Thanks are also due to Mollie Tearne and Lindley Paul Bullen for reading and commenting on parts of the text, and to Nicki Davis for her editorial care and patience.

Picture Credits

Fictitious names as **Exonbury**
Real names as **Portsmouth**

Cliff without name
Targan Bay
Dundagel
Barwith Strand
Endlestow
Castle Boterel
St. Laun

Bristol

Mendip Hills

Fa

Prospect Hotel
Bristol Channel
Stancy Castle

Cliff Martin
Exon Moor
Fountall

Downstaple
Dunkery Beacon
Quantock Hills
Will's Neck
Poldon Hills
Marshal's Elm
Glaston

O W

Toneborough Deane
Sedgemoor River
Parret

Toneborough
Nelchester

Tvell
She
Abb
Vale
The Hint

L O W E R
King's Hintock
Evershead
Grimmerrock Lane
Chalk Newton

W E S S E X
Emminster

River Otter
River Axe
Pilsdon
Teller Down
Frome
SOUTH
Casterbridge

Exonbury
Port Bredy
Blackon
Wacton Vale
Pebble Beach

Deadmans Bay
Street of Wells
Isle of Slingers
The Bea